Stevie Smith and the Aphorism

OXFORD ENGLISH MONOGRAPHS

General Editors

NANDINI DAS   SANTANU DAS   PAULINA KEWES
MATTHEW REYNOLDS   FIONA STAFFORD   MARION TURNER

Stevie Smith and the Aphorism

Hard Language

NOREEN MASUD

Great Clarendon Street, Oxford, OX2 6DP,
United Kingdom

Oxford University Press is a department of the University of Oxford.
It furthers the University's objective of excellence in research, scholarship,
and education by publishing worldwide. Oxford is a registered trade mark of
Oxford University Press in the UK and in certain other countries

© Noreen Masud 2022

The moral rights of the author have been asserted

Impression: 1

All rights reserved. No part of this publication may be reproduced, stored in
a retrieval system, or transmitted, in any form or by any means, without the
prior permission in writing of Oxford University Press, or as expressly permitted
by law, by licence or under terms agreed with the appropriate reprographics
rights organization. Enquiries concerning reproduction outside the scope of the
above should be sent to the Rights Department, Oxford University Press, at the
address above

You must not circulate this work in any other form
and you must impose this same condition on any acquirer

Published in the United States of America by Oxford University Press
198 Madison Avenue, New York, NY 10016, United States of America

British Library Cataloguing in Publication Data
Data available

Library of Congress Control Number: 2022943689

ISBN 978–0–19–289589–9

DOI: 10.1093/oso/9780192895899.001.0001

Printed and bound by
CPI Group (UK) Ltd, Croydon, CR0 4YY

Links to third party websites are provided by Oxford in good faith and
for information only. Oxford disclaims any responsibility for the materials
contained in any third party website referenced in this work.

I have started the preceding paragraph with the word
'nevertheless' ... I believe myself to be fairly indoctrinated
by the habit of thought which calls for this word. In fact I
approve of the ceremonious accumulation of weather
forecasts and barometer-readings that pronounce for a fine
day, before letting rip on the statement: 'Nevertheless, it's
raining.' I find that much of my literary composition is based
on the nevertheless idea. I act upon it. It was on the
nevertheless principle that I turned Catholic.

— Muriel Spark, 'What Images Return'

Acknowledgements

This book is about unhearability. I have been heard and enjoyed. I owe bigger debts to Laura Marcus, Sally Bayley, Freya Johnston, and Sos Eltis than I think they can know. Laura died before this book came out; much of what she taught me took me years to understand.

The Arts and Humanities Research Council, and the Paul Slack Studentship at Linacre College, Oxford, funded the original thesis. Grants from the AHRC, the English Faculty of Oxford, Linacre House Trust, and Santander let me visit archives and speak at conferences. Time and space to adapt the thesis were granted by the Leverhulme Trust, and Durham University's Department of English.

For reading with careful attention, sometimes over and over again: Patrick Hayes, Kate McLoughlin, Erica McAlpine, Sophie Ratcliffe, Jacob Lloyd, Aliyah Norrish, Richard Kendall, Lucy Whelan. Deryn Rees-Jones and Seamus Perry were kind examiners; Hamish MacGibbon a gracious executor; Aimee Wright a patient and tolerant editor. My agent Matt Turner had my back. Thank you to the three anonymous readers at OUP, for intellectual generosity. Bryony Armstrong was a brilliant proofreader and reference-checker, and Venetia Bridges helped with the Greek, but any errors, in any language, are mine alone.

For intellectual community: Will May, Holly Laird, Matthew Bevis, Michael Shallcross, Chris Robson, Jasmine Jagger, Frances White, and the attendees of 'Aphoristic Modernity' in 2015 and the Stevie Smith conference in 2016. *Essays in Criticism* published a version of Chapter Five in 2018, and its editors have kindly allowed me to reprint points of overlap here.

Thanks to Faber and Faber, New Directions, the McFarlin Library, and the estates of Stevie Smith, James Thurber, and Muriel Spark for permission to quote and reproduce images. Especial thanks to Jeremy Noel-Tod for helping.

Staff at the Bodleian Library, British Library, Bill Bryson Library, McFarlin Library, Houghton Library, Cadbury Research Library, National Library of Scotland, Brotherton Library, Hull History Centre, and Oxfordshire History Centre went out of their way to help me. Special bibliographic thanks to Fiona Richardson at Linacre College, Marc Carlson at the McFarlin, Anne George at the Cadbury, Sally Harrower at the National Library of Scotland, Kristen Marangoni and her family, Audrey Granger Perry at *Regarding Arts and Letters*, Susan Proctor, JC Proctor, Holly and Natalia.

Aphorism can make space to declare love which would embarrass its recipients. For wisdom and friendship: Jacob Lloyd, Ben Morgan, Liz Peretz, Millie Schurch,

Kristin Grogan, Robert Sowden, Stephen Blanchard, Agota Marton, Dan Sperrin, Tom Cook, Suzie Hanna, Faye Green, Marion Turner, Venetia Bridges, Dan Grausam, Clare Deal, Hannah Ashman.

I moved to the UK when I was sixteen. Since then, I have been vaulted 'into enormous rooms' by systems whose generosity now seems unimaginable: they face existential threat or are gone altogether. Aphorism calls out to a world which it knows cannot heed it. In that anechoic space, I thank Madras College Endowment Trust, Education Maintenance Allowance, Oxford Opportunity Bursaries, Jesus College Access Bursaries, the Student Awards Agency for Scotland, and the AHRC, again, for giving me choices which today's teenagers might not feel able to risk.

Nuzhat Saleem saw me through Pakistan; Sally Bayley cared for me after that. Katie Murphy turned the light on, ten years ago, with 'Thoughts about the Person from Porlock'. Fiona Grace tolerated years of Stevie Smith talk; I remember Mary Grace at the end of this book. Sarah Pethybridge gave me a garden. Dennis Harrison made me a space. This book is for Aliyah: the base on which my life's bowl stands.

Contents

List of Illustrations	x
List of Abbreviations	xii

Introduction: Smith's Hard Language	1
Smith's Aphoristics	2
Usefulness, Eccentricity, and the Aphorism	11
'Strong Communication': Foregrounding the Aphorism's Internal Contradiction	19
Reading Smith through Aphorism	25

1. Unnecessary Aphorisms	30
Aphorism's Empty Shapes	32
Half Truths: One and a Half Truths	38
'A Strong Way Out': To and From the Aphorism	50

2. Aphoristic Messages, Too Late	55
Smith and the Classics	57
Carrying Hard Aphoristic Messages in *Novel on Yellow Paper*	61
The Undelivered Message	65
Epitaph as Belated Aphorism	72
In a Bit	75

3. Proverbs through Fairytale	78
Circling the Fairytale	82
Repositioning the Proverb	87
The Proverb as Fairytale Core	92
A Lion is in the Street	95
Three and Four	98

4. Captions and the 'Appropriate'	103
Smith's Drawings	105
Caption and Euphemism	112
The Caption's Social Life	115
The Too-Appropriate Caption	122

5. Fragments 'Going On'	129
Fragment and Aphorism	133
Collecting Fragments	139
Aphorism: Going On	144
Thoughts about the Person from Porlock	151
Conclusion: To Go On	159
Bibliography	173
Index	188

List of Illustrations

I.1. Gesturing figure, 'How Cruel is the Story of Eve'. Stevie Smith, *The Collected Poems and Drawings of Stevie Smith*, ed. Will May (London: Faber & Faber, 2015), 557. By permission of Faber and Faber Ltd and New Directions Publishing Corp.   17

I.2. 'Moi, c'est moralement que j'ai mes élégances—' Stevie Smith, *Some Are More Human Than Others* (London: Peter Owen, 1990). © Stevie Smith 1958. Copyright © James MacGibbon 1989. Reprinted by permission of Faber and Faber Ltd and New Directions Publishing Corp.   18

I.3. 'Love is everything'. Stevie Smith, *Some Are More Human Than Others* (London: Peter Owen, 1990). © Stevie Smith 1958. Copyright © James MacGibbon 1989. Reprinted by permission of Faber and Faber Ltd and New Directions Publishing Corp.   18

1.1. Croft, in the loft. Stevie Smith, *The Collected Poems and Drawings of Stevie Smith*, ed. Will May (London: Faber & Faber, 2015), 218. By permission of Faber and Faber Ltd and New Directions Publishing Corp.   34

1.2. The Weak Monk. Stevie Smith, *The Collected Poems and Drawings of Stevie Smith*, ed. Will May (London: Faber & Faber, 2015), 286. By permission of Faber and Faber Ltd and New Directions Publishing Corp.   37

1.3. Figure and flowers, 'How Slowly Time Lengthens'. Stevie Smith, *The Collected Poems and Drawings of Stevie Smith*, ed. Will May (London: Faber & Faber, 2015), 142. By permission of Faber and Faber Ltd and New Directions Publishing Corp.   39

1.4. 'Father, I have had enough'. Series 2, Box 1, Folder 11. Stevie Smith papers, 1924–1970. Coll. No. 1976.012. McFarlin Library. Department of Special Collections and University Archives. The University of Tulsa. By permission of Faber and Faber Ltd, New Directions Publishing Corp, and the McFarlin Library.   42

4.1. 'Such an animal is not responsive to love'. Stevie Smith, *Some Are More Human Than Others* (London: Peter Owen, 1990). © Stevie Smith 1958. Copyright © James MacGibbon 1989. Reprinted by permission of Faber and Faber Ltd and New Directions Publishing Corp.   108

4.2. 'So what!' Stevie Smith, *Some Are More Human Than Others* (London: Peter Owen, 1990). © Stevie Smith 1958. Copyright © James MacGibbon 1989. Reprinted by permission of Faber and Faber Ltd and New Directions Publishing Corp.   115

LIST OF ILLUSTRATIONS   xi

4.3. 'If you can keep a secret, I'll tell you how my husband died'. By permission of Cartoon Collections www.CartoonCollections.com. First published *New Yorker* 10, 9 June 1934, 26.   116

4.4. 'These girls are full of love'. Stevie Smith, *Some Are More Human Than Others* (London: Peter Owen, 1990). © Stevie Smith 1958. Copyright © James MacGibbon 1989. Reprinted by permission of Faber and Faber Ltd and New Directions Publishing Corp.   117

4.5. 'I will tell you everything!' Stevie Smith, *Some Are More Human Than Others* (London: Peter Owen, 1990). © Stevie Smith 1958. Copyright © James MacGibbon 1989. Reprinted by permission of Faber and Faber Ltd and New Directions Publishing Corp.   118

4.6. 'Lord Say-and-Seal'. Stevie Smith, *Some Are More Human Than Others* (London: Peter Owen, 1990). © Stevie Smith 1958. Copyright © James MacGibbon 1989. Reprinted by permission of Faber and Faber Ltd and New Directions Publishing Corp.   119

4.7. 'My mother was a fox'. Stevie Smith, *Some Are More Human Than Others* (London: Peter Owen, 1990). © Stevie Smith 1958. Copyright © James MacGibbon 1989. Reprinted by permission of Faber and Faber Ltd and New Directions Publishing Corp.   120

4.8. 'I could eat you'. Stevie Smith, *Some Are More Human Than Others* (London: Peter Owen, 1990). © Stevie Smith 1958. Copyright © James MacGibbon 1989. Reprinted by permission of Faber and Faber Ltd and New Directions Publishing Corp.   121

4.9. 'His eyes are blue'. Stevie Smith, *Cats in Colour* (London: Batsford, 1959), 24.   122

4.10. 'Sometimes it holds its head on one side'. Stevie Smith, *Some Are More Human Than Others* (London: Peter Owen, 1990). © Stevie Smith 1958. Copyright © James MacGibbon 1989. Reprinted by permission of Faber and Faber Ltd and New Directions Publishing Corp.   126

C.1. Miss Pauncefort. Stevie Smith, *The Collected Poems and Drawings of Stevie Smith*, ed. Will May (London: Faber & Faber, 2015), 20. By permission of Faber and Faber Ltd and New Directions Publishing Corp.   169

List of Abbreviations

CP   Stevie Smith, *The Collected Poems and Drawings of Stevie Smith*, ed. Will May (London: Faber & Faber, 2015)

Novel   Stevie Smith, *Novel on Yellow Paper* (London: Virago, 2015)

Frontier   Stevie Smith, *Over the Frontier* (London: Virago, 1980)

Holiday   Stevie Smith, *The Holiday* (London: Virago, 1979)

MA   Stevie Smith, *Me Again: The Uncollected Writings of Stevie Smith*, ed. Jack Barbera and William McBrien (London: Virago, 1981)

Introduction
Smith's Hard Language

Nobody heard him, the dead man,
But still he lay moaning:
I was much further out than you thought
And not waving but drowning. (CP, 347)

Not waving but drowning. The dead man goes on moaning out Stevie Smith's most famous phrase, long after his voice ceases to be hearable ('Nobody heard him'). He speaks even though his words can do nothing to save his life.

But the line survives him. It outlasts Smith, and (in the public mind) so much of her idiosyncratic, startling poetry and prose. While Smith's other writing remains obscure, 'not waving but drowning' creeps into headlines and the speeches of politicians. Even readers unfamiliar with Smith and her mid-twentieth-century milieu recognize the phrase. It is a piece of hard language, like bone, which survives the picking currents of the sea. It stands on its own, long after the poem's surrounding soft tissue has rotted away, with a contained dignity: seeming, as aphorism often seems, to sum up and express a shattering general revelation in one striking line.

Twelve years after the poem was first published, Smith's reviewer Rodney Ackland was still marvelling over the stubborn independence of that phrase:

> whether out of context or back in the poem where it belongs, Stevie Smith's famous 'not waving but drowning' must be one of the few absolutely indelible, absolutely ineradicable single lines in the English language ... should I ever find myself a wandering victim of amnesia with total non-recall of all my reading, the solitary exception would be those forlornly and forever echoing words of Stevie Smith ... 'not waving but drowning' would be the phrase which would refuse entirely to be obliterated from the records of my mind.[1]

Smith's 'absolutely indelible, absolutely ineradicable' line survives, like a cockroach, after a cognitive apocalypse. It is 'solitary', maddening, compelling. In its singularity, the line becomes indelibly associated with Stevie Smith, a cipher for her and for her startling, resistant aesthetic. 'Not waving but drowning' has the

---

[1] Rodney Ackland, 'Bear up Chaps', *Spectator* 223, 30 August 1969, 272.

Stevie Smith and the Aphorism. Noreen Masud, Oxford University Press.
© Noreen Masud (2022). DOI: 10.1093/oso/9780192895899.003.0001

'epigrammatic incisiveness' that Calvin Bedient associates briefly with Smith,[2] the 'emphatic aphoristic edges' that Michael Horovitz finds in her work.[3] The phrase's elegant construction, based around a startling turn ('waving' to 'drowning') and verbal symmetry (the mirroring present-continuous tense) give it a neatness which predisposes the reader to agree: it appears to epitomize Ben Grant's definition of aphorism, 'a short statement which encapsulates a truth'.[4] It has the unarguable elegance of, for instance, the quip by Seneca which Smith liked to quote: '*Fata nolentuem trahunt, volentem ducunt* (the fates drag the unwilling, the willing they lead)' ('What Poems Are Made Of', MA, 128), where the accomplished polish of the Latin rhyme and contrast imply that the line is making an irrefutable truth-claim.

But if we can identify a truth-claim in the line 'not waving but drowning', what good does it do for that amnesiac mind in which it echoes, forlornly? In Ackland's account, the line's hard rhetoric insists on its importance, but that rhetoric can never be penetrated; no revelation useful in the circumstances can be extracted. The line repeats precisely because it can never lead to resolution. It lingers in the mind, insistently, but does nothing helpful for the bewildered amnesiac, just as it did not aid Smith's original 'dead man'. Its imperious style promises truth, but never casts light on anything. This book finds in that paradoxical gesture of aphorism— revealing and withholding in the same moment, compulsively spoken though it changes nothing—an interpretative lens for Stevie Smith's writing. Aphorism, it argues, lets Smith showcase difficult feelings fully, in the same motion as it prevents them from being apprehended.

Smith's Aphoristics

> Oh no categories I pray.
> (Stevie Smith, 'No Categories!', CP, 294)

The word 'aphorism' derives from the Greek: ἀφορίζειν, 'to define', parsable as ἀπό ('off') and ὁρίζειν ('to set bounds').[5] It dates back to Hippocrates, whose *Aphorisms* (*c.* 400 BCE) sums up established rules for medical practice.[6] In the 1600s, Francis Bacon used aphorism in *The Advancement of Learning* (1605) to present scientific findings in the form of 'a knowledge broken', in little aphoristic snippets of insight, in order to refute an earlier model of science as complete and wholly

---

[2] Calvin Bedient, *Eight Contemporary Poets* (London: Oxford University Press, 1974), 140.
[3] Michael Horovitz, 'Of Absent Friends', in *In Search of Stevie Smith*, ed. Sanford Sternlicht (Syracuse: Syracuse University Press, 1991), 150.
[4] Ben Grant, *The Aphorism and Other Short Forms* (London and New York: Routledge, 2016), 1.
[5] 'aphorize, v,' OED Online, June 2017, Oxford University Press. http://www.oed.com/view/Entry/9152 (accessed 19 September 2017).
[6] See Joel E. Mann, *Hippocrates, On the Art of Medicine* (Leiden and Boston: Brill, 2012), 57–64.

known, and encourage further inquiry.[7] A century later, a separate German line of aphorism began to emerge through writers such as Georg Lichtenberg, Friedrich Nietzsche, Franz Kafka, and, later, Karl Kraus. German aphorism presents as an eccentric mode: speaking truth from the margins, refusing to participate in its social context.[8]

From one perspective, then, 'aphorism' refers to a series of particular traditions: the Hippocratic medical, the Baconian scientific, the German isolationist. These coexist with, and are at various times critically differentiated from, the satirical Renaissance epigram (such as those of John Donne, Ben Jonson, and Thomas More),[9] the French salon maxims of writers such as François de La Rochefoucauld,[10] the folk-proverb, and the seventeenth-century *pensées* of Blaise Pascal, as well as a host of forms occasionally discussed in opposition to aphorism: axioms,[11] dicta, riddles,[12] parables,[13] and slogans.[14] Yet these traditions—spanning social integration as well as solitary marginality—have influenced each other indelibly, which has given rise to the second position: that aphorism is a broad term encompassing all of these short forms. All of them, at various times, are asked to do each other's work. Gray differentiates maxim and aphorism, for instance, by suggesting that while the French maxim aims to win its author social acceptance and approval in the salon—embedding itself in the heart of society, a brilliant interpersonal glue—the German aphorism is an isolationist form: written independently of social context, and aiming to draw its reader out of the mainstream current of life.[15] Yet in style, tone, and purpose, the German aphorisms of Karl Kraus, Kafka, and Nietzsche in fact continually display the influence of maxim's sociable

---

[7] Francis Bacon, 'The Advancement of Learning', in *Francis Bacon: The Major Works*, ed. Brian Vickers (Oxford: Oxford University Press, 2002), 234–235.

[8] Richard T. Gray, *Constructive Destruction: Kafka's Aphorisms: Literary Tradition and Literary Transformation* (Tübingen: Niemeyer, 1987), 44.

[9] See, for instance, W. H. Auden and Louis Kronenberger, 'Foreword', in *The Faber Book of Aphorisms* (London: Faber and Faber, 1970), vii; for a refusal to distinguish between the forms, see John Dominic Crossan, *In Fragments: The Aphorisms of Jesus* (San Francisco: Harper & Row, 1983), 22. On Renaissance epigrams as offering an insider perspective, satirizing a particular context, see James Doelman, 'Epigrams and Political Satire in Early Stuart England', *Huntington Library Quarterly* 69, no. 1 (2006): 36. Auden and Kronenberger define the aphorism as stating a universal truth (in contrast to their view that epigrams need only be true of a single occasion). Despite this apparent strictness of definition, Auden and Kronenberger include a range of short texts (quotations from Woolf's diaries, for instance) which stretch their own terms, being extremely specific to a particular situation. The rules of aphorism, here as always, seem laid down only in order to be broken.

[10] The maxim's primary function is often held to be social integration; their second, the establishment of rules of conduct. Gray, 41–42; Barbara Spackman, 'Machiavelli and Maxims', *Yale French Studies* 77 (1990): 140.

[11] Grant, 57.

[12] Gary Saul Morson, 'The Aphorism: Fragments from the Breakdown of Reason', *New Literary History* 34, no. 3 (2003): 416, 413.

[13] See Jacobus Liebenberg, *The Language of the Kingdom and Jesus* (Berlin: Walter de Gruyter, 2001), 512.

[14] See Giorgio Agamben, *Infancy and History: On The Destruction of Experience*, trans. Liz Heron (London and New York: Verso, 2007), 17.

[15] Gray, 44.

4 STEVIE SMITH AND THE APHORISM

salon context.[16] Equally, the French maxims of La Rochefoucauld are in many cases dark, solitary, and uninstructive.[17] The eccentric, isolationist form of aphorism turns out to be more 'centric' than it appears, just as the apparently sociable maxim keeps drawing itself away from view.

Gary Saul Morson argues that aphorism and its variant forms have no single definition, and are in practice used in overlapping ways.[18] While this book unpacks Stevie Smith's particular relationship to individual variants—proverb, caption, and Romantic fragment, among others—I follow Morson here in using the term broadly. I understand aphorism inclusively: as writings which convey a dismissive sense of finality, whether through formal devices, arrangement on the page, social and literary context, or description by the author.

What unites these forms is a dependence upon style.[19] Beverly Coyle identifies the aphorism's regular deployment of formal devices which bolster its characteristic sense of 'closure ... finality and stability', including rhyme, metre, scansion, repetition, predicative sentence structure, unqualified assertion, and a lack of adjectives.[20] Aphorisms may not always be brief, expanding frequently beyond a single sentence.[21] But they tend as a rule to be self-contained,[22] though Jacques Derrida exaggerates when he notes, tongue in cheek, that aphorisms should be

---

[16] La Rochefoucauld's tendency to compare one's inner self and one's social self, and his diagnostic treatment of human qualities (displaying their unrecognized motivations clearly to view), emerges in several of Nietzsche's aphorisms: for instance, 'Man is more sensitive to contempt from others than to contempt from himself' (Friedrich Nietzsche, *Human, All Too Human*, trans. Marion Faber and Stephen Lehmann (London: Penguin, 1994), 242). See Alexander Nehamas, *Nietzsche: Life as Literature* (Cambridge, MA, and London: Harvard University Press, 1985), 14.

[17] For instance, 'It is hard to judge whether a straightforward, sincere, honorable deed has resulted from integrity or cleverness.' François de la Rochefoucauld, *Collected Maxims and Other Reflections*, trans. E. H. and A. M. Blackmore and Francine Giguère (Oxford: Oxford University Press, 2007), 49. See also Philip E. Lewis, *La Rochefoucauld: The Art of Abstraction* (Ithaca and London: Cornell University Press, 1977), 17 on the failure of La Rochefoucauld's maxims to provide direct moral guidance or commands, another attribute often used to define the form, as described in Spackman, 140.

[18] Morson, 409. Critics who conflate maxim and aphorism include Grant, 17; Mary J. Muratore, 'Deceived by Truth: The Maxim as a Discourse of Deception', in *La Princesse de Clèves*, *Zeitschrift für Französische Sprache und Literatur* 104 (1994): 30–31; Marion Faber, 'The Metamorphosis of the French Aphorism: La Rochefoucauld and Nietzsche', *Comparative Literature Studies* 23, no. 3 (1986): 209; Harold E. Pagliaro, 'Paradox in the Aphorisms of La Rochefoucauld and Some Representative English Followers', *PMLA* 79, no. 1 (1964): 42–50.; Simon Reader, 'Social Notes: Oscar Wilde, Francis Bacon, and the Medium of Aphorism', *Journal of Victorian Culture* 18, no. 4 (2013): 454.

[19] On aphorism defined in terms of a 'resistance to fluent reading', relying on antithesis, see J. P. Stern, *Lichtenberg: A Doctrine of Scattered Occasions* (Bloomington: Indiana University Press, 1959), 191; on the importance of stylistic density to aphorism, see Gray, 4. See also Nehamas, 23, on the importance of hyperbole to aphoristic style.

[20] Beverly Coyle, *A Thought to Be Rehearsed: Aphorism in Wallace Stevens's Poetry* (Ann Arbor: UMI Research Press, 1983), 2–8.

[21] On the association of aphorisms with brevity, see, to give just a few examples, John Fagg, *On the Cusp: Stephen Crane, George Bellows, and Modernism* (Tuscaloosa: The University of Alabama Press, 2009), 129; James Geary, *The World in a Phrase: A Brief History of the Aphorism* (New York: Bloomsbury, 2005), 9–11. On the capacity of aphorisms to grow to whatever size they like, without renouncing their genre, see Morson, 412.

[22] Alvin Snider, 'Francis Bacon and the Authority of Aphorism', *Prose Studies* 11, no. 2 (1988): 60.

entirely self-enclosed and never refer to one another.[23] Importantly, this gesture of enclosure comes as a corollary to another aspect of aphoristic form: its impression of summing everything up,[24] making a general declaration,[25] and, importantly, issuing a claim to be expressing some universal truth.[26] Aphorism's style revolves around the creation of a hardened carapace of language: a rhetorical unassailability which shuts the reader out even as it dictates to them. Its pithy announcement of what is generally true, in a way which disdains the need for any further information or explanation, is the work that the aphorism has come to claim for itself. Despite Bacon's use of aphorism to house uncertainty or fragmentation, its stiff imperious form nevertheless promises a striking, commanding communication of distilled wisdom, potted ready for memory and use.

Such a rhetorical gesture implies both sincerity and a confidence that communicable, useful truth exists. Both notions sit awkwardly within narratives of modernism. Aphorisms became key to modernist acts of self-definition in the early twentieth century: through, for instance, the aphoristic tendencies of modernist magazines,[27] the brief, cutting poems of D. H. Lawrence's *Pansies* (1929),[28] and the manifestos of movements such as Vorticism. Aphorism is a form ideal for declaring singularity and uniqueness, as an artistic movement must do; as its etymology suggests, aphorism offers a way of self-defining which involves a performance (albeit doubtful) of putting up boundaries, setting oneself apart—creating something hard and definite, rather than something which might softly dissolve into another movement or a crowd. These aphoristic experiments informed the careers of figures such as Ezra Pound and Wyndham Lewis, as they sought to establish their distinctiveness through their Vorticist phase and into the 1930s.[29] However, it is a critical commonplace to observe that the aphorisms in Vorticism's manifestos fail to yield the definitional uniqueness they seem to promise. Instead, their hard forms become board-game pieces, swapped in self-contradictory play

---

[23] Jacques Derrida, 'Fifty-two Aphorisms for a Foreword', in *Psyche: Inventions of the Other*, ed. Peggy Kamuf and Elizabeth Rottenberg, trans. Andrew Benjamin (Stanford: Stanford University Press, 2008), 2: 117–126, 121. The series's constituent aphorisms do refer to each other.

[24] Derrida, 124.

[25] See John Gross, ed., *The Oxford Book of Aphorisms* (Oxford: Oxford University Press, 1983), viii.

[26] See Fagg, 129.

[27] See Chris Mourant, 'We Moderns: Katherine Mansfield and Edwin Muir in the *New Age*', in *Aphoristic Modernity: 1880 to the Present*, ed. Kostas Boyiopoulos and Michael Shallcross (Leiden: Brill, 2020). Mourant argues that the *New Age* 'positioned the aphorism as a form synonymous with modernity', inviting young contributors to write aphorisms (94).

[28] Lawrence was a fundamental influence on Smith's 'aphoristic vein'; an early reviewer called her first collection *A Good Time Was Had By All* (1937), the 'feminine counterpart' of *Pansies* (G. W. Stonier, 'The Music Goes Round and Round', *New Statesman*, 17 April 1937). She copied snippets of Lawrence's writing into her reading notebooks, and afterwards adapted them for inclusion, unacknowledged, in *Novel on Yellow Paper* (*Novel*, 172).

[29] Peter Robinson, 'Aphoristic Gaps and Theories of the Image', in *Aphoristic Modernity*, 32. See also Alan Munton, '"You must remain broken up": Wyndham Lewis, Laughter and the Subjective Aphorism', in *Aphoristic Modernity*, 113–132.

6 STEVIE SMITH AND THE APHORISM

(alternately blasting and blessing the same things).[30] Poets like Robert Frost, in contrast, seem to draw less ironically on the aphorism's promise of compact, portable truth; as Leonard Diepeveen notes, they therefore occupy critically suspect places within a narrative of modernism which valorizes obscurity.[31] Texts such as Frost's 'Mending Wall' trade hard on the memorable resonance of their bookending aphorisms—'Something there is that doesn't love a wall', 'Good fences make good neighbors'—even as the substance of that poem pokes gentle fun at the idea of the all-purpose maxim.[32] Aphorism's penchant for repetition, rhyme, and pleasing rhythms makes it a seductive candidate for the poetic line. Yet poetry which steers too close to the aphorism's promise of communicative or rhetorical use, which makes too many deals with its apparent capacity to change minds or convey a philosophical truth, risks critical demotion to the status of propaganda or Sunday-school rhyme. Aphorism may deploy hard, insistent rhetoric, but modernist poetry's abstruseness and difficulty—hardness in another sense—works to exceed the aphorism's definitional promise of a contained, summed-up truth. Aphorism presents as a tool, in other words, in a particular way that high modernist poetry does not.

Scribbling little poems in the early 1930s, these already-complexed aphoristic tendencies pervaded Smith's work, as she sought to stake out artistic territory for herself. Reviewers marvelled at the two- to four-line 'epigram[s]' in her first collection *A Good Time Was Had By All* (1937), with *Granta* quoting examples of her 'freshness and incisiveness'.[33] Poems such as 'From the County Lunatic Asylum', 'Beware the Man' and 'Poet!' bite hard in their brevity:

> The people say that spiritism is a joke and a swizz,
> The Church that it is dangerous—not half it is. (CP, 32)

> Beware the man whose mouth is small
> For he'll give nothing and take all. (CP, 89)

> Poet, thou art dead and damned,
> That speaks upon no moral text.
> I bury one that babbled but;—
> Thou art the next. Thou art the next. (CP, 190)

This note of imperious pithiness stiffens Smith's rhetoric, even in longer poems. Her concluding lines often seal texts off with ringing aphoristic finality.

---

[30] *BLAST 1* (London: John Lane, 1914), 11, 22.

[31] On Frost's contested place within modernist literature, see Leonard Diepeveen, *The Difficulties of Modernism* (London and New York: Routledge, 2003), 189.

[32] Robert Frost, *The Poetry of Robert Frost*, ed. Edward Connery Lathem (London: Vintage, 2001), 33–34.

[33] P. G. B. K, *Granta* 46, 5 May 1937; the *TLS* also called her poem 'Alfred the Great' an 'epigram' ('Humour', *Times Literary Supplement*, 8 May 1937).

Ride he never so fast he'll not cast her off.

> ('Behind the Knight', CP, 265)

You hear the north wind riding fast past the window? He calls me.
Do you suppose I shall stay when I can go so easily?

> ('Lightly Bound', CP, 305)

And a devil's voice cried: Happy
Happy the dead.

> ('Mr Over', CP, 299)

Yes they will have a lord and it matters not who
Be he hollow as a drum he will do, do, do.

> ('The Leader', CP, 332)

Smith's aphoristic tendencies mesmerize, but also perplex. Her pronouncements seem at first to sit strangely alongside the irreverence, humour, and surrealism of so many of the rest of her poems, based as they often are around mishearings, japes, dancing, unnerving digressions, and sharp tonal twists. 'Not Waving but Drowning' describes a tragic death in comically deadpan tones:

> It must have been too cold for him his heart gave way,
> They said. (CP, 347)

These wild swerves of tone, subject, form, and mode characterize her whole output. No hierarchy of significance separates poems such as 'The Dedicated Dancing Bull and the Water Maid', a dramatic monologue spoken by a dancing bull; 'How do you see?', a lengthy, serious discursion on Christianity and its evils; and 'My Hat', a fantasy of escape from society via a flying hat. They all come jumbled in together—tragedy, laments, comedy, and song alike leavened by little sketchy doodles, presented as equally important, perpetually disrupting any sense of how Stevie Smith is to be read or interpreted. If aphorism 'encapsulates a truth', as Grant puts it, Smith's contexts can make it difficult for readers to locate or grasp that truth. We cling on to the hard bones of her memorable lines without knowing what they amount to collectively.

Stymied by this lack of any convincing and reassuring paradigm for Smith's writing, and faced with a chaotic mingling of the important and the unimportant, the reader can only pick out and hold on to scraps. Smith's work tends therefore to be conducted—as Rodney Ackland discovered—via small memorable phrases, like 'not waving but drowning'. This tendency holds across both her shorter and lengthier writing. In the *New Statesman*, G. W. Stonier contrasted *A Good Time Was Had By All* with the longer, free-flowing prose of *Novel on Yellow Paper*: this, he suggested, was 'her briefer, more caustic, aphoristic vein'.[34] As Stonier hints,

---

[34] Stonier, 643.

8 STEVIE SMITH AND THE APHORISM

Smith does have veins other than the aphoristic, and when she slits them they tend to bleed right out. Many of her later poems spill over multiple pages, and three full-length novels testify to her ability to sustain textual duration. Yet the sense of her as an essentially, or most characteristically, epigrammatic or aphoristic writer remains. Elizabeth Bowen offers an explanation in a review of Smith's novel *The Holiday* (1949). Though *The Holiday* is a full-length novel, Bowen remarks that several of the protagonist Celia's reflections 'might well be cut out and pasted up on walls'. The remarks have, in other words, the 'portability and detachability' which John Fagg associates with the aphorism, allowing the text to be lifted and recycled into different contexts.[35] A note of flusteredness in the face of wayward genre, or slight irony, emerges when Bowen observes, '"The Holiday" being a novel, not a book of *pensées*, it behoves the reviewer to give some idea of set-out and plot'.[36] Bowen hints that *The Holiday* resists this treatment; that it tends always towards the status of compendium of short-texts. What lingers in the reader's mind, after finishing this temporally and narratively disjointed novel, are the pithy observations and resounding one-liners:

> So Tiny, I cry, listen, Tiny, love is everything, it is the only thing, one looks for it. Yes, everybody is hankering after it and whining. This hunger we have is a good thing, it is the long shin bone that shows the child will grow tall.
>
> (*Holiday*, 50)

> Caz, I cry, Caz. How long will the post-war last, Caz, shall we win the post-war, how does it go?
>
> (*Holiday*, 90)

So by 1963, a review of Smith's *Selected Poems* in *The Tablet* considers the selection with confident, condescending approval: the book includes 'sufficient of the really dotty epigrams to satisfy the most exigent'.[37] If you are a Stevie Smith fan, in other words—a properly dedicated fan—then you will want what is most characteristic and opinion-dividing of her work: namely, 'the really dotty epigrams', the texts which mark themselves most clearly as eccentric. This 'dottiness' can be prized as collectable and worth preserving. John Gross includes two of Smith's short poems in *The Oxford Book of Aphorisms*:

> Ceux qui luttent ce sont ceux qui vivent,
> And down here they luttent a very great deal indeed.

---

[35] Fagg, 136.
[36] Elizabeth Bowen, 'Bright-Plumaged Brood', *The Tatler and Bystander*, 5 October 1949, 33.
[37] 'Angle Shot', *The Tablet* 217, 15 June 1963, 656.

But if life be the desideratum, why grieve, ils vivent.
STEVIE SMITH, 'Ceux qui luttent ... ', *The Frog Prince*, 1966

Sin recognized—but that—may keep us humble,
But oh, it keeps us nasty.
STEVIE SMITH, 'Recognition not Enough', *Selected Poems,*
1964[38]

And Geoffrey Grigson includes five of Smith's poems in *The Faber Book of Epigrams and Epitaphs* (1977), including 'This Englishwoman':

This Englishwoman is so refined
She has no bosom and no behind.[39]

Stevie Smith, then, is a poet who tends to be heard as aphoristic, with even her longer writing remembered that way, or surviving that way.

Smith writes always in response to the question of brevity—whether to hold short or run long, as I'll suggest in the final chapter—and the communicative limits that either choice entails. For if aphoristic brevity can offer Smith penetration and charisma—the spellbinding fascination conferred by confident assertion—it can also become a reason not to take her seriously. Even at their most dignified, aphorisms often seem funny. Their declarations of certainty seem either suspect or pompous, in need of deflation, or camp in their casual privileging of form over content.[40] Aphorism as a form easily accommodates absurdity, play, the tongue-in-cheek, and the poker-face.[41] It is funny because of its powerful allegiance to seriousness; its brief but earnest insistence on itself transforms almost immediately into humour.

Stevie Smith's work at the publisher Pearson's embedded her in a journalistic tradition which emphasized this perpetual precarious aphoristic wobble

---

[38] Gross, *Oxford Book of Aphorisms*, 30, 198.
[39] Geoffrey Grigson, ed. *The Faber Book of Epigrams and Epitaphs* (London: Faber & Faber, 1977), 232–233.
[40] Thus Gary Saul Morson and Jacques Derrida write their essays on aphorism in aphorisms, capitalizing for humour on the form's capacity for self-contradiction and urbane slickness. Morson, 409–429; Derrida, 117–126. The relationship can reverse: if aphorism tends towards the camp, the camp equally tends towards the verbal artistry, memorable speech and resistance to direct knowing associated, as John Gross suggests (*Oxford Book of Aphorisms*, viii), with the aphoristic. So Susan Sontag writes her 'Notes on "Camp"' in aphorisms, and other writers on camp (Allan Pero, for instance) have followed suit (Susan Sontag, 'Notes on "Camp"', in *Against Interpretation* (London: Vintage, 2001), 275–292; Allan Pero, 'A Fugue on Camp', *Modernism/modernity* 23, no. 1 (2016): 28–36).
[41] The humour of aphorism—based on brevity, pomposity, and surprise—underpins the Victorian tradition of quick comic verse, represented by texts such as Harry Graham's *Ruthless Rhymes for Heartless Homes* (1899), Edward Lear's limericks, and Hilaire Belloc's cautionary tales. This comic tradition offers a rich touchpoint for Smith's work. In her last novel *The Holiday* (1949), for instance, she invokes Lear's man of Thermopylae who never did anything properly (*Holiday*, 127); she also misquotes Belloc's 'Henry King' in a letter to Rachel Marshall in 1964: 'I fear it will be a case of "They murmured as they took their fees, there is no cure for this disease"', (MA, 312).

10 STEVIE SMITH AND THE APHORISM

towards comedy.[42] 'Snippet journalism' magazines such as *Tit-Bits*—the weekly magazine launched in 1881, composed of extracts from other books, newspapers, and periodicals—took serious aphoristic texts out of their sober habits and habitats, and repositioned them in contexts where their insistent self-announcements became, if not quaint, at least less thunderously resounding. Imitators such as *Rare Bits* levelled different kinds of short texts into mutually equivalent diversions, placing quotations, jokes, proverbs, and howlers on an equal footing:[43]

> Never confide in a young man—new pails leak. Never tell your secret to the aged—old doors seldom shut closely.
>
> ---
>
> 'Come here, Johnny, and tell me what the four seasons are.'—Young Prodigy: 'Pepper, salt, mustard, and vinegar.'[44]

Pearson's participated in this tradition, as it stretched into the twentieth century. *Pearson's Weekly,* for instance, had as its first pages in the early 1920s a tissue of jokes and anecdotes in the *Tit-Bits* tradition:

> LADY: 'Are you the same man who ate my mince-pie last week?'
> TRAMP: 'No, mum. I'll never be th' same man again!'[45]

Smith's pithy poems emerged against this journalistic backdrop. While in one breath, her reviewers praised her characteristic epigrams, in another they acknowledged that brevity might become disposability. A poem like 'All Things Pass' demonstrates the boundary-effects which Beverly Coyle sees as fundamental to the aphorism:[46]

---

[42] Smith's background in this magazine world positions her alongside Dorothy Parker, whose 'hard-boiled' quips Louis MacNeice compared to Smith's own poems (Louis MacNeice, *Modern Poetry* (Oxford: Oxford University Press, 1938), 187. Like Smith, Parker had to earn her living soon after leaving school: both writers found employment in the publishing industry. While Smith did secretarial work, Parker wrote brief, witty captions at *Vogue* and *Vanity Fair*—influenced, perhaps, by La Rochefoucald, whose maxims she had discovered at school (Arthur F. Kinney, *Dorothy Parker* (Boston: Twayne, 1978), 27–28). Parker's poetry bears the marks of this aphoristic training. Its quick brevity casts the heavy into flippancy and lightness, as in her sarcastically named, four-line 'Two-Volume Novel'. Smith read Parker's stories, and acknowledged that their chatty colloquial style influenced *Novel on Yellow Paper* (Jack Barbera and William McBrien, *Stevie: A Biography of Stevie Smith* (London: Macmillan, 1986), 75; Frances Spalding, *Stevie Smith: A Critical Biography* (London: Faber and Faber, 1988), 111; Kay Dick, *Ivy and Stevie* (London: Allison & Busby, 1983), 73).

[43] On the history of *Tit-Bits*, see Bob Nicholson, 'Jonathan's Jokes: American Humour in the Late-Victorian Press', *Media History* 18, no. 1 (2012): 38. The practice of including snippets predated *Tit-Bits*, whose first issue excused its practices by claiming 'There is scarcely a newspaper which does not give some extracts'; the novelty resided in the extent of *Tit-Bits*' reliance on the technique. 'Tit-Bits', *Tit-Bits* 1, 22 October 1881, 1.

[44] *Rare Bits* 36, 5 August 1882.

[45] *Pearson's Weekly* 1539, 10 January 1920.

[46] Coyle, 3.

All things pass
Love and mankind is grass. (CP, 53)

The stressed, monosyllabic rhyme binds the poem into a sealed, conclusive-sounding couplet; the predicative structure sweeps away the possibility of disagreement. Smith's superlative 'all', the poem's very first word, underlines the text's claim to aphoristic irrefutability. Yet, looking back at her career in the sixties, a review of *Selected Poems* spoke of her 'casual throwaway lines'.[47] The tiny poem 'Pearl', for instance, appeared in *The Frog Prince and Other Poems* in 1966:

Then cried the American poet where she lay supine:
'My name is Purrel; I was caast before swine'. (CP, 530)

Like the joke, the poem is 'throwaway': it elicits only a moment of attention and a (very) weak laugh before being 'caast' aside. Reviewing *The Frog Prince*, Bernard Bergonzi thought the book had 'strong hints of the cracker-motto',[48] and a review in the *Spectator* noted the 'lines suitable for a Christmas cracker'.[49] Stevie Smith's poetry becomes something to be read with interest, laughed (or groaned) at, and then thrown away without further thought.

The disposability of Smith's poems does not prevent them, for her reviewers, from being interesting. John Gross acknowledged this in his review of *The Frog Prince,* describing Smith's writing as 'poems, squibs, jottings, thumbnail elegies, call them what you will'. For Gross, her poems are equally small explosive 'squibs', all bright light and noise and no lasting substance, and 'thumbnail elegies', exquisitely condensed monuments to something lost.[50] They can be both earth-shaking and transient.

Usefulness, Eccentricity, and the Aphorism

Smith's unsettling, ambivalent aphoristic bent was fascinating enough to catch the eye of David Wright, coeditor of the literary magazine *X: A Quarterly Review,* which ran from 1959 to 1962. In an undated letter, he asked Smith:

to contribute ... aphorisms being to do with the nature of poetry & the business of writing it. Or if not aphorisms, pensees [sic] ... A few words from practising poets

---

[47] 'Wastrels, Pirates, Poets in Paperbacks', *San Francisco News-Call Bulletin*, 6 June 1964.
[48] Bernard Bergonzi, 'Tones of Voice', *The Guardian*, 16 December 1966.
[49] C. B. Cox, 'Scots and English', *Spectator*, 17 February 1967.
[50] John Gross, 'Ruthless Rhymes', *Observer*, 11 December 1966. On aphorism and the belated or lost, see Chapter Two.

12   STEVIE SMITH AND THE APHORISM

would do much to dispel the mystic boredom woven about the whole subject of Poetrah by the New Critics and all the other hardworking little dons.[51]

Smith obliged Wright with a series of aphorisms, which he published in March 1960. These texts embody the declarative tone of absolute finality which often identifies an aphorism; the superlatives ('All', 'at all'); the characteristic brevity; the repetition of an imperious 'is' which permits no argument:

> Poetry is like a strong explosion in the sky. She makes a mushroom shape of terror and drops to the ground with a strong infection. Also she is a strong way out. The human creature is alone in his carapace. Poetry is a strong way out ...
> ... Poetry is very strong and never has any kindness at all. She is Thetis and Hermes, the Angel, the white horse and the landscape. All Poetry has to do is to make a strong communication. All the poet has to do is to listen. The poet is not an important fellow. There will always be another poet.[52]

Despite their imperious tone, Smith's aphorisms in fact stress her own insignificance, her own humble relegation as a poet to society's margins. 'The poet is not an important fellow.' Smith reiterates this view in a 1961 interview by Peter Orr:

> [INTERVIEWER]: So you don't think that the poet should occupy a unique or favored place in society?
> SMITH: No, I don't think he should at all. I think he should be just made to get on with his writing: put in a room with pencils and pen or a typewriter; and then if his poems are no good, then he must just be thrown out, I think.[53]

Smith's severity appears puzzling: such enforced solitude and peace (put out of the way, in a room of one's own) seem like a form of special treatment, for which a poet might be grateful. However, being out of the run of life, detached and solitary, represents for Smith a way of being ordinary. Spending her life with her aunt, unmarried, commuting into London from the suburbs to work as a secretary, writing in her dead office hours, Smith lived not exactly a double life, but one which disrupts the opposition between the sparkling and the humdrum, the invisibly normal and the visibly, strikingly unusual.[54] She was born in unromantic Hull,

---

[51] Letter from David Wright to Stevie Smith, Series 1, Box 11, Folder 7, Stevie Smith papers, 1924–1970. Coll. No. 1976.012. McFarlin Library. Department of Special Collections and University Archives. The University of Tulsa.

[52] Vernon Watkins, Patrick Kavanagh, Hugh MacDiarmid, Stevie Smith, 'Poets on Poetry', in *An Anthology from X: A Quarterly Review of Literature and the Arts, 1959–1962*, ed. David Wright (Oxford: Oxford University Press, 1988), 68–69.

[53] Peter Orr, 'Stevie Smith', in *In Search of Stevie Smith*, 37.

[54] Geographically, the suburb, where Smith lived since she was three, stands as a symbol of this paradox: a space out of (what is viewed as) the main sway of life, which simultaneously represents

but spent most of her life just outside London; she was a middle-class woman who had experienced both privilege and suffering; she maintained both a dull secretarial job and a sparkling literary correspondence. This was both an unexceptional private life and an eccentric one: literally off-centre, outside central London, but still in greater London; different from the lives her literary friends lived, but by no means unusual for the time. Romantically, too, hers was a common story imagined as outlandish, because it existed outside the norms of the heterosexual romance narratives which Smith's publishing company churned out in magazines such as *Peg's Paper*. While the women in these magazine stories found husbands and generated lovely '*kiddies*' (*Novel*, 115), Smith broke off her engagement to Eric Armitage, and lived unmarried with her aunt.

Instead of marriage, she opted for a lifelong public and private performance. Many poets do. But while Edith Sitwell, for instance, based her theatricality around exaggeratedly ornamental trappings, Smith's costume was more mundane, tending in the latter part of her life towards outfits such as tunic dresses with white stockings.[55] Getting up on stage and singing her poems in the 1960s, in what John Gross called 'a queer, flat voice',[56] off-key and unsettling, Smith drew her weirdness for viewers, contradictorily, from the very everyday image she evoked: the dutiful little girl doing her school performance piece.[57] Her gesture is striking, but nevertheless constitutes itself through a trope so quotidian as to efface itself from vision.

Smith's interplay between being special and eccentric, and being ordinary, average, invisible—and in fact deriving that eccentricity from a particular kind of performative normality, an inconsequentiality which refuses to sustain its own grandeur—runs through her poetry. It can be critically tempting, since 'eccentric' is a loaded and gendered word, to argue that Smith is not eccentric but integrated into her social and poetic milieu.[58] On the contrary, her integration and her eccentricity produce each other, and their mutuality provides the basis for her complex poetics. Edith Sitwell offered a model for this kind of eccentricity in

---

a ground-zero of the normal. Palmers Green (disguised as 'Syler's Green' and 'Bottle Green') enters her poems, novels, and essays (see *Novel*, 110; Stevie Smith, 'Syler's Green', *MA*, 83–99); it lets Smith position herself outside the prominent and public, mirroring for Kristin Bluemel her 'out-of-place' persona and writing (Kristin Bluemel, '"Suburbs are not so bad I think": Stevie Smith's Problem of Place in 1930s and '40s London', *Iowa Journal of Cultural Studies* 3, no. 1 (2003): 104. See also Simon Dentith, 'Thirties Poetry and the Landscape of Suburbia', in *Rewriting the Thirties: Modernism and After*, ed. Keith Williams and Steven Matthews (London and New York: Longman, 1997), 120, and Ged Pope, *Reading London's Suburbs: From Charles Dickens to Zadie Smith* (London: Palgrave Macmillan, 2015), 112).

[55] Barbera and McBrien, 251.

[56] Gross, 'Ruthless Rhymes', 26.

[57] Spalding quotes Seamus Heaney's impression of Smith's performance as 'an embarrassed party-piece by a child half-way between tears and giggles'. Spalding, 293.

[58] Laura Severin, *Poetry Off the Page: Twentieth-Century British Women Poets in Performance* (Farnham: Ashgate, 2004), 46.

English Eccentrics (1933) (published three years before Smith's first novel), where it comes to seem simply 'the Ordinary carried to a high degree of ... perfection.'[59]

This derivation of eccentricity from ordinariness describes, as I'll suggest in a moment, the workings of aphorism. It also underlies Stevie Smith and her work. Smith manages her relationships with other poets to make herself seem ordinary, just 'another poet' visibly influenced by a stream of other writers, past and present.[60] Nevertheless, even as her work positions her in a tradition, Smith situates her poetry as different and eccentric. Will May outlines how Smith establishes her connection with the illustrated nonsense poetry of Edward Lear only in order to minimize it, in a bid to highlight her own uniqueness.[61] On other occasions, Smith employs conventional verse forms and imagery, inhabiting Victorian and Modern styles, but mingles these with the casually grisly, out-of-place, or colloquial. In 'The Bereaved Swan', she interrupts Tennysonian melancholy by comparing the titular swan to 'a cake / Of soap' (CP, 35). The outlandish occupies the same space as the nondescript, the two absorbed so thoroughly into each other that our capacity to notice the disjunction is disrupted.[62]

Both Smith's life and Smith's work, then, participate at once in the eccentric and in the average, the prominently displayed and the modestly effaced. Her self-portrayal as eccentric, as *sui generis*, derives from the normality at the heart of eccentricity itself. Eccentricity becomes a stiffening into or of oneself, the normal made unusually prominent: into, as Sitwell puts it, a 'rigid, and even splendid, attitude of Death, some exaggeration of the attitudes common to Life.'[63] When ordinary life is exaggerated, it hardens into an austerely magnificent gesture.

This, crucially, is the self-insistent thrust which underlies aphoristic utterance: ossifying into a nugget of hard, stubborn language. Aphoristic declarations originate from an impulse towards eccentricity: to fully inhabit a posture which may be socially alarming (or at least, may set one apart), but to do it safely. The eccentric

---

[59] Edith Sitwell, *English Eccentrics* (London: The Folio Society, 1994), 4. Sitwell's own performances of eccentricity depended strongly on the aristocratic. Her singular appearance and costume were in themselves anything but ordinary (see Victoria Glendinning, *Edith Sitwell: A Unicorn Among Lions* (London: Phoenix, 1993), 52). But when Sitwell depicted the phenomenon in *English Eccentrics*, a book of brief biographies of eccentric characters, she did not produce an eccentric volume. Making no claim to originality, it situates itself comfortably in the nineteenth century's tradition of eccentric biographies (see Richard Greene, *Edith Sitwell: Avant-Garde Poet, English Genius* (London: Virago, 2011), 226).

[60] On Smith's engagement with Movement poetry, see Alice Ferrebe, *Literature of the 1950s: Good, Brave Causes* (Edinburgh: Edinburgh University Press, 2012), 110; as representative of women's post-war writing, see Jane Dowson and Alice Entwistle, *A History of Twentieth-Century British Women's Poetry* (Cambridge: Cambridge University Press, 2005), 107. See Paul Muldoon, *The End of the Poem: Oxford Lectures on Poetry* (London: Faber & Faber, 2006), 141–153, on powerful echoes of Keats, Hardy, and Edward Thomas in Smith's writing.

[61] Will May, 'Drawing Away from Lear: Stevie Smith's Deceitful Echo', in *Edward Lear and the Play of Poetry*, ed. James Williams and Matthew Bevis (Oxford: Oxford University Press, 2016), 316–338.

[62] See Noreen Masud, '"Ach ja": Stevie Smith's Escheresque Metamorphoses', *Cambridge Quarterly* 45, no. 3 (2016): 251.

[63] Sitwell, 4.

can be indulgently laughed at; the aphorism can earn a respectful nod before the topic is changed. For certain subject positions, the aphorism's eccentricity offers not powerful dictation but self-protection: one may gloriously declare a conviction, unconcerned how it may be received. Issued by an 'ex-centric' individual, on the margins which are both vantage-point and site of invisibility, the aphorism in fact makes a declaration too sonorous, too strange and risky and weighty, to be fully heard.

Smith's poems of all lengths often insist heavily on the weight of their own announcements, delineating a message or a sentiment clearly and passionately. 'How Cruel is the Story of Eve' is starkly tendentious in its delivery of an opinion:

> How cruel is the story of Eve
> What responsibility
> It has in history
> For cruelty.
> ...
> Ah what cruelty,
> In history
> What misery.
> ...
> It is only a legend
> You say? But what
> Is the meaning of the legend
> If not
> To give blame to women most
> And most punishment? (CP, 556–558)

Yet what is the relationship of that powerful rhetoric to its audience? The poem takes and inhabits a position, for three pages, without doing much more than insisting on its own case. But the poem signals that it is untroubled about its reception. All objections have been foreseen and dealt with; the 'you' addressed is invoked and swept aside in rebuttal. The speaker may simply nod and agree with herself, again and again: 'Ah what cruelty', 'Oh what cruelty', 'Oh what cruelty' (CP, 556–557). The text is self-sufficient. Its bluster and power are untrammelled, and can be, precisely because they are undirected, or directed at a slant (like the safely sheathed sword in the illustration) to their audience. Smith has placed significant and unignorable rhetorical fuel behind the statement of opinion in this poem, but it does not quite hit home.

It is in religious poems like this that Smith is most clearly propositional in her statement of an authoritative perspective, of the sort that we associate with the content of aphorisms:

When we want to think of God, is there nothing which turns us aside, tempts us to think of other things? All that is bad, and it is born with us.

(Pascal)[64]

People are most dishonest in relation to their god: he *must* not sin!

(Nietzsche)[65]

Pascal and Nietzsche's aphorisms state their content lucidly, in short and emphatic words. Yet as Smith's poems take a similarly clear position, they further supply a clue to what her propositional statements might be doing:

There is a god in whom I do not believe
Yet to this god my love stretches,
This god whom I do not believe in is
My whole life. My life and I am his.

('God the Eater', CP, 390)

'God the Eater' adopts, and describes the adoption of, a position with serious and ardent dedication: the act of loving a god and devoting everything imaginable to his service. As it does so, it sweeps aside the very grounds on which it stands. The speaker states that there is a god, and also that she does not believe in him. Neither fact negates the other. Smith's speaker actively and baldly takes up a position which she understands to be invalid, which cannot be justified or argued for, and inhabits it with absolute commitment. She is indifferent to her reception, to any audience which might reason with her. What matters is the *shape* of that position, its rhetorical shell and posture.

Such rhetorical stiffening is everywhere in Smith's writing. It is particularly observable in her aphoristic moments, with their hard, stylized language. As a declaration, the aphorism is rigid, splendid and deathly, insisting on its own urgent importance even as its absolutist tone tips it over into absurdity. Take, for instance, the aphoristic opening to Smith's poem 'Parents': 'Parents who can barely afford it / Should not send their children to public schools ill will reward it' (CP, 408). Even without those comic rhymes, the lines balance on the edge of ridiculousness, because of that emphatic, doom-laden, archaic warning: 'ill will reward it'. Stiff, absolute statements encode their own bathos.

This exaggerated self-insistence of the aphorism, so uncompromising as to be absurd, identifies Smith's ec-/ex-centric drawings, lurking in the margins of her texts. Splayed on the ground or tragically posed, hands outspread, mouth open, her

---

[64] Blaise Pascal, *Pensées and Other Writings*, trans. Honor Levi, ed. Anthony Levi (Oxford: Oxford World's Classics, 1999), 7.
[65] Friedrich Nietzsche, *Beyond Good and Evil*, ed. and trans. Marion Faber (Oxford: Oxford University Press, 1998), 58.

Figure I.1 Gesturing figure, 'How Cruel is the Story of Eve'. Stevie Smith, *The Collected Poems and Drawings of Stevie Smith*, ed. Will May (London: Faber & Faber, 2015), 557. By permission of Faber and Faber Ltd and New Directions Publishing Corp.

melancholy doodled figures embody stiff postures of silent lament or exclamation. 'How Cruel is the Story of Eve' (see Figure I.1) backs itself up with an indignantly tearful and gesturing figure sketched alongside it: declarative, passionate, but eccentric enough to be dismissed as merely diverting.

Such figures (see Figures I.2 and I.3, for example) abound in *Some Are More Human Than Others* (1958), Smith's book of drawings captioned with pithy, frequently aphoristic lines. Her strange, often big-hatted characters inhabit postures—raised hands, narrow eyes, imperious glares, and bodies surrendered wholly to a sentiment—which mirror, in their rigid dignity, aphoristic statements which brook no disagreement.

The remarks these dowdy but self-possessed characters deliver are as grand and as absurd as Smith's own poems, calling attention to themselves with the over-weighted brevity of the aphorism.[66] In the second captioned drawing, gravity topples into comedy: 'Love is everything. One looks for it.' The line is a version of

---

[66] See Chapter Four on the difficulty of attributing these lines uncomplicatedly to the figures in the drawings.

Figure I.2 'Moi, c'est moralement que j'ai mes élégances—' Stevie Smith, *Some Are More Human Than Others* (London: Peter Owen, 1990). © Stevie Smith 1958. Copyright © James MacGibbon 1989. Reprinted by permission of Faber and Faber Ltd and New Directions Publishing Corp.

Figure I.3 'Love is everything'. Stevie Smith, *Some Are More Human Than Others* (London: Peter Owen, 1990). © Stevie Smith 1958. Copyright © James MacGibbon 1989. Reprinted by permission of Faber and Faber Ltd and New Directions Publishing Corp.

one of Celia's aphoristic laments in *The Holiday*, quoted above: 'Tiny, I cry, listen, Tiny, love is everything, it is the only thing, one looks for it' (*Holiday*, 50). As in the novel, the line-as-caption insists seriously on its own urgency. The pithy interjection seems to issue from a place of supreme, authoritative isolation, distancing itself from the crowd as it ostensibly addresses them. Nevertheless, the solitary drawn figure's waving legs, encased in schoolgirl knee-socks, undercut this grandeur absurdly. Smith's inclusion of the drawing guides her readers to notice how the urgent, emotional lament dissipates its own force. It exaggerates its lofty, austere insistence into an excess which is quotidian (the overwrought cry of the adolescent) and embarrassing. Therefore it is ignorable. Its affective appeal has inscribed itself too fervently, and has lost the right to be heard. The reader turns the page to the next image.

These aphoristic captions stage-manage a cancellation of embarrassing emotions, so highly emphasized that they sink under the weight of their own insistence. Eccentricity can consist of giving oneself wholeheartedly to the normal: embracing one's role as 'not an important fellow' so strongly that one stands out starkly. And Stevie Smith, as the next section will suggest, arranges her aphorisms in X to magnify the deep and paradoxical inhabitation of the neutralized quotidian normal by the eccentric (and the) aphorism.

'Strong Communication': Foregrounding the Aphorism's Internal Contradiction

In his letter to Smith, requesting some aphorisms, Wright imagines her aphorisms silencing 'all the ... hardworking little dons', whose industry conjures only a miasma of 'mystic boredom'. Aphorisms, in this imaginary, cut through and 'dispel' that cloud of waffle. With their incisive 'few words', they seem to clear spaces around them, in which they can resound in exquisite solitude.

Yet in the piece she writes for him, Smith makes it her business to complicate the capacity of her own rhetorical gestures to resound with convincing force. A broader look at X: A Quarterly Review shows that Smith sabotages the aphorism's emphatic solitude, in a treatment of the form which differs starkly from her contemporaries. In the March 1960 issue of X, David Wright also published aphorisms by Vernon Watkins, Hugh MacDiarmid, and Patrick Kavanagh; their contrast with Smith's work highlights the particularity of her aphoristic project. Vernon Watkins, for instance, takes seriously the propensity of aphorism to resound in silence. He spaces his short one- or two-line units across the page, presenting each separately:

Natural speech may be excellent, but who will remember it unless it is allied to something artificial, to a particular order of music?

Criticism projects its high tone, its flattering responses, but of what man-made echo does the mind not weary, as it turns endlessly round the Earth?[67]

Patrick Kavanagh's 'aphorisms' are longer than Watkins', but still divided by white space. Hugh MacDiarmid alternates between longer musings and aphorisms as

---

[67] Watkins, Kavanagh, MacDiarmid, Smith, 64.

20 STEVIE SMITH AND THE APHORISM

short as 'Deeper than opinions lies the sentiment that predetermines opinion'.[68] Stevie Smith's aphorisms (or pensées) are the shortest and most emphatic of all. Unlike the other poets, however, she arranges her texts in almost completely continuous prose.

> All Poetry has to do is to make a strong communication. All the poet has to do is to listen. The poet is not an important fellow. There will always be another poet.[69]

In her presentation of these aphorisms as a prose passage, Smith disowns their capacity to resound authoritatively in solitude. She eliminates the white space which usually frames and privileges an aphorism, so that one of her aphorisms immediately supplants another.[70] Allowing no airy-fairy nonsense or 'mystic boredom' from pretentiously over-admiring critics, Smith hurries us along, forces us to go on to the next aphorism before we have a chance to pause and digest the first. She dulls the impact of her own texts, even as they express painful feelings around despair, escape, and self-criticism. Like the poets she describes, her aphorisms do not seem to be important fellows. There will always, she insists, be another aphorism.

What makes this hurrying, embarrassed gesture so opaque is that in themselves, Smith's aphorisms in X are absolutely assertive. They communicate their points in brusque nuggets. These are not, in other words, texts which apologize for themselves; they fully inhabit the imperious, compelling communication which their aphoristic form permits. Smith's aphorisms are hard pieces of language which insist rhetorically on themselves, and on their own survival. Why, then, do they whisk themselves so quickly away, one allowing the next to replace it without pause? Why might a text frame itself as at once crucially important and not worth attending to?

Each aphorism in Smith's piece says something explosive which is at the same time unimportant and replaceable, as the next one appears immediately afterwards without separation by white space. They gesture towards an emphatic significance, which nevertheless vanishes too quickly into the textual crowd. That *overt* challenge to aphorism's claim to resound—to echo emphatically and powerfully in its frame of empty space—can take many forms in Smith's work. It may involve an elimination of white spaces, as in X; at other times, it involves inane statements presented with aphoristic finality (see Chapter 1) burial in longer texts

---

[68] Watkins, Kavanagh, MacDiarmid, Smith, 63.

[69] Watkins, Kavanagh, MacDiarmid, Smith, 69.

[70] On the significance of the white space surrounding an aphorism, see, for instance, Clare Kennedy, *Paradox, Aphorism and Desire in Novalis and Derrida* (London: MHRA, 2008), 80; Morson, 423; Grant, 55; Spackman, 152.

(see Chapter 2), acts of misuse (see Chapter 3), unsettling text-picture couplings (see Chapter 4) and incongruous poetic continuations (as Chapter 5 suggests). It may involve a modification of pompous authority through humorous or Ogden-Nash-esque rhymes, jaunty or mismatched metrical choices, as in the examples below:

> Man is a spirit. This the poor flesh knows,
> Yet serves him well for host when the wind blows,
> Why should this guest go wrinkling up his nose?
>
> ('Man is a Spirit', CP, 271)

> Parents who can barely afford it
> Should not send their children to public schools ill will reward it
>
> ('Parents', CP, 408)

I want to emphasize, however, that in these examples and in *X*, it is not that Smith undercuts the 'authoritative' aphorism. Witty flourishes of devices such as rhyme, as showcased in 'Man is a Spirit', are key to the workings of many aphorisms. Rather, Smith's arrangement of aphorisms in *X* highlights the aphorism's inherent doubleness, in a way that Watkins, Kavanagh, and MacDiarmid do not. Aphorism already builds that undercutting gesture into its own form, because its slickness, polish, and self-sufficiency (as I will suggest in Chapter 1) make the text just as elusive as it is didactic. Aphorism gives the impression of whisking itself away before it has been fully apprehended or unpacked. The aphoristic resides in making full revelation unreceivable by its reader—as something unnecessary, or redundant, or even socially embarrassing—even as it signals, as a point taken for granted, that such revelation is entirely possible, indeed has already been bestowed, and the reader should earnestly seek it. I stress firstly this double motion (sending its reader after something unfindable), and secondly the fact that very often, with the aphoristic short text, there is nothing more to find than what is there—that the form of the aphorism permits and enables an openness which, strangely, the form of the aphorism prevents us from apprehending. Its very slickness of style cauterizes our exegetical impulse even as it seems to invite it.

This aesthetic emerges in the work of some of the twentieth century's most significant aphorists. Although Nietzsche positions exegesis as fundamental to a reading of the aphorism in *On The Genealogy of Morals* (1887),[71] his aphorisms in *Beyond Good and Evil* (1886) (making the most of the aphorism's capacity to accommodate different perspectives) can express a weariness at the core of deep understanding, an indifference to exegetical effort:

---

[71] Friedrich Nietzsche, *On The Genealogy of Morals*, trans. Douglas Smith (Oxford: Oxford University Press, 1996), 10.

22 STEVIE SMITH AND THE APHORISM

Once a matter has been clarified it no longer concerns us.[72]

We no longer love our knowledge enough, once we have communicated it.[73]

Developing his thoughts on reading Nietzsche in *Minima Moralia* (1951), Theodor Adorno recasts this aphoristic withholding of full discursion, which is also a refusal of the responsibility of urgent, powerful, and world-changing communication, as a moral imperative. *Minima Moralia* consists of a series of short texts which Adorno himself calls aphorisms in his dedication, although most are several sentences long.[74] Many were written during Adorno's exile from Germany, before and during the Second World War: they originate from, reflect on and embody, in the phrase of the subtitle, a 'damaged life'. Adorno uses aphorisms as many Modernist writers used fragments: to represent a shattered world which resists cohesion.[75] Their 'disconnected and non-binding character' allows Adorno to reject 'explicit theoretical cohesion', in favour of subjective experience as a lens on philosophy.[76] Yet this does not entail an aimless laying out of scraps of writing which may or may not possess value. Adorno dwells on the social responsibilities of short-form writing in his reflections on Anatole France's *Jardin d' Épicure*:

> ... one cannot help feeling [when reading France], despite gratitude for enlightenment dispensed, an uneasiness ... It stems from the contemplative leisureliness, the sermonizing, however sporadic, the indulgently raised forefinger. The critical content of the thought is belied by that air of having all the time in the world ...

> His mode of delivery contains, beneath the poised humanity, a hidden violence: he can afford to talk in this way because no-one interrupts the master.

> ... the impossibility of uttering thoughts without arrogance, without trespassing on the time of others. The most urgent need of exposition, if it is to be in the least serviceable, is to keep such experiences always in view, and by its tempo, compactness, density, yet also its tentativeness, to give them expression.[77]

What is significant about Adorno's criticism of France's diction as leisurely and self-indulgent is that, in form at least, France tends to keep his meditations at least as brief as Adorno's. The difference, Adorno thinks, is that France makes no effort to manage what he says: he brings forth platitudes 'as if no-one may dare to notice

---

[72] Nietzsche, *Beyond Good and Evil*, 60.
[73] Nietzsche, *Beyond Good and Evil*, 70.
[74] Theodor Adorno, *Minima Moralia: Reflections on a Damaged Life*, trans. E. F. N. Jephcott (London and New York: Verso, 2005), 16.
[75] See Chapter Five on the modernist fragment.
[76] Adorno, 18.
[77] Adorno, 98–100.

their triteness'.[78] Adorno emphasizes that the act of expressing a thought at all signals the privilege of presuming a right to speak and a right to take up the time of one's listener. The theorist, he suggests, must express a thought; it must be rich and solid. Yet it must also waver, must shyly seek a hearing without expectation or entitlement; it must take up no more space than it merits. If Nietzsche espouses frugality of expression because revelation can never be heeded with interest and understanding, Adorno adds an uncertainty about whether one's revelation in fact deserves to be listened to at all. Aphorism's proper work is to keep its truth-claim contained: to state itself flatly, but to manage its own boundaries so that it makes no demands. The writer does not take for granted his or her right to be attended to, retreating from the scene in good time. Such an ethos and rhetoric, as Chapter 1 will suggest, becomes visible throughout Stevie Smith's poetics. They embody, I suggest, a propositional, clear declaration of feelings and ideas, which nevertheless not only becomes indifferent to its own hearing, but defuses its own hearability.

The process is visible in Smith's 'All Things Pass'. In contrast to other texts which describe the giving-over of human life to grass—the repetitive cadences of Isaiah 40:6–8 in the Bible, for instance, as well as Walt Whitman's vast, sprawling *Leaves of Grass*—Smith's poem ends almost as soon as it begins, leaving only a smooth grassy expanse to view. So much happens in eight words, and yet nothing remains afterwards: no hope, no result, and above all no interpretative handle. Smith's quick, brutal dispatch of love and mankind hovers between comedy and tragedy. She leaves her reader unsure how to react, unsure even of what has happened. Revelation and concealment happened in the same gesture. Something has been disclosed and yet it is smoothed over: by the snappy rhyme and triply stressed first three syllables, the accomplished aphoristic form of the text, as much as that image of flat unyielding ground. Nothing more, the aphorism signals, is necessary. And yet what was granted to the reader seems to embody an indifference to communication, to understanding and to interpretative endeavour. Aphorism's accomplished elegance casts its message as self-evidently true—but at the same time, that polished dismissive tone makes itself impenetrable to further enquiry, and ensures that each will ultimately be bypassed in favour of the next maxim. That double gesture is key to Smith; it is the aspect of aphorism she foregrounds.

Smith uses aphoristic gestures to create texts which urgently declare their messages, and yet whose hard insistence can become the hardness of impenetrability: we hear those messages as though through a closed door. It is that perpetual sense of broken communicative promises—of a striking revelation rhetorically promised and displayed in simple language, and nevertheless by turns impenetrable, belated, unusable, inane, and inappropriate—which structures my reading of Stevie Smith's writing. The contention of this book is that Smith's particular acrobatics of communication and withholding, where the two do not alternate but

---

[78] Adorno, 99.

24 STEVIE SMITH AND THE APHORISM

become identical, is deeply imbricated in her inclination towards aphorism and aphoristic forms. Romana Huk feels that Smith is 'tempt[ed]' by a Blakean style of 'oracular prophecy and denouncement', but implies that she resists it: 'a romantic rhetoric of hieratic authority that she abhorred and undermined when aware of its takeover of her lines'.[79] But Smith's aphoristics are not, I argue, a refusal of didacticism and of its gendered, classed structures (which place authority implicitly in the hands of wealthy men).[80] Instead, her clear relish of the aphoristic mode, throughout her writing, leads me to contend that Smith is doing something specific and important with the aphorism: she is being fully didactic—making a 'strong communication'—and yet simultaneously (as this book will unpack), she is fully minimizing that communication. Her poems and novels, like her aphorisms, are starkly propositional, and yet multiply structured to prevent them from having a deep impact. I argue that Smith deliberately employs an aphoristic aesthetic, like many of her forebears and contemporaries, but to unique effect: in order to simultaneously announce something, and deface that announcement.

I ask, therefore, whether aphoristic writing—didactic, dignified, imperious; entirely poised in its sense of its own rightness—might nevertheless be fundamentally oriented away from the listening audience; it might not set out to be heard, understood, or heeded. By positioning this phenomenon at the heart of the workings of so many aphorisms, as a gesture not just of ambiguity but of self-sabotaging withdrawal, this monograph offers a new theory of the aphorism: as a form which may often be based not so much on rhetorical claims to discursive authority or promises of useful, tool-like bits of insight, as on a simultaneous double gesture of exposure and withdrawal, which enables a kind of self-protection. Though this intricate movement gives the aphorism its distinctiveness, it has evaded critical description. The consensus has focused on the form's authoritative communication and confident power-seizing: these performances by the aphorism are indeed so compelling that its subtle self-cancellation has been easy to overlook. Persuasive to critics, too, has been its pretence of being open to dialogue:[81] an ideal form for responding to other writers.[82] This monograph takes a different stance: that while the aphorism appears to invite dialogue and answer, it simultaneously freezes any possible response. Its glacial tone often repulses overtures of intimacy between text and text, or between text and reader.

This rebuffing of affective and intellectual engagement means that aphorism—and this is the heart of my theorization—offers a safe form in which dangerous

---

[79] Romana Huk, *Stevie Smith: Between the Lines* (Basingstoke: Palgrave, 2005), 64.
[80] On the misogyny of aphorism, see Grant, 78; on aphorism as a form which presents as aristocratic, see Susan Sontag, *As Consciousness is Harnessed to Flesh: Diaries 1964–1980*, ed. David Rieff (London: Penguin, 2012), 512.
[81] Kostas Boyiopoulos and Michael Shallcross, 'Introduction', in *Aphoristic Modernity*, 12.
[82] Mourant, 94.

feelings and claims might be allowed to survive. Ideas which are too provocative or upsetting, emotions which are too strong or embarrassing, sentiments which might outrage authority, or which are irrational or indefensible, are appropriate to be expressed in aphorisms, because the exquisite aloofness of the form sabotages their conveyance to the listener. The strong sentiment—outrage, despair, hatred, complaint—can be expressed without risk, since, in its polish and finish, the aphorism becomes too assured to be dug into, questioned, or retaliated against. As a result, lucid as the aphoristic statement may seem, the reader is cut off from experiencing and interrogating it fully. Aphorism is therefore, in fact, best understood as a tool for the social management of emotion. It displays and effaces ideas in a single gesture, leaving nothing to argue with, or to punish.

And that very self-effacement gives the aphorism its longevity. It survives precisely because it is impenetrable: because it cannot be digested and used. So, as Chapter 1 describes, it offers a site for hopeful return in Smith's work: where a reader can revisit its unassimilable truth-claim over and over again, in a posture of interpretative optimism which may console in itself, even as the aphorism does not. Or, as Chapter 2 outlines, it offers a model for a sense of illumination which exists only in hindsight: an impression of revelation (accurate or otherwise) which cannot be used because it has been reached too late, because the aphoristic utterance has outlasted the context to which it referred.

Against a twentieth-century background where a wide range of writers use aphorism—W. H. Auden, D. H. Lawrence, Katherine Mansfield, Mina Loy, Dorothy Parker, Ivy Compton-Burnett, Wallace Stevens, to name just a few—this reading has the potential to reframe the aphoristic announcements that these authors make. To take Stevie Smith seriously as an aphoristic writer, in particular, opens up and complicates the notion of any political or feminist stance she might seem to adopt, and illuminates her writing's strange illegibility. Aphorism offers a route through Smith's often oblique, though variously and emphatically stated, intellectual stances, and through the critical debates which surround these questions. Understanding the aphorism's acrobatics of display and effacement offers access to a mode of poetic communication which cannot be read easily as either subversion of an idea, or affirmation of it. It illuminates another way that those who navigate between the centre and the margins might choose to speak: a safely self-concealing mode of protest, common and yet under-theorized.

Reading Smith through Aphorism

Aphorism's simultaneous inhabitation of the significant and the frivolous, the emphatic and the self-dismissive, frames the difficulty of Smith's poems. They

26 STEVIE SMITH AND THE APHORISM

can appear to be unnecessary, discardable fritters. Philip Larkin described her mode as '*fausse-naïve*, the "feminine" doodler or jotter who puts down everything as it strikes her'.[83] Whether she should therefore be read as a writer of 'light verse' remains a matter of critical debate.[84] But Smith both resisted and encouraged this image as a light or childlike writer. While she decorated her poems with doodly drawings, she also complained that the poetic value of her writing remained unappreciated.[85] Accordingly, Smith requested once that a write-up remove descriptions of her work as 'whimsical' and 'primitive'.[86] A letter to Anna Kallin encapsulates the poet's (not uncomplicated) counter-argument:

> It [a lecture mixing in her own poetry] is not *at all whimsical*, as some asses seem to think I am, but serious, yet not aggressive, & fairly cheerful though with melancholy patches. (MA, 304)

The thorough and discursive simplicity of this self-judgement in fact drains away any stable critical standpoint. It offers Smith's sympathetic commentators two (not necessarily incompatible) approaches to her work.

One option has been to take the first part of her statement at face value. She is not whimsical, she is serious. Her work contains a serious message which can be revealed if read properly, and which exists under (and often separate from) its lighter elements. So Smith can be read as a rebellious feminist, resisting the confines of domesticity, interrogating the category of 'woman' and underlining the performativity of gender.[87] Her doodles emerge as a route for female presence

---

[83] Philip Larkin, 'Frivolous and Vulnerable', in *Required Writing: Miscellaneous Pieces 1955–1982* (London: Faber & Faber, 1983), 153.

[84] See Eleanor Risteen, 'Daddy, Mummy and Stevie: The Child-Guise in Stevie Smith's Poetry', *Modern Poetry Studies* 11 (1983): 243, arguing for a manipulative 'child-guise' in Smith's work, versus Mark Halliday, 'Stevie Smith's Serious Comedy', *Humor* 22, no. 3 (2009): 306, arguing that she seldom allows her moments of frivolity to develop fully into comedy, and James Najarian, 'Contributions to Almighty Truth: Stevie Smith's Seditious Romanticism', *Twentieth-Century Literature* 49, no. 4 (2003): 472, presenting Smith's appearance of lightness as deceptive.

[85] See May, 'Drawing Away from Lear', 316–317, on Smith's complex relationship with Lear, as one in which Smith causes her reader to misrecognize her poetry as nonsense. It was in her interests to elide her connection to Lear, May suggests, in order to be taken seriously

[86] Spalding, 259.

[87] Julie Sims Steward, 'Pandora's Playbox: Stevie Smith's Drawings and the Construction of Gender', *Journal of Modern Literature* 22, no. 1 (1998): 82; Julie Sims Steward, 'The Problem of the Body in Stevie Smith's Body of Work', *South Atlantic Review* 70, no. 2 (2005): 80; Julie Sims Steward, 'Ceci n'est pas un Hat: Stevie Smith and the Refashioning of Gender', *South Central Review* 15, no. 2 (1998): 19; Laura Severin, *Stevie Smith's Resistant Antics* (Madison: University of Wisconsin Press, 1997), 4, 14; Laura Severin, 'Becoming and Unbecoming: Stevie Smith as Performer', *Text and Performance Quarterly* 18, no. 1 (1998): 29. On a clash between literary and legal interpretive regimes in one of Smith's short stories, ending on the silencing of a site of male power, see Bryony Randall, '"Give him your word": Legal and Literary Interpretation in Stevie Smith's "The Story of a Story"', *Law and Literature* 21, no. 2 (2009): 238–40.

and unregulated energy to re-enter the text while escaping its disciplinary norm.[88] Though some critics locate Smith's 'serious message' beyond a feminist approach, the watchword for these approaches is still subversion. Even Lauryl Tucker's psychoanalytic account of Smith's poetry suggests that Smith, via her child characters, subverts repetitive cultural narratives of narcissism.[89]

As early as 1993, however, Romana Huk complicated this account of Smith's subversive feminist poetics, pointing out that as a female subject Smith is constituted within the very (patriarchal) discourses which she subverts.[90] Four years later, Huk argued that Smith's reworking of familiar modes 'disrupt[s] without redefining', and does not, in contrast to critics who see Smith as offering an alternative way for women to live, prescribe a new way of living and writing.[91] Attending to this embeddedness of Smith within her cultural discourses, several critics have focused on Smith's unsubversive relationship to tropes which are troubling to the present-day reader. Most disconcertingly, this emerges in a number of anti-Semitic episodes in her writing. Pompey carols 'Hurrah to be a goy!' in *Novel on Yellow Paper*, and Smith's depiction of Aaronsen in *Over the Frontier* trades heavily in Jewish stereotypes (*Novel*, 2; *Frontier*, 196).[92] Gill Plain, focusing on how Smith's stream-of-consciousness writing mirrors the manipulative language of fascism, argues that Smith divides form and content to numb the reader into 'a false sense of poetry' which disguises the implications of its own narrative.[93] In *Stevie Smith: Between the Lines* (2005), Huk positions Smith's novels as exploring how such self-delusion leads to entrapment within oppressive political discourses, most prominently fascism and anti-Semitism. She reads Smith's texts as building

[88] Linda Anderson, 'Gender, Feminism, Poetry: Stevie Smith, Sylvia Plath, Jo Shapcott', in *The Cambridge Companion to Twentieth-Century Poetry*, ed. Neil Corcoran (Cambridge: Cambridge University Press, 2007), 174–179.

[89] Lauryl Tucker, 'Progeny and Parody: Narcissus and Echo in Stevie Smith's Poems' *Twentieth-Century Literature* 60, no. 3 (2014): 337.

[90] Romana Huk, 'Eccentric Concentrism: Traditional Poetic Forms and Refracted Discourse in Stevie Smith's Poetry', *Contemporary Literature* 34, no. 2 (1993): 244–245.

[91] Romana Huk, 'Poetic Subject and Voice as Sites of Struggle: Toward a "Postrevisionist" Reading of Stevie Smith's Fairy-Tale Poems', in *Dwelling in Possibility: Women Poets and Critics on Poetry*, ed. Yopie Prins and Maeera Shreiber (Ithaca and London: Cornell University Press, 1997), 154, 165.

[92] Phyllis Lassner proposes that Smith's Jews test the other characters' contradictory attitudes towards war, bringing out the best and worst in them. Phyllis Lassner, 'A Cry for Life: Storm Jameson, Stevie Smith, and the Fate of Europe's Jews', in *Visions of War: World War II in Popular Literature and Culture*, ed. M. Paul Holsinger and Mary Anne Schofield (Bowling Green: Bowling Green State University Popular Press, 1992), 182. On how Smith's characters deploy anti-Semitism to shore up their own subject positions, see Phyllis Lassner, *British Women Writers of World War II: Battlegrounds of their Own* (London and Basingstoke: Macmillan, 1998), 198, and Kristin Bluemel, *George Orwell and the Radical Eccentrics: Intermodernism in Literary London* (New York: Palgrave Macmillan, 2004), 27.

[93] Gill Plain, *Women's Fiction of the Second World War: Gender, Power and Resistance* (Edinburgh: Edinburgh University Press, 1996), 73. See also Adam Piette, 'Travel Writing and the Imperial Subject in 1930s Prose: Waugh, Bowen, Smith, and Orwell', in *Issues in Travel Writing: Empire, Spectacle, and Displacement*, ed. Kristi Siegel (New York: Peter Lang, 2002), 60, on Smith's fascistic fascination with speed and destructive movement.

28 STEVIE SMITH AND THE APHORISM

gradually to climactic revelations of how her protagonists are trapped within the political currents of the 1930s (anti-Semitism, fascism), even as they attempt to distance themselves.[94]

Huk's work acknowledges, and absorbs, Smith's unstable viewpoints and tones. In her reading, the perspectives and stated views of Smith's characters fluctuate as they try (and, ultimately, fail) to evade the realization of their own implication within coercive ideologies.[95] What Huk illuminates so well is that Smith's tendency to expound sharply differentiated positions within and between her texts complicates attempts to interpret her work as a legibly singular assertion of particular views on politics or gender. And this instability of perspective and ideology in Smith's work forms the basis for the second critical alternative: to read Smith's work in terms of shifting personae. For critics such as Frances Spalding and Sheryl Stevenson, multiple personae allow Smith to explore different, contradictory points of view.[96] Will May argues that Smith herself shrewdly curates the failure of cohesive readings of her texts, framing the reader in continuous acts of misreading through the 'mixed messages' she deliberately supplies.[97] May emphasizes how rapidly Smith's tone can switch from one mode to another;[98] keeping her poetry in flux between possible interpretations, she repeatedly unseats her readers, forcing the conscientious among them to 'return again and again to her work, always conscious of their fallible attempts to decode her writing.'[99]

Critics therefore seem to have two options. Either one reads Smith's work as not light but secretly weighty (in other words, her poems seem frivolous but can conceal an important message), or one can read her as alternately light and weighty at varying moments (rapidly switching modes, so that she is sometimes frivolous and sometimes doing important poetic or philosophical work). This monograph finds a critical position beyond this binary. Acknowledging the range of possibilities in the aphoristic aesthetic, and paying particular attention to certain variants which Smith deploys in her writing, this book offers a new angle on the work of aphorism, in itself and in Smith's hands, to ask whether Smith can be fruitfully read as a poet who may in the same moment be simultaneously, concomitantly light and weighty. Smith's work resists analysis because it exemplifies a mode of clear declaration which nevertheless makes itself critically and practically unavailable to an

---

[94] Huk, *Stevie Smith*,168, 119–121.

[95] Huk, *Stevie Smith*, 4.

[96] Spalding, xvii; Sheryl Stevenson, 'Stevie Smith's Voices', *Contemporary Literature* 33, no. 1 (1992): 27. See also J. Edward Mallot, 'Not Drowning But Waving: Stevie Smith and the Language of the Lake', *Journal of Modern Literature* 27, no. 1/2 (2003): 186, who positions Smith in a 'sea of words' (competing voices or modes, perhaps) which endanger communication.

[97] William May, *Stevie Smith and Authorship* (Oxford: Oxford University Press, 2010), 54. See also Will May, 'An Eye for an I: Constructing the Visual in the Work of Stevie Smith', in *From Self to Shelf: The Artist Under Construction*, ed. Sally Bayley and William May (Newcastle: Cambridge Scholars Publishing, 2007), 76–86.

[98] May, *Stevie Smith and Authorship*, 36.

[99] May, *Stevie Smith and Authorship*, 136.

enquiring readerly mind. She uses aphorism and aphoristic gestures to weightily declare the world's unacceptability to her, safe in the knowledge that the revelation laid out, in clear and compelling language, cannot be acted upon: that ultimately it will be lightly received and passed by. Aphorism allows its speaker to express something fully while cauterizing the reader's emotional or intellectual response to what she says: it unburdens the speaker of the need to be useful, or even audible.

1

Unnecessary Aphorisms

> Yet not light always is the pain
> That roots in levity. Or without fruit wholly
> As from this levity's
> Flowering pang of melancholy
> May grow what is weighty,
> May come beauty.
>
> ('The Poet Hin', CP, 634–635)

Smith's archives include a report laying out the perplexed reaction of one of the publisher Curtis Brown's readers, 'E.B', to a submission of Smith's poetry in 1934. E.B describes a page of 'several short verses', including texts not extant elsewhere: 'Casual copulation / Cheats the heart and the imagination'. Calling Smith's writing 'bitty', 'ultra-1934', and (in pleasingly faint praise) *so many*, E.B ends her review in telling terms:

> The reader very much doubts the literary quality of most of the poems but feels there may be some power in them which she has failed to find.[1]

Here, brusquely outlined, is the Smith-dilemma. The poet's brevity might easily be cast as light-heartedness, disposability—but even a reviewer as unsympathetic as E.B remains uneasy, suspecting a weight to the poems which she cannot find or access. The 'bitty' little poems which seem to claim little or no 'literary quality' manage nevertheless to signal a palpable but unlocatable 'power': to move, to transform, to reveal.

E.B's choice of the word 'power' matters here. This is not simply a question of 'quality' or 'value': words which do fall within the jurisdiction of a publisher's reader, whose job is to discern whether or not Smith's poems are any good. The bigger issue E.B has sensed is that, despite their lack of 'literary quality', these poems are nevertheless poised with a latent 'power': the ability to act or have an effect. Smith's poems make, in other words, the promise of the aphoristic short form, offering themselves as tools to communicate, reveal, clarify.

---

[1] 'E.B', reader's report, Series 2, Box 4, Folder 17, Stevie Smith papers, 1924–1970. Coll. No. 1976.012. McFarlin Library. Department of Special Collections and University Archives. The University of Tulsa.

Stevie Smith and the Aphorism. Noreen Masud, Oxford University Press.
© Noreen Masud (2022). DOI: 10.1093/oso/9780192895899.003.0002

E.B's sense, reading Smith's submission, is of a capacity to have an (emotional, transformative) effect on the world which can be 'felt'—to repurpose E.B's chosen words—but not quite 'found'. What does it mean to feel something but not find it? Two forms of writing where sensation (sound, impression, image) may come prior to findable, definable meaning are, variously, poetry and aphorism. The short verse that E.B quotes from Smith's submission straddles both:

> Casual copulation
> Cheats the heart and the imagination.

Modernist poetry privileges form and impression over any informational 'nugget of pure truth',[2] to quote Virginia Woolf, which may be extracted and held up as the poem's 'meaning'. This positions it in a curious relationship to aphorism. In contrast to Ezra Pound's 'Image', offering 'an intellectual and emotional complex in an instant of time' which cannot be further reduced or translated,[3] aphorism claims, implicitly, to offer Woolf's tidy 'nugget' of truth, addressing a matter pithily and directly. In practice, though, as it draws on the rhyme, rhythm, and verbal symmetry which align it with the poetic line, aphorism often presents in a form attractive and compelling enough to become the text's most memorable quality. With Smith's little poem, what her readers remember, and dwell on, is the ingenious rhyme (copulation/imagination), whose cheerful Ogden-Nash-style verbal play eclipses the poem's po-faced warning against casual sex. Here, the wit of aphoristic form works in fact to sideline, rather than enhance, the text's message.

Aphorists have freely confessed to this trick for centuries. If a maxim was 'startling' in its verbal play, as the moralist Vauvenargues knew, any content could pass, however false:

> What is called a brilliant maxim is generally merely a misleading statement which, by the aid of a little truth, imposes on us a startling falsehood.[4]

And for Thoreau, if a sentence presents as ironclad in its rhetorical self-confidence, it does not have to be wise to be convincing:

> The most attractive sentences are not perhaps the wisest, but the surest and soundest.[5]

---

[2] Virginia Woolf, *A Room of One's Own and Three Guineas*, ed. Morag Shiach (Oxford: Oxford World's Classics, 2008), 4.

[3] Ezra Pound, 'A Retrospect', in *Modernism: An Anthology of Sources and Documents*, ed. Vassiliki Kolocotroni, Jane Goodman, and Olga Taxidou (Edinburgh: Edinburgh University Press, 1998), 373–382, 374.

[4] Luc de Clapiers, Marquis of Vauvenargues, *The Reflections and Maxims*, trans. F. G. Stevens (London: Humphrey Milford, 1940), 91.

[5] John Gross, ed., *The Oxford Book of Aphorisms* (Oxford: Oxford University Press, 1983), 1.

32 STEVIE SMITH AND THE APHORISM

The list continues: Malesherbes admits 'A new maxim is often a brilliant error'.[6] Aphorists confess shamefacedly—over and over again, since their admission is too outrageous to be heeded—to their form's rhetorical capacity for charlatanry. Stiffened and purified by brevity, by assertiveness, and by the formal *sprezzatura* of rhyme, repetition, and predicative structure, aphorism automatically sounds true: the reader is halfway to accepting it before they have stopped to think about what it might mean. Aphorism's bullet-like polish forces itself past the reader's passive defences. But easy come, easy go: accepted effortlessly, aphorism is only provisionally absorbed, and as this chapter will suggest, its 'pure truth' slips from the mind just as easily as it came.

This chapter argues that the effect of the style and structure of aphorisms (particularly those which make the promises of isolationist brilliance, by figures such as Kafka, Kraus, and Auden), whose accomplished rhetorical suaveness allows them to imprint on the mind then quickly depart from it, offers a model of reading for Stevie Smith's shorter and longer poetry. It asks how Smith's pieces of hard language position themselves in relation to the reader's hearing and use. Are they received as frivolous or full of aphoristic truth? Can the two be separated, given the contestability of 'aphoristic truth'? And might they in fact be too full of truth to be received as anything *but* unusable and discardable? As the introduction argued, despite its useful appearance aphorism is ultimately, and necessarily, an unusable tool, in terms of the insight it promises to offer. At once airily lightweight and insistent on their own importance, Smith's poems over-engineer their own communicative emphasis to prevent absorption of their content, and to slip away from attempts to assimilate them: they must therefore be returned to repeatedly.

Aphorism's Empty Shapes

Smith's aphoristic aesthetic falls, broadly, into two kinds, which nevertheless have the same impact on the reader. On one side, her texts may proffer a recognizable truth-claim, but that truth-claim is too hardened (by style, gnomicism, or self-insistence) for the reader to fully assimilate, understand, or use. On the other side, her texts may encode no truth claim, despite a stiff aphoristic rhetoric, and this makes them too lightweight to use or interpret. Her readers respond to both kinds of texts in the same way: uneasy, half-laughing acknowledgement, and a movement onwards to the next text.

In the former camp, punchy poems like 'If I lie down' from *Mother, What is Man?* (1942) encode a message, about the difference between death and sleep:

[6] Gross, *Oxford Book of Aphorisms*, 1.

If I lie down upon my bed I must be here,
But if I lie down in my grave I may be elsewhere. (CP, 196)

'Reversionary', from *Tender Only to One* (1938), is a clearly content-dense epigram, exploring an idea about shame:

The Lion dishonoured bids death come,
The worm in like hap lingers on.
The Lion dead, his pride no less,
The world inherits wormliness. (CP, 132)

'Reversionary' privileges its own form. It shores up its message by combining recognizable fabular types and metaphorical implications with rhyme, repetition, and assertion. These formal techniques come under the heading of Beverly Coyle's aphoristic boundary-effects: a cluster of devices which contribute to the pithy convincingness of aphorism or epigram.[7]

The slickness of such boundary-effects, which should make the message conveniently swallowable and assimilable, in fact work to create a time-lag between form and content. Aphorism insists that it has a truth-claim to make, but that claim is, in John Fagg's phrase, 'based on form rather than content'.[8] Faced with aphorisms, the reader experiences, as Harold E. Pagliaro argues, an 'immediacy and intensity of response ... [which makes] them seem incontrovertible'.[9] Aphorism's first effect is asemantic, a wordless impression made on the reader before the content catches up. It promises a particular kind of utility: some universal and paradigm-shifting truth, potted into a small compass and delivered with a sharpness and sleekness which penetrates through to a reader's assent before they have grasped it intellectually.

In her other mode of aphorism, Smith foregrounds and intensifies this effect: boundary-effects become all that there is. 'Croft', from *Mother, What is Man?* (1942), conveys its initial impression of significance through a form which claims profundity far beyond its content:

Aloft,
In the loft,
Sits Croft;
He is soft. (CP, 218)

---

[7] Beverly Coyle, *A Thought to Be Rehearsed: Aphorism in Wallace Stevens's Poetry* (Ann Arbor: UMI Research Press, 1983), 3.

[8] John Fagg, *On the Cusp: Stephen Crane, George Bellows, and Modernism* (Tuscaloosa: The University of Alabama Press, 2009), 142.

[9] Harold E. Pagliaro, 'Paradox In The Aphorisms Of La Rochefoucauld And Some Representative English Followers', *PMLA* 79, no. 1 (1964): 45.

Figure 1.1 Croft, in the loft. Stevie Smith, *The Collected Poems and Drawings of Stevie Smith*, ed. Will May (London: Faber & Faber, 2015), 218. By permission of Faber and Faber Ltd and New Directions Publishing Corp.

Each line in this poem is predicatively unassailable: truth-claims whose very brevity permits no space for argument, knitted tightly together with an AAAA rhyme scheme. Even Smith's accompanying drawing (see Figure 1.1) shores up the text's status as self-sufficient: showing an androgynous figure, sitting in a small boxy loft space, the walls of the room enclosing the image into a tight-sealed unit (CP, 218).

Tantalizingly drawn-out, buttressing its imperiousness with predicative structure and rhyme, 'Croft' builds, line by short, assertive line, to a position of 'aloft' authority. As Croft sits on high, like an anchorite in his tiny cell, we feel he is preparing to declaim a revelation. This never materializes. 'He is soft' deflates the poem's gravitas, albeit with convincing firmness; the destabilizing dress worn by the figure in the image is never acknowledged or dealt with. Caught between laughter and awe, we give in to receiving the text as authoritative, even as 'Croft' empties out the truth-claim which it promises.

Smith's work places apparently 'serious' poems like 'Reversionary', whose aphoristic construction embeds an at least partially apprehensible meaning, alongside texts such as 'Croft', whose tight and sombre form convinces us, as readers and critics, to seek a message which was, we eventually suspect, never there at all. 'Croft' signals significance without meaning: a solid assertion, bolstered by formal boundaries, whose claim to truth is overemphasized into impenetrability. Yet Smith insisted in a letter to Kay Dick on Croft's role as a self-portrait (MA,

288). She does not elaborate. Is she isolated (in the loft)? 'Aloft' with an angel's detached, haughty wisdom? Or simply 'soft', with all that word's ambiguity? Smith's claim positions us on the brink of accessing authoritative revelation from the poem, but restrains us from quite reaching it. We are kept on our toes, scanning for a significance or absolute communicable truth which seems promised by the poem's form, but which—despite the baldly revelatory quality of the text's simple remarks—remains unfindable.

In this sense of meaning as both promised and withheld by imperious aphoristic form, Smith has impressive pedigree. Though the aphorism insists on its capacity to transmit truth, meaning, in the aphoristic encounter, is always ultimately deferred. Gary Saul Morson describes how each aphorism 'points beyond itself, step by potentially endless step. It is a mystery'.[10] Like Smith, James Joyce's *Finnegans Wake* (1939) repeatedly offers its reader the shape of aphorism without powerful content, or with only minimal content: 'a nod to the nabir is better than wink to the wabsanti' echoes the proverb 'A nod is as good as a wink to a blind horse', but to little discernible end.[11] As Pagliaro acknowledges, aphorism may make the reader feel 'that he has been shown a more extensive truth than in fact he has'.[12]

And this cognitive sensation characterizes our encounter with an aphorism: a sense that absolute truth lies within its boundaries, although we inevitably fail to marshal a set of terms which helps us comprehend it. Texts like 'Croft' flag themselves up as at once authoritative and frivolous, with equal and irresolvable fervour. Weight becomes concomitant with weightlessness: we cannot read this text securely. Smith builds in lightness, so thoroughly but lightly identical with the text's own imperiousness that it unsettles almost imperceptibly.

It is this very aesthetic, in which a text presents itself as at once highly significant and completely dismissable, which I term aphoristic, and which runs throughout Smith's work, including her longer poems and novels. The same drive led Karl Kraus to title his aphorisms in *Die Fackel* 'Waste', and brought Lichtenberg's books of aphorisms to be called *Sudelbücher* (Waste Books).[13] Aphorisms always teeter on the verge of waste, of discardability, despite their apparent declaration of unassailable authority. Aphorism demands the right to be dissipative, uncommunicative, discardable, spared from thorough interrogation, in the same moment that it establishes its own weighty significance. Countless examples offer themselves:

---

[10] Gary Saul Morson, 'The Aphorism: Fragments from the Breakdown of Reason', *New Literary History* 34, no. 3 (2003): 413.

[11] James Joyce, *Finnegans Wake*, ed. Robbert-Jan Henkes, Erik Bindervoet, and Finn Fordham (Oxford: Oxford University Press, 2012), 5.

[12] Pagliaro, 50.

[13] Steven Tester, 'Introduction', in Georg Christoph Lichtenberg, *Georg Christoph Lichtenberg: Philosophical Writings*, ed. and trans. Steven Tester (Albany: State University of New York Press, 2012), 4; Karl Kraus, 'Abfälle', *Die Fackel* 198, 12 March 1906.

The cherubim know most; the seraphim love most.[14]

The rat, the mouse, the fox, the rabbit, watch the roots.
The lion, the tiger, the horse, the elephant, watch the fruits.[15]

This deflating of revelatory value operates visibly in ambiguous or enigmatic short texts, such as Smith's 'If I lie down': its meaning cannot be fully and finally accessed. Yet it operates more strikingly, if more elusively, in texts which seem at first to offer a balder and clearer communication: whether that declaration seems inane, as in 'Croft', or starkly legible, such as the closing lament of Smith's brief 'The Repentance of Lady T':

I wish to change,
How can that be?
Oh Lamb of God
Change me, change me. (CP, 225)

In her movement between the semi-informative epigrammatic text (like 'Reversionary'), and the short text that promises a significance which eludes the reader (like 'Croft'), Smith foregrounds the aphorism's own inherent impenetrability: its claim to be intellectually weighty, to have something important to say, even as it offers only the banal, the impossible, the opaque, or the unknowable.

Such an aesthetic of substance which signals its arresting solidity, but which cannot be finally or fruitfully delved into for meaning or function, runs through Smith's longer and shorter poetry. The monk in 'The Weak Monk' (*Harold's Leap* [1950]) writes 'till he was ninety years old'—but buries the book immediately, making his ideas inaccessible:

... he shut the book with a clasp of gold
And buried it under the sheepfold.

... he thought he'd a right to expect that God
Would rescue his book alive from the sod.

Of course it rotted in the snow and rain,
No one will ever know now what he wrote of God and Men.
For this the monk is to blame. (CP, 286)

Smith's illustration to 'The Weak Monk' in May's edition (CP, 286) shows a distrustful-looking monk holding in his left hand a large blank square (see Figure 1.2). If this is the book, it has no title and no pages are visible. This

---

[14] Ralph Waldo Emerson, 'Intellect', in *Essays* (Boston: Houghton Mifflin, 1883), 321.
[15] William Blake, *Blake: The Complete Poems*, ed. W. H. Stevenson (Harlow: Pearson Education, 2007), 115.

UNNECESSARY APHORISMS 37

Figure 1.2 The Weak Monk. Stevie Smith, *The Collected Poems and Drawings of Stevie Smith*, ed. Will May (London: Faber & Faber, 2015), 286. By permission of Faber and Faber Ltd and New Directions Publishing Corp.

is an idea of a book, a place-holder: no message is visible or legible within or on it. It is one of Smith's many unreadable messages: the 'missing text[s]' upon which May builds his reading of her work as resisting determinacy.[16] Picture and poem, together, present a hermetic, ultimately inadequate reading experience, identified by only partial interpretative access.

The monk's book embodies an authoritative statement about 'God and Men'. He shores up his text's physical boundaries with a gold clasp, before ritually burying it. In other words, an assertive truth-claim is made and then cancelled or discarded.

More subtly, however, Smith envisages the burial as at once preservation and disposal. The monk's gesture prevents others from accessing his truth-claim, even as it creates the necessary preconditions for a miraculous revelation of that claim: God would, he thought, 'rescue his book alive'. The monk's treatment of his text both ensures (he hopes) and withholds enlightenment. Stern locates precisely this mode of blocked illumination in the way an aphorism 'preserves and thus also

---

[16] William May, *Stevie Smith and Authorship* (Oxford: Oxford University Press, 2010), 2.

38 STEVIE SMITH AND THE APHORISM

arrests the flow of life'.[17] We experience the text, but only partially; we cannot get beyond its 'clasp of gold' to discover 'what he wrote'.

Stevie Smith structures her oeuvre through the modes of speech and storytelling by this aphoristic acrobatic. Even through texts which present themselves as loose, chaotic, and discursive, we perceive a model of authority which repeatedly stops, withdraws, and cancels itself—in a way characteristic of the aphoristic form. While James Najarian finds that Smith's poetry 'pretends not to aspire to authority even as it quietly seizes it', I locate Smith's poetic effects in a *staged* seizure, and abrupt abandonment, of authority through the aphoristic mode.[18] Heavy with authority but resistant to interpretation, the aphorism makes itself weightless by destroying the mechanisms which would render its revelation accessible.

Half Truths: One and a Half Truths

Aphorism's incomplete enlightenment runs deeper than its boundary-effects which weigh down or conceal an intact truth.[19] Unsuccessful or incomplete epiphany is, in fact, built into the aphorism's truth-value. The form promises a communicable insight, but simultaneously it does not deliver it as promised. Aphorism derives monadic 'sufficiency' from its refusal to reveal the process of its own genesis: its insistence, perhaps, on its own eccentric self-performance, which means that it therefore remains aesthetically and referentially accountable only to itself. It employs the terms of its own originary universe, which it builds from scratch, letting the reader guess how to understand it. Smith's 'How Slowly Time Lengthens' functions in this way. Its four lines withhold all contextual details, presenting its mini-narrative as self-evidently comprehensible even as it remains obscure:

> How slowly time lengthens from a hated event.
> In my youth I was humiliated in a guilty association—
> Insinuator, flatterer, Board of Trade Surveyor, hypocrite,
> Aha, Hildreth Parker, how have the years dealt with you? (CP, 142)

'How Slowly Time Lengthens' invokes a named individual, epigram-like, whose context has been lost. The 'hated event' remains unspecified, the 'guilty association' unexplored. The drawing appended to the poem (see Figure 1.3) offers no

---

[17] J. P. Stern, *Lichtenberg: A Doctrine of Scattered Occasions* (Bloomington: Indiana University Press, 1959), 218.

[18] James Najarian, 'Contributions to Almighty Truth: Stevie Smith's Seditious Romanticism', *Twentieth-Century Literature* 49, no. 4 (2003): 472.

[19] On the aphorism's multiplicity, see for instance Morson, 'The Aphorism', 412; Alvin Snider, 'Francis Bacon and the authority of aphorism', *Prose Studies* 11, no. 2 (1988): 65.

Figure 1.3 Figure and flowers, 'How Slowly Time Lengthens'. Stevie Smith, *The Collected Poems and Drawings of Stevie Smith*, ed. Will May (London: Faber & Faber, 2015), 142. By permission of Faber and Faber Ltd and New Directions Publishing Corp.

illumination (CP, 142). It shows a bent old woman, surrounded by towering flowers and leaves, which we assume to be the poem's speaker remembering her youth (in which Hildreth Parker played a part). The picture provides detail (the gender of the speaker, perhaps) but does not clarify the narrative; the unexplained vast flowers obfuscate. In its complex of poem and picture, Smith's text has severed its own genealogy, 'dissociated' itself, even as it insists on the existence of that originary context. It demands our questions, but forestalls them, with a rhetorical question which shuts down the possibility of answer.

Smith's poems seem, aphoristically, to promise communicable potted truths. In the same gesture, they withhold those truths, holding themselves just above or below the status of informational usefulness. Karl Kraus summed up this contested capacity for revelation in his aphorism: 'An aphorism never coincides with the truth: it is either a half-truth or one-and-a-half truths'.[20] The aphorism either possesses not enough truth (to reposition this in the terms of one of Smith's poems, perhaps Hildreth Parker never existed; the narrative is a baffling fabrication and we are unsure why we are hearing it) or it contains too much truth: too many interpretations, more than one can cause mentally to cohere. At both sides of the

---

[20] Karl Kraus, *Half Truths and One-and-a-Half Truths: Karl Kraus: Selected Aphorisms*, ed. and trans. Harry Zohn (Manchester: Carcanet, 1986), 67.

binary, the result is a text which cannot live up to the extent of the revelation which its form promised.[21]

This sense of both an aphorism's ambiguous import and its partially deflated revelation carries as an aesthetic into Smith's 'Never Again' from *A Good Time Was Had By All*:

> Never again will I weep
> And wring my hands
> And beat my head against the wall
> Because
> Me nolentem fata trahunt
> But
> When I have had enough
> I will arise
> And go unto my Father
> And I will say to Him:
> Father, I have had enough.[22]

The pacing and line lengths in the second half suggest that the text is building to a definite and significant climax. The repetition, the Biblical language, and the penultimate colon all inscribe that final line with dramatic weight. But what we get is anticlimax: the frank but weightless 'Father, I have had enough'.

'Having enough', in its first appearance in the poem, seems to be the stimulus which will lead causally to action and conclusion: reaction, suicide, escape. What really happens, however, is startlingly undramatic: subtle and hard to define. Action is replaced by repetition, a restatement of the status quo ('I have had enough') which seems, in its content, to confirm it as inescapable.

To have enough, moreover, is a scarcely palpable act, implying modesty of desire both past and present. It suggests both that much has been silently endured, and hints in its phrasing at an asceticism latent in the refusal of more (anything). The speaker makes a declaration to God which contains no demand and involves no threat: it is a quiet statement, barely in itself 'enough' even to constitute a complaint. The announcement seems to have little to do with her Father. We never witness his reply. It is unclear what, if anything, she could expect him to say.

---

[21] On the uselessness of proverb, as a mode which can be deployed to support any possible decision, see Ben Grant, *The Aphorism and Other Short Forms* (London and New York: Routledge, 2016), 63, who suggests nevertheless that 'the comfort proverbs provide' means that they offer their own kind of use-value (64).

[22] Stevie Smith, *A Good Time Was Had By All* (London: Jonathan Cape, 1937), 64.

And yet it is hard to see this ending as unsatisfactory. It is 'enough'. It is enough for the speaker—making the announcement seem itself sufficiently satisfying—and for us as readers. It is enough to end the poem—and, it is at least partly implied, the speaker's existence. In Smith's hands, the phrase hardens into a piece of language charged with an omnipotent imperiousness. A drawing in her archive in Tulsa lifts it from the poem and presents it on its own, an aphoristically-contained caption for an image (see Figure 1.4).[23] As so often (as the introduction outlined), this shows a girl frozen in an act of declaration, fingers spread emphatically.

'Father, I have had enough' is both over- and underdetermined, in form and content respectively. We sense that it has power, and the fact that we never find out how or why seems of secondary importance even as we are entirely aware of Smith's sleight of hand.[24] We are content to view it as revelatory in the full knowledge that no successful revelation is made.

The dilemma of 'Never Again', then, has multiple parts. Firstly, we are surprised that the closing statement has been made at all: its anticlimax dismantles our narrative expectations. But more, our difficulty as readers lies in grasping that a statement of unhappiness which should have had no effect has somehow managed to claim a (contestable) degree of victory. A woman going to her God and saying with great and quiet dignity that she has had enough would in any other situation be interpreted as an event which has no effect and serves no purpose. Here, though, it is (ambiguously) enough. Something utterly light has simultaneously laid claim to real weight.

And this leads to the poem's third striking discharge: this demand is meaningful precisely in the sense that it is prepared to have no real effect. Though an 'I' speaks in this poem, imagining addressing God directly, this is not, I suggest, a lyric 'I'.[25] The polyvocality of these poems, channelling various and unpredictable voices, means that they resist a lyric voice which might intimately address an other; in which, to adopt Jonathan Culler's phrase, 'poets call on a universe they hope will prove responsive, and their demands often prove seductive'.[26] If lyric makes

---

[23] Series 2, Box 1, Folder 11. Stevie Smith papers, 1924–1970. Coll. No. 1976.012. McFarlin Library. Department of Special Collections and University Archives. The University of Tulsa. The line is scribbled out, apparently with a different implement; it is impossible to speculate on why, given Smith's repurposing of her drawings in different contexts, but it is clear that at one point she thought the line a suitable caption for this image.

[24] I am indebted to Anne-Lise François' study of the 'reticent assertion' (*Open Secrets: The Literature of Uncounted Experience* (Stanford: Stanford University Press, 2008), 22). Her argument delineates a mode of speech which presents itself as utterly light. But while François focuses on texts which do not mark themselves, Smith's texts flag themselves up, rhetorically emphasize themselves, even while they force the reader to consider them entirely lightweight. Such self-presentation is inherent in the aphorism; as I suggest, the form of the aphorism makes it dismissable even as it presents itself as unignorably significant and eternal. Its formal effects therefore sharpen the vexation of its 'reticent assertion': when something presents as reassuringly solid, we are frustrated to find it weightless.

[25] Mark Sandy suggests certain parallels between the aphorism and the lyric: both are distilled and concise, and can cross genre boundaries. See '"A Ruin Amidst Ruins": Modernity, Literary Aphorisms, and Romantic Fragments', in *Aphoristic Modernity:1880 to the Present*, ed. Kostas Boyiopoulos and Michael Shallcross (Leiden: Brill, 2020), 37–52.

[26] Jonathan Culler, *Theory of the Lyric* (Cambridge, MA, and London: Harvard University Press, 2015), vii.

42 STEVIE SMITH AND THE APHORISM

Figure 1.4 'Father, I have had enough'. Series 2, Box 1, Folder 11. Stevie Smith papers, 1924–1970. Coll. No. 1976.012. McFarlin Library. Department of Special Collections and University Archives. The University of Tulsa. By permission of Faber and Faber Ltd, New Directions Publishing Corp, and the McFarlin Library.

requests of the world in the faith that they will or could be heard and fulfilled, as Culler suggests, 'Never Again' showcases how Smith's writing repudiates both lyric's voice and its secure orientation towards an (imagined) responsive other.

In its refusal to have an effect, in its derivation of value precisely from its withdrawal from eliciting change and response from the world, 'Never Again' participates in the aphoristic. Aphorism overlaps with the poetic, in its use of rhyme and rhythm; fundamentally, however, it is anti-lyric. It is starkly original, and in that way carrying the trace of its originator, yet in its formal self-sufficiency shaking its skirts clear of dependence on the mind which produced it, and on any postulated audience. It refuses to make an address in faith of a hearing, and it therefore cannot be attended to. In his journal, the (aphoristic) poet Wallace Stevens explored how part of the aphoristic encounter derives from the fact that it is impossible really to permanently heed aphorism in the way that its delivery seems to command:

> There are no end of gnomes that might influence people—but do not. When you first feel the truth of, say, an epigram, you feel like making it a rule of conduct. But this one is displaced by that, and things go on in their accustomed way.[27]

The aphorism claims a truth which we nevertheless inevitably fail to implement. One aphorism is displaced by another, as in Smith's stream of aphorisms in 'My Muse', so that each cannot be heard and heeded fully. Things go on in their accustomed way. The aphorism is sealed: for Derrida, a 'totality that claims self-sufficiency', 'dissociated' both from the reader and from real-world utility.[28] It is independent of us, and therefore indifferent to us. Derrida's language, in the same essay, unpacks how the very absoluteness of the aphorism's authority allows it to withdraw from readers:

> ...authoritative, peremptory, dogmatic eloquence, self-legitimating to the point of complacency, when it does everything to save itself a demonstration.[29]

Derrida's aphorism is 'complacent': self-satisfied, needing or expecting nothing beyond itself. It is willing to share no more than its brusque, delimited substance with the reader. Refusing dialogue, it denies access both to the context which created it and to any further explanation which might aid understanding and enable it to have an impact (on the reader, on the world). Saving itself 'a demonstration', the aphorism trades on the implicit assertion that its epiphanic potential, conveyed formally through Coyle's 'boundary-effects', is self-evident. This is the verbal

---

[27] Quoted in Coyle, 15.

[28] Jacques Derrida, 'Fifty-two Aphorisms for a Foreword', in *Psyche: Inventions of the Other*, ed. Peggy Kamuf and Elizabeth Rottenberg, trans. Andrew Benjamin (Stanford: Stanford University Press, 2008), 2: 124.

[29] Derrida, 124.

44   STEVIE SMITH AND THE APHORISM

frugality of a knowledge whose magnitude, ironically, allows it to hold itself 'in reserve'.[30] Self-cancellation or self-minimization is built into the aphorism's truth-claim—which is, crucially, no less insistent for that. And because it is so detached from and indifferent to us, it renounces lasting power over its audience. The aphorism's impact in the moment of encounter does not cross over into real-world results. As Stevens implies, the knowledge it provides seldom leads to action.

Pompey's key epiphany in *Novel on Yellow Paper* (1936)—the moment, perhaps, on which this fugitive text turns—hinges on such an idea of revelatory but unusable knowledge. Pompey recounts how, at eight, she was sent to a convalescent home. Wildly unhappy, the child cries and refuses to eat, hoping she will die. When this plan fails, she has a revelation: she does not need to court Death passively, weeping and hoping he will come. She can simply commit suicide whenever she likes:

> ... when I sat up and said: Death has got to come if I call him, I never called him and never have.
>
> (*Novel*, 123)

Smith repositions this epiphany into aphoristic respectability, by adding it, in almost the same imperious terms, to the end of her version of Dido's final speech in the *Aeneid*:

> Come Death, you know you must come when you're called
> Although you're a god. And this way, and this way, I call you.
> ('Dido's Farewell to Aeneas', CP, 379)

When eight-year-old Pompey accesses that revelation, it is presented as a turning point in her life, though it leads to no action and no palpable change. In fact, it is precisely because she has had this revelation that she does not need to use it. Her knowledge that Death is her slave frees her from the burden of trying to die. As a result of her epiphany, '[she] never called him' and was, obliquely, reconciled to her own existence.

Such an epistemology of unusable revelation is difficult to access critically. Eve Kosofsky Sedgwick suggests that, as readers, our current 'paranoid' Ricoeurean schema places:

> ... an extraordinary stress on the efficacy of knowledge per se—knowledge in the form of exposure ... as though to make something visible as a problem were, if

---

[30] Derrida, 125.

not a mere hop, skip, and jump away from getting it solved, at least self-evidently a step in that direction ...[31]

This is a model in which real-world impact is assumed to be built into knowledge, and in which revelation that fails to provide impact is seen as excessive. From this perspective, it is tempting to sum up Smith's poems with the striking word chosen by her aunt to describe one of her early efforts. The poem 'Spanky Wanky', Aunt said, was 'unnecessary' ('Syler's Green', MA, 94).

> *Spanky Wanky had a sister*
> *He said, I'm sure a black man kissed her*
> *For she's got a spot just here*
> *Twas a beauty spot my dear*
> *And it looks most awfully quaint*
> *Like a blob of jet black paint ...* (MA, 94)

Aunt may of course have meant that the poem's sexual content (or, indeed, its racism) was unnecessary, but Smith presents the word as a criticism of the poem as a whole. In that light, 'unnecessary' seems an extraordinarily tangential descriptor. One could imagine many alternative criticisms, but 'unnecessary' underlines Aunt's inclination to gauge 'Spanky Wanky''s textual value in terms, of all things, of utility and of excess. There is too much of the poem (we are reminded of the '*so many*' of 'E.B') and none of it is any use.

The absurdity of Aunt's remark obviously derives from the fact that 'Spanky Wanky' stages a rejection of utility. Not only do the poem's rhythms assimilate it into the tradition of playground skipping chants, designed to mark time rather than convey semantic content, but Spanky Wanky's observations are ultimately pointless:

> *But when he told his sister that*
> *She threw at him her gorgeous hat*
> *And with airs that made her swanky*
> *Said, I hate you Spanky Wanky.* (MA, 94)

The poem ends irresolutely: in anti-climax, with a simper and an ineffectual hat-toss. Much of Smith's writing undermines attempts to use it within a wider interpretative frame. This judgement is distinct from labelling her work 'play'; Martin Pumphrey's influential chapter suggests that 'Smith's poetry ... exploits the interrogative play signal to challenge conventional literary and cultural frames',

---

[31] Eve Kosofsky Sedgwick, 'Paranoid Reading and Reparative Reading; or, You're So Paranoid, You Probably Think This Essay Is About You', in *Touching Feeling: Affect, Pedagogy, Performativity* (Durham and London: Duke University Press, 2003), 138–139.

46 STEVIE SMITH AND THE APHORISM

identifying her work with the subversive Bakhtinian carnivalesque.[32] But calling Smith's poetry 'play' continues to work within the strategies of paranoid reading which Sedgwick identifies (it still assumes that Smith is writing in order to subvert authority) and is doubly overwriting as a result. Not only does this designation minimize the truth-claim of her work, and its (complex) weightiness: it also, ironically, involves an attempt to reclaim play as important, with purposes beyond itself.

Smith's aphoristic aesthetic allows her, then, to sabotage utility of the sort which the aphorism, ironically, promises through its tool-like form: both to the reader and to the critic who would integrate her into a broader analysis. 'Spanky Wanky' is disturbing but ultimately ignorable. Its pacey weight and urgent rhythm are belied by its 'unnecessary' excess—too tasteless, too violent, too formally overdetermined—which encourages us to treat the text as discardable.[33] Smith's work is aphoristically excessive, like Karl Kraus's 'Waste' aphorisms.[34] The sense is of aphorisms as the residue of an oversized idea, too big to handle, which had to be discarded. Both weighty and weightless, the aphorism, like Smith's poems, can only be read and then abandoned.

The tonal flatness of 'Never Again' encourages us to hover on this borderline between mental assimilation of the text, and its dismissal. 'Father, I have had enough' refuses melodramatic inflection. Its very reticence allows it to stand highly emphasized. We simultaneously feel that we must stay and try to understand further, and that there is no more to be said: the only possible response is to pass on by.[35] Smith has highlighted, here, the crucial gap in the aphorism's claim to authority, which Wallace Stevens hinted at in his journal. When he writes 'this one is displaced by that, and things go on in their accustomed way', Stevens builds dismissability into the heart of the aphoristic project.

Oscar Wilde's writing makes visible this rhythm of self-cancelling textual authority. His aphorisms use brief, clear words to make self-contained sentences:

The artist is the creator of beautiful things.

To reveal art and conceal the artist is art's aim.

The critic is he who can translate into another manner or a new material his impression of beautiful things.[36]

---

[32] Martin Pumphrey, 'Play, Fantasy, and Strange Laughter: Stevie Smith's Uncomfortable Poetry', in Sanford Sternlicht, *In Search of Stevie Smith* (Syracuse: Syracuse University Press, 1991), 100, 112.

[33] Discardability also derives from lightness: too casual or glibly dashed-off to be worth keeping. See Stern, 111: 'the aphorism is written as it were casually'.

[34] Kraus, 'Abfälle'.

[35] Compare with Marion Faber's description of how one reads La Rochefoucauld: 'savoring provocations and putdowns, mulling them over, and going on'. Faber, 'The Metamorphosis of the French Aphorism: La Rochefoucauld and Nietzsche', *Comparative Literature Studies* 23, no. 3 (1986): 207.

[36] Oscar Wilde, *Complete Works of Oscar Wilde*, intr. Merlin Holland (London: HarperCollins, 2003), 17.

They claim the dignity of confident clarity: their message, they signal, is so evidently worth revealing that they need not seek an audience's reaction. The act of announcement is enough in itself. The certainty of Wilde's copulas, the elegance of the alternating 'reveal' and 'conceal' in the second aphorism, create an impression of a writer wholly in control of his subject, needing no assistance from a responding reader.

With that assured polish comes a slipperiness. Because every word is perfectly placed, into an impeccably smooth surface, they exercise no friction; because the aphorisms want nothing from the reader, they exercise no traction. Elegance of style and comparative brevity gives them speed; even Wilde's longer aphorism, in this set of three, darts past the reader quickly. The aphorism's audience marvels first at the text's technical brilliance, and thinks later.

This process becomes especially visible when Wilde puts his aphorisms into dialogue. Both his plays and the early parts of *The Picture of Dorian Gray* (1890) present aphorisms as swappable currency, in the tradition of the French salon maxim.[37] Nevertheless, they possess the same discardability, the same resistance to declaring absolute truth, as Smith's writing. Wilde's aphorisms often conceal their strangeness, reworking clichés to reverse their meanings in a way which takes time to process.[38] But in his writing, one aphorism immediately follows another, or else a change of subject. The reader's attention is constantly elicited, and overstimulation leads to boredom, a withdrawal from a context which demands too much.[39]

Wilde's characters help to call into question the idea that aphorisms invite or enhance dialogue.[40] They may counter with aphorisms of their own (each neutralized by the next), ignore each other's aphorisms, or tell their interlocutors that they talk nonsense. Characters respond to witty wisecracks with the same banal inconsequence which, we suppose, the aphorisms are satirizing.

ALGERNON: Relations are simply a tedious pack of people, who haven't got the remotest knowledge of how to live, nor the smallest instinct about when to die.

---

[37] On Wilde's aphorisms, see Grant, 104, and Sandra Siegel, 'Wilde's Use and Abuse of Aphorisms', *Newsletter of the Victorian Studies Association of Western Canada* 12, no. 1 (1986): 22) who consider whether Wilde's aphorisms are true; and Simon Reader's discussion of how Wilde's aphorisms act 'like individuals, actors, appearing in different works and voiced by different characters' (Simon Reader, 'Social Notes: Oscar Wilde, Francis Bacon, and the Medium of Aphorism', *Journal of Victorian Culture* 18, no. 4 (2013): 461).

[38] On Wilde's reworking of clichés, see Umberto Eco, 'Wilde: Paradox and Aphorism', in *On Literature*, trans. Martin McLaughlin, 62–83 (London: Vintage, 2006).

[39] Despite (in fact, I suggest, because of) their aphorisms, Wilde's characters are always bored. *Dorian Gray*'s Basil Hallward is 'listless', and in *A Woman of No Importance* (1894), Lord Illingworth talks constantly about being bored. Oscar Wilde, *The Picture of Dorian Gray*, in *Complete Works of Oscar Wilde*, 18–23; Wilde, 'A Woman of No Importance,' in *Complete Works of Oscar Wilde*, 487, 493.

[40] See for instance Kostas Boyiopoulos and Michael Shallcross, 'Introduction', in *Aphoristic Modernity*, 1–20.

48 STEVIE SMITH AND THE APHORISM

JACK: Ah! I haven't got any relations ...[41]

This dialogue pre-empts G. K. Chesterton's criticism of conversations in 'the new novel' in 1901: 'it is not conversation at all, but a kind of savage competition ... the new comment is not meant as a cap, but as an extinguisher'.[42] Dialogue, such as it is, happens not because of the aphorism, but in spite of it. Each aphorism flattens the conversation, which must then pick itself back up and limp on. These aphorisms sink without trace; they have no impact. When aphorism follows aphorism, all are reduced to the same bloodless tonal flatness.

Something similar occurs in Smith's long poem 'The House of Over-Dew', about the Minnim family's decision to establish a retreat for missionaries. She describes this text, in a performance introduction, in terms of flatness:

> The House of Over-Due is a very long poem indeed, and flat. It is meant for several voices, say half a dozen, each playing in with each, as people do in conversations about friends they have in common who are not there. So there will be a flat statement, and then another voice coming in with something else they have remembered, to fill it out.[43]

This sense of 'flatness' (as in 'a flat statement') as self-sufficiency, as the refusal to ask questions or answer them other than in the most gnomic and lateral way, takes us back to Derrida's definition of the aphorism: a mode of speech offering nuggets of information, 'dissociated' from each other.[44] 'The House of Over-Dew' calls on us to receive each of its paratactically-offered nuggets, each 'flat statement', as significant:

> Mrs Minnim had courage and was cheerful
> But she was by now an old lady. Suddenly
> There was the gift of a little money. Mr Minnim
> Bought chasubles for visiting priests. But at first
> There were no visitors at all ... (CP, 641)

The voices loom authoritatively out of the darkness; their lack of mutual connection presents them as absolute—the imperious happenings of a fable or fairytale, mappable on to infinitely broad human concerns as the aphorism

---

[41] Wilde, 'The Importance of Being Earnest', in *Complete Works of Oscar Wilde*, 370.

[42] G. K. Chesterton, 'Critics and Conversation', in *G. K. Chesterton at the Daily News: Literature, Liberalism and Revolution, 1901–1913*, ed. Julia Stapleton, vol. 1 (London: Pickering & Chatto, 2012), 86.

[43] Stevie Smith, introduction to 'The House of Over-Dew', Series 2, Box 1, Folder 4, Stevie Smith papers, University of Tulsa. Smith moved, in drafts, between the spellings 'Due' and 'Dew'.

[44] Derrida, 117.

seems to be—rather than situational or contextually valid truths. To say something 'flatly' insists on its undeniability. It stresses that it has said everything necessary—spreading everything out to view on a flat surface, revealing everything no matter how distasteful—and that no further argument or response is possible. The only thing that can follow a 'flat statement' is another 'flat statement', just as aphorism follows aphorism in an aphoristic series, or a Wildean dialogue. Succeeding units do not respond to those which came before, and they do not build up into a larger cohesive whole. It appends events, one after the other, without adjudicating on how we are to assign emotional and narrative significance. The responsibility for excitement and tangible event lifts: the flatness of this plot resides, to quote Adorno's description of Hölderlin, in the 'supreme passivity' of seriation, with each new event proffered as self-evidently enough in itself.[45] Here, this lack of responsiveness—where a statement is made but not followed up, not graced with the explicit recognition as significant, as worth attending to and recuperating, which absorption into a cohesive and connected narrative would offer—foregrounds the sadness of the poem. 'The House of Over-Dew' is about repeated failed attempts to get what one wants. Cynthia loses Georgie, the Minnims lose their savings on their wild scheme, Georgie does not get the post at Oxford that he hopes for. The final line of the poem is part of a Latin prayer which Cynthia reads to her class. 'Come, love of God', she cries. But (as with 'Father, I have had enough' in 'Never Again') no love is forthcoming; the cry remains there, baldly unanswered, on the page.

Mirroring this indifferent world, Smith's disconnected aphoristic delivery of a family's tragic downfall deflates the affective potential of what she describes, limiting the reader's ability to feel or express pity. To sing this poem as one 'flat' statement after another reflects its aesthetic of unsuccess: the way one abortive bid for advancement follows another. Flatly presenting flat statements attenuates our emotional reaction to the very average disappointments which this poem describes, caused by nothing and of no real significance to the world: failed engagements, failed careers, the loss of savings, the drudgery of washing dishes. These descriptions of quotidian heartbreak are not allowed to build into anything greater. Each remains contained both physically and emotionally, in the extent of the affective demand they make on the reader, and things—as Stevens observes—can go on in their accustomed way.

---

[45] Theodor W. Adorno, 'Parataxis: On Hölderlin's Late Poetry', in *Notes to Literature*, ed. Rolf Tiedemann, trans. Shierry Weber Nicholsen (New York: Columbia University Press, 1992), volume 2: 135.

'A Strong Way Out': To and From the Aphorism

It would be easy to read the aphoristic aesthetic's lightness and dismissability as catastrophic: to suggest that Smith is emphasizing the pointlessness of truth-claims such as the speaker's in 'Never Again'. Instead, her poetry drives towards a model of value which constructs itself in the moments of lapse implicit in the rhythm of aphoristic engagement. In its dissociated stops and starts, the aphoristic text demands to be simply passed by. Yet this tendency to be ignored, or not quite read, permits the reader brief, merciful escapes from truth-claims which exceed immediate comprehension. In this system, the weightlessness of the aphorism's function does not negate its value. It becomes, in contrast, the source of that value. Aphorism offers a model of reading which can accommodate impossible and illegitimate extremes of feeling, by allowing the reader to depart from them and return to them as necessary.

For Smith, things 'go[ing] on in their accustomed way' can assume the scale of a triumph. Pompey's revelation in the *Novel on Yellow Paper* nursing home makes nothing happen, but it is essential. Although weightless, it assumes a weight in Pompey's life which is difficult either to quantify or to underplay. The aphoristic assertion, then, continues to stand on some level even though it is inevitably dismissed. Admitting a truth too big to assimilate in one reading, one's capacity to respond to the aphorism is exhausted before the text's potential has been used up. Yet the necessity of then passing it by does not negate its validity. Smith's 'The English Visitor' from *Not Waving But Drowning* (1957) delineates this complex value of the aphoristic encounter. It portrays an experience no less striking for being passed by, half-forgotten. A widow mourns by her husband's grave:

> Oh my darling why did you leave me
> To lie so cold where I cannot come,
> I only wished to have you by me
> In the busy town.
>
> How beautiful are the Scottish mountains
> Their backs are like ancient mammoths so quiet
> And I should like to walk on the mountain
> While it is light. (CP, 348)

A moment of grief is followed, seamlessly, by a meditation on beauty. The thoughts are discrete: presented in aphoristically self-contained stanzas, their language is precise and declarative ('Their backs are like ancient mammoths'; 'I only wished to have you by me'). Identical rhymes (me/me, mountains/mountain) stall the verses, sealing them conclusively back into themselves. Indeed, the first stanza reads as an account of aphoristic impenetrability: it nods to a place 'where I cannot come'.

Equally, however, Smith complicates this weightiness, concluding each stanza with a half-line ('In the busy town', 'While it is light'). Like Kraus's aphorism, this half-line termination presents itself as simultaneously half a truth and one-and-a-half truths. The 'halfness' suggests incompleteness—but also an absolute economy which uses no more words than needed; complete simplicity which nevertheless states everything necessary, with the resistance to demonstration which characterizes the Derridean aphorism.

Formally, then, these stanzas are at once generously expressive, insisting on their own significance, and reticent. The simultaneity of these impulses reflects the balance between deep, emphasized emotion, and a carefully delimited modesty of desire. The widow's grief is underscored ('Oh my darling why did you leave me / To lie so cold where I cannot come'), but her love's expression is imagined in undemanding terms ('I only wished to have you by me'). Paralleling this experience of grief is her response to the mountains' beauty: expressed in superlatives ('so quiet', 'How beautiful'), but enacted in a humbly small wish against this sublime landscape ('I should like to walk on the mountain / While it is light').

This is, in each case, an expansive emotional reaction with a small outcome: magnitude modulated into something simple. It is both one-and-a-half and half; both potent and dismissable. Because of this, and because the stanzas reflect each other in their tonal and structural self-sufficiency, the widow can grieve and then pass, almost impalpably, from her grief. Very gently, the Englishwoman transitions from mourning to forgetfulness.

Becoming alert to this rhythm enables us to rehabilitate the aphorism's frustratingly unassimilable revelation. The failure of a reader or character to fully grasp a form of knowledge which is (or claims to be) defined by excessive magnitude and significance can comprise a benevolent relief-offering: the Englishwoman passes from her grief because it is unsustainably severe. The aphoristic aesthetic involves both a swelling into (emotional, semantic) excess, and the construction of an escape-route out of that burdensome excess: the aphorism's excessive truth-claim can be abandoned because its brevity offers us reprieve. It enables the exit service which Smith, strikingly, places at the centre of the poetic function in her aphorisms in 'My Muse': 'The human creature is alone in his carapace. Poetry is a strong way out' (MA, 126).

Accordingly, Smith's aphoristic aesthetic stages a build-up of untapped, untappable, troublingly excessive significance (bulging, perhaps, under that carapace) from which escape is cast as relief. Pompey performs this most obviously in *Novel on Yellow Paper*. She tells the story of Karl, slowly and digressively, landing at one point at a question whose terrible answer is dimly beginning to take form:

I too can see that idea of sleeping, dreaming, happily dreaming Germany, her music, her philosophy, her wide fields and broad rivers, her gentle women. But the dream changes, and how is it to-day, how is it to-day in this year of 1936, how is it to-day? (*Novel*, 33)

52 STEVIE SMITH AND THE APHORISM

Without answering, Pompey changes tack. The story has become too troubling, she suggests: 'gentle reader you have been very patient very kind and forbearing indeed in this matter of Karl'. So we are treated to 'some ... nice little quotations' (*Novel*, 33) instead: the narrative breaks off to offer the reader a collection of striking asides, cribbed from magazines and textbooks:

> Let everything that creeps console itself, for everything that is elevated dies ...
> The Dead Sea is very fortunately situated as compared with the German potash deposits inasmuch as its waters for practical purposes contain no sulphates. The sulphates though delightful from the theoretical point of view of the academic chemist have the habit of forming a large number of double salts, which would be the despair of many people.
> Jessie: What is a love apple? A love apple is just another name for the tomato.
> (*Novel*, 33–34)

In other words, aphoristic interjections, erupting into the text like the explaining angel in 'The English Visitor', become themselves the rupturing means of escape, the agent of the text's own dismissal. These are ready-made conclusions which do nothing to conclude. Yet somehow, as in 'Never Again', they are 'enough'. I am reminded of how Smith summed up her own poems in the most banal analytic terms. In her recitations, when she chanted or sang her poems, she sometimes closed them off with flatly empty observations: 'Oh, that's awfully good, isn't it?' or 'Oooh, that's terrific!'[46] Smith's bland formulations seal her poems into aphoristic impenetrability, discouraging further comment or interrogation. Climax and conclusion are replaced by simple termination: an empty summary which apologizes neither for its own simplicity, nor for anything which has preceded it. In its economy, the gesture is analogous to the non-revealing revelation of Smith's 'Never Again'. The transition from building climax to non-fulfilment is slight, yet entirely unapologetic. Rather than evading a terrible, important truth, these movements of the aphoristic aesthetic constitute the quiet lapses palpable in 'The English Visitor'. In *Novel on Yellow Paper*, this lapse is a small rest, a brief period of relief, which eventually allows the story of Karl to be finished. Similarly, 'The English Visitor''s interludes of quiet oblivion in fact enable the widow to remember and return to her grief. A passing angel instructs us, explicitly, not to read her passing-by mourning as callous:

> And the people said she would never think of Alan again
> And it was typical of Englishwomen.
> But No, said an angel, you are wrong
> She will think of him freely and frequently
> She is not less sorry than you are ... (CP, 349)

---

[46] Spalding, 194.

Her sorrow remains—she will return to thoughts of her husband 'freely and frequently'—but her grief needs to be characterized by periods of interruption and lapse. Instead of being less potent for that, this rhythm speaks of an emotion too intense to sustain for a long duration. A period of intensely-experienced grief does not work itself out in a single encounter. It does not, if pursued intently, reach a climax, decline, and conclude forever. Its endings are always temporary. It may finish for a while, when one is too tired to continue experiencing it. Then, presently, it resumes again. A pattern emerges where, as in our engagement with the aphoristic, we can only negotiate intense (intellectual or emotional) experience through alternating departure and return. Since the aphorism's potential outstrips the reader's cognitive capacity, the reader can pass by in the knowledge that they can always—and will, 'freely and frequently'—come back.[47] Stern hints at this potential in the aphorism, suggesting that such texts:

> ... spur us on, every time anew, to the discovery of ... new insights ... yet, when we have surveyed the landscape which the aphorism illuminated for us we do return to it once again ...[48]

In this light, Smith's recurring set-piece phrases, such as Death who comes when we call, take on new significance. Seeing these repetitions as aphoristic acknowledges that they constitute epiphanies which are absolute, but which both Smith's characters and Smith's readers need nevertheless to have again and again. In every moment of encounter, the epiphanic phrases exceed one's cognitive capacity: they must be left unused, and later returned to.

Stylistically accomplished, aphoristic and epigrammatic texts possess (or claim) the smoothness and wit which repel further interrogation. Unable to penetrate aphorism's boundaries, the reader skims instead over the surface, and eventually abandons the attempt to get further. And yet, despite its refusal to yield insights, that polished imperviousness of style nags at the reader's attention. The reader pauses in a space configured to insist that it is worth attending to, but which does not instruct them, specifically, on how to attend or to what. Failing to penetrate the text, the reader passes on from aphorism to aphorism, over smooth surfaces which balance between weighty significance and light dismissability.

In Smith's hands, aphorism acts as a form from which nothing—neither moral lessons nor applicable wisdom—can be derived; to which one returns again and again without result. An aphorism may be apposite to a situation, but it does nothing to change that situation. It has no effect beyond the immediate shock of pleasure at how well it fits. Aphorism may therefore become affectless: an emblem

---

[47] Brian Dillon gestures towards this aphoristic rhythm of return and departure: 'the aphorism is a sharp or pointed thing, violently deployed—though this action can never be definitive, but must be repeated time and again.' Brian Dillon, *Essayism* (London: Fitzcarraldo Editions, 2017), 74.
[48] Stern, 221.

54 STEVIE SMITH AND THE APHORISM

for emotional flatness, or withdrawal from an inhospitable world. It shrinks from explanation: it says its piece, and then folds itself away. Appropriately, John Gross bookends *The Oxford Book of Aphorisms* with texts which testify to their own uselessness, their own exempt status from the run of everyday life:

> Everything has been said before, but since nobody listens we have to keep going back and beginning all over again.
> ANDRÉ GIDE, *Le traité du Narcisse*, 1891[49]
> All the good maxims already exist in the world; we just fail to apply them.
> PASCAL, *Pensées*, 1670[50]

Aphorism, in Smith's hands, defies engagement and use. Reading Smith involves becoming sensitive to an aphoristic 'flatness', clearest in her shorter poems but emerging into view throughout her writing: a statement of fact which refuses argument or sympathy, denying anything further beyond what is explicitly stated. Her flattening-out of bold declarations allows her, as the next chapter will suggest, to position them beyond hearing and heeding. The classical narratives which she so often reworks offer a model for revelation which either does not materialize at all, or which—in the case of the messenger-speech of Greek tragedy, with its aphoristic core—arrives too late to be attended to. By the time it becomes audible to the audience and to the other characters, they find that they have already passed by that aphoristic moment of revelation. Receiving it too late, they cannot penetrate its hard surface for guidance.

---

[49] Gross, *Oxford Book of Aphorisms*, 1.
[50] Gross, *Oxford Book of Aphorisms*, 365.

2
Aphoristic Messages, Too Late

Smith's key figures, as the next three chapters will suggest, are people who rule themselves out of being attended to. They misbehave, they are embarrassing; they listen to the wrong things and say the wrong things, and always in the wrong way. Unheeded, they are like Cassandra in Greek mythology: cursed with a prophetic vision to which no one will pay mind. Smith's speaker, in the poem 'I had a dream ... ', fancies herself a bit of a Cassandra. She travels back to the siege of Troy in a dream, from the present day, knowing everything about how the story goes: 'I saw everywhere, as Cassandra saw too' (CP, 491). But Paris is too 'stupid' to listen to her, and when she says that Troy will inevitably be sacked—for she knows her classics well—Hector grows angry. Stung, the speaker 'laughed / But I felt more like crying' (CP, 490–491). Cassandra would wail and gnash, as she does in Aeschylus's *Agamemnon*; Smith's speaker, in contrast, knows enough to manage the situation away with a laugh. She forestalls the embarrassment of (inevitably) not being heard.

Listening to her would change nothing, anyway. Even as they stand on the walls of Troy, looking towards the Greek tents, Troy has already been sacked: the speaker has read the texts and knows how they go. Every warning the speaker issues is already too late. This trope of belated declarations—issued with ringing force, but uselessly tardy—becomes the aspect of classical literature on which Smith puts most pressure, in her extensive engagement with Greek and Roman texts. Belatedness offers the poem 'Oh stubborn race of Cadmus' seed ... ' its dramatic force. Young Antigone orders Orcus not to let her sister suffer—but she only makes that lordly, imperious declaration after she herself is dead.

> And when they have killed me I shall stand in the Dark Hall
> And cry: Orcus, see that my sister does not suffer at all. (CP, 281)

Antigone is dead. Her declaration empties itself of power, as she cannot enforce it. In performance introductions to this poem, Smith specifically emphasized the belatedness of Antigone's statement:

> It is heartrending, is it not, this backward looking cry, too late, to her sister the soft Ismene.

Stevie Smith and the Aphorism. Noreen Masud, Oxford University Press.
© Noreen Masud (2022). DOI: 10.1093/oso/9780192895899.003.0003

56   STEVIE SMITH AND THE APHORISM

From Hades, with the fire-flush of hell upon her cheeks comes the young
Antigone, with a loving thought—now too late—for her sister, the soft Ismene.[1]

Too late it may be, a now-useless cry, yet Antigone articulates it anyway. It feigns
an impossible certainty, rhetorically reinforcing its impact despite its untrustwor-
thiness in making a command which cannot be obeyed. Drawn by the glamour of
this declaration, Smith presents the lordly sentence with admiration. An equally
grand version recurs in *Some are More Human than Others* (1958). Smith captions a picture of a forcefully-glaring woman, 'I am Antigone and I shall bury my
brother!'[2] These announcements derive their impact from their staginess, absolute language and brevity: their smallness and density allow them to survive their
speakers' deaths, penetrating through from the underworld.

What is at stake in Smith's constant return to the characters and modes of classical literature, as she offers them new ways to survive through literary history?
Reworkings of mythical narrative along feminist lines may subvert patriarchal
norms or reveal new possibilities for lived female experience. Hélène Cixous connects mythic images with the imperative to write for and through the female body,
connecting one's life with the whole of feminine history.[3] Susan Sellers underlines this drive towards real-world function when she notes how rewritings by
women tend to alter their source myths, setting them to different purposes.[4] These
purposes centre around reclamation. This can be of myth itself as a particularly
feminine force, reclaiming the term in the gendered opposition between rational-
ity and the mythical.[5] More specifically, rewritings of myth by women privilege
female voices, allowing them to be heard. Myth, in this work, becomes a means of
challenging authority.

Accordingly, Virginia Woolf's *Three Guineas* (1938), published two years after
Smith's *Novel on Yellow Paper*, uses the figure of Antigone to illustrate the male
desire to control women and resist their power. She maps Creon's abuse of
Antigone on to the 'picture of dead bodies and ruined houses' which stands in
for the atrocities of the Spanish Civil War.[6] Along similar lines, therefore, critics
often begin from the stance that Smith uses myth to resist oppressive systems, since
Smith rewrote classical narratives (as in 'Oh stubborn race of Cadmus' seed ... ')

---

[1] Stevie Smith, performance introductions to 'Oh stubborn race of Cadmus' seed ... ', Series 2, Box
2, Folder 11, Stevie Smith papers, 1924–1970. Coll. No. 1976.012. McFarlin Library. Department of
Special Collections and University Archives. The University of Tulsa.

[2] Stevie Smith, *Some Are More Human Than Others* (London: Peter Owen, 1990), n. pag.

[3] Hélène Cixous, Keith Cohen, and Paula Cohen, 'The Laugh of the Medusa', *Signs* 1, no. 4 (1976):
882–883.

[4] Susan Sellers, *Myth and Fairy Tale in Contemporary Women's Fiction* (Basingstoke: Palgrave,
2001), 128.

[5] Vanda Zajko and Miriam Leonard, *Laughing with Medusa: Classical Myth and Feminist Thought*
(Oxford: Oxford University Press, 2008), 10.

[6] Virginia Woolf, *A Room of One's Own and Three Guineas*, ed. Morag Shiach (Oxford: Oxford
World's Classics, 2008), 363.

from the viewpoint of female protagonists.[7] Yet Smith's reworkings hold short of overthrowing patriarchal structures to enable escape. Jan Montefiore notes how, while Anne Sexton, for example, reinterprets the stories she retells, Smith instead 'shift[s] the emphasis of the story so that the result is an entirely new plot'.[8] This is not subversion. We are not being encouraged to view a known, lasting story in a new light. Smith, I suggest in this chapter, is interested precisely in the failure of new interpretative angles on the classics to struggle into vision. Her sustained engagement with Greek epigram and Euripides' *Bacchae*, in *Novel on Yellow Paper* (1936) and her poetry, centres on the idea that a message might be missed until it is too late to heed. By the time the aphoristic messages within these texts survive into the present-day, they may already feel outdated or irrelevant. Or else they may be too deeply known already to be of use; or perhaps they become too buried under the detritus of history to pick out.

What Smith adds to the twentieth-century literary history of women rewriting the classics is to foreground, rather than to reverse, the unheedability of aphoristic speakers who move to and from the margins. Smith's classical lines reveal and effect nothing; they come too late to be used or heeded. In inhabiting that mode deeply and curiously, without explicit resistance, she finds a particular narrative schema for her *Novel on Yellow Paper*, in which everything that might happen has already occurred, too late to change. In that novel, excess detail swallows up the aphorism, preventing its revelatory promise from being located, let alone listened to or allowed to have an impact. The aphorism's failure to reveal what it promised means that it lingers on, impenetrable as a monument—just as the phrase 'not waving but drowning' lingered, as described in the introduction, for Rodney Ackland—standing in for the never-achieved revelation in the form of epitaph.

Smith and the Classics

Smith's interest in the classics ranges widely. *Novel on Yellow Paper* revolves around Euripides' *Bacchae*, 'Dido's Farewell to Aeneas' (1957) translates Dido's final speech from Book IV of Virgil's *Aeneid* (CP, 379), and a recently-collected poem is entitled 'Professor Snooks Does His Worst with a Grecian Fragment' (CP, 708). Her *Batsford Book of Children's Verse* includes neo-classical pieces such S. T. Coleridge's 'Catullan Hendecasyllables', as well as quotations from Sophocles' *Oedipus Coloneus*, presented and framed as poems in their own right:

[7] See Laura Severin, *Stevie Smith's Resistant Antics* (Madison: University of Wisconsin Press, 1997), 18.
[8] Jan Montefiore, *Feminism and Poetry: Language, Experience, Identity in Women's Writing* (London and New York: Pandora, 1987), 49.

58   STEVIE SMITH AND THE APHORISM

> Chorus: Not to be born at all
> Is best, far best that can befall,
> Next best, when born, with least delay
> To trace the backward way.[9]

Smith drew her knowledge of Latin and Greek poetry largely from school impositions for infractions, which on at least one occasion took the form of a passage of Catullus to learn.[10] Her engagement with the classics stabilized, therefore, at a schoolgirl's point of entry, which prioritized grandeur and recitability. Brief poems such as 'From the Greek' are compactly dramatic:

> To many men strange fates are given
> Beyond remission or recall
> But the worst fate of all (tra la)
> 's to have no fate at all (tra la). (CP, 22)

Smith's epigrammatic presentation of these lines underscores the fact that her reception of the classics often privileges the memorable aphorisms or 'gnomes' for which ancient Greece was known.[11] Hippocrates' pithy medical precepts acted as a mnemonic allowing symptoms and treatments to be easily remembered and repeated,[12] while epigrams originated as engravings on monuments to mark an event or occasion, before developing into a literary genre. Roman epigrams were pointed and satirical. Catullus, of whom Smith learned so much as a punishment, wrote many epigrams which have survived; he influenced Martial's epigrams—brief, addressed to a pseudonymized individual, often witty and cutting—which have come to exemplify the contemporary sense of the epigrammatic.[13]

Smith writes several poems which participate in this epigrammatic tradition: carrying compact little messages far past their temporal origin-points. 'Lord Say-and-Seal', for instance, addresses a named individual with satirical, critical brevity:

> Lord Say-and-Seal, Lord Say-and-Seal
> Why not for once say and *reveal*
> All the dark thoughts your words go over
> To make a pretty bog-hole cover. (CP, 528)

---

[9] Stevie Smith, ed. *The Batsford Book of Children's Verse* (London: Batsford, 1970), 23.

[10] Frances Spalding, *Stevie Smith: A Critical Biography* (London: Faber and Faber, 1988), 28.

[11] See Ben Grant, *The Aphorism and Other Short Forms* (London and New York: Routledge, 2016), 6–7.

[12] Richard T. Gray, *Constructive Destruction: Kafka's Aphorisms: Literary Tradition and Literary Transformation* (Tübingen: Niemeyer, 1987), 24.

[13] On Catullus's influence on Martial, see Bruce W. Swann, *Martial's Catullus: The Reception of an Epigrammatic Rival* (Zürich and New York: George Olms, 1994). Swann notes that Martial mentions a 'Catullus' at least twenty-five times in his writing (33).

More widely, Smith builds her favourite aphoristic tags, over and over again, into her classical adaptations. The first two lines of 'Dido's Farewell to Aeneas' echo the phrasing of a 'schoolroom tag' which Smith enjoyed and quoted frequently: *Fata nolentuem trahunt, volentem ducunt* (The fates drag the unwilling, the willing they lead) ('What Poems Are Made Of', MA, 128). Dido, Smith suggests, is being led; she is one of the willing, accepting her externally-imposed fate:

> I have lived and followed my fate without flinching, followed it gladly
> And now, not wholly unknown, I come to the end. (CP, 379)

To the end of the poem, Smith adds two lines which have no precedent in the classical original:

> Come Death, you know you must come when you're called
> Although you're a god. And this way, and this way, I call you.
> (CP, 379)

The sentiment lasts across Smith's writing. It turns up in *Novel on Yellow Paper*, as Chapter 1 described, when eight-year-old Pompey realizes she can summon death whenever she likes, and in Smith's last poem, 'Come, Death (2)'.

> Ah me, sweet Death, you are the only god
> Who comes as a servant when he is called, you know ... (CP, 658)

Smith adds a conclusion to 'Dido', in other words, which has survival value: the 'portability' which John Fagg attributed to the aphorism, capable of being lifted out of a longer text and circulated in its own right.[14] The brief punchiness of these lines enables them to survive across texts, being quoted and requoted.

This survival of the classically-configured invocation, through Smith's writing—pulled out of contexts and reborn in new ones—echoes Jacques Derrida's description of how aphorisms work. 'Despite their fragmentary appearance', he writes, 'they signal toward the memory of a totality, at the same time ruin and monument'.[15] Lines attest to something larger from which they were excerpted; they stand in, stonily, for that monumental wholeness. Derrida's description of aphorism connects to the epigram's classical origin as an engraving on a monument, testifying to the memory of a person or event.[16] That aspect of classical writing

---

[14] John Fagg, *On the Cusp: Stephen Crane, George Bellows, and Modernism* (Tuscaloosa: The University of Alabama Press, 2009), 136.

[15] Jacques Derrida, 'Fifty-two Aphorisms for a Foreword', in *Psyche: Inventions of the Other*, ed. Peggy Kamuf and Elizabeth Rottenberg, trans. Andrew Benjamin (Stanford: Stanford University Press, 2008), 2: 125.

[16] Niall Livingstone and Gideon Nisbet, *Epigram* (Cambridge: Cambridge University Press, 2010), 5.

60 STEVIE SMITH AND THE APHORISM

was key to the hard, small poems of the Imagists, twenty years before Smith's first book, which signal their affiliation to this epigrammatic and monumental tradition. Richard Aldington's 'To a Greek Marble' (1912) summons up a silent statue, and H.D.'s 'Epigram' (1913) rewrote an engraving on a tomb. Subtitled 'After the Greek',[17] it sits as a precursor to Smith's 'From the Greek':

> The golden one is gone from the banquets;
> She, beloved of Atimetus,
> The swallow, the bright Homonoea:
> Gone the dear chatterer;
> Death succeeds Atimetus.[18]

The speaker's declaration is public yet intimate. They describe Homonoea in terms fully legible only to those who knew her, tying her directly and indissolubly to a particular individual in a certain time and place. This is how Manuel Baumbach, Andrej Petrovic, and Ivana Petrovic sum up the particular workings of the public epigram:

> ... fixed both in time and space: the passer-by comes, sees, reads, reacts and—eventually—passes by. Epigrams, in particular, which are closely in dialogue with 'their' material monuments ... are not meant to leave their place and be 'taken away' by the passer-by, as they would lose parts of their meaning.[19]

The contradiction is that epigrams demand to be decontextualized—their handy, pithy form begs to be taken away, quoted and requoted—even as, in their classical usage, they remained physically immovable. Ultimately, they can only be passed by. Even as the epigram evolved, in the Renaissance, into a more mobile form,[20] its stony origin means that it retained what Niall Livingstone and Gideon Nisbet call a 'playful ambivalence' between mobility and stasis. Literary epigrams, they claim, 'know they come from stone, and are forever throwing out hints of making the return trip'.[21] They liaise constantly, therefore, with the possibility of irrelevance to the present moment in which they find themselves. Epigrams carve themselves insistently into vision, though the events they describe may be long over. They continue bringing their messages, cryptically, to listeners who may not know how to deploy them.

---

[17] See Eileen Gregory, *H.D. and Hellenism: Classic Lines* (Cambridge: Cambridge University Press, 1997), 55, for a suggestion that Pound, not H.D., assigned this title to the poem.

[18] H.D., *Collected Poems 1912–1944*, ed. Louis L. Martz (New York: New Directions, 1983), 309.

[19] Manuel Baumbach, Andrej Petrovic, and Ivana Petrovic, 'Archaic and Classical Greek Epigram: An Introduction', in *Archaic and Classical Greek Epigram*, ed. Manuel Baumbach, Andrej Petrovic, and Ivana Petrovic (Cambridge: Cambridge University Press, 2010), 15.

[20] See James Doelman, 'Epigrams and Political Satire in Early Stuart England', *Huntington Library Quarterly* 69, no. 1 (2006): 31.

[21] Livingstone and Nisbet, 8.

Carrying Hard Aphoristic Messages in *Novel on Yellow Paper*

Smith's *Novel on Yellow Paper* (1936) revolves around the delivery of messages which may or may not be usable or hearable. The author had played the Second Messenger in a school production of Euripides' *Bacchae*; in an interview with Patrick Garland, she describes the 'terrific effort' involved in learning her lines, but that she then never forgot them.[22] Smith's interest in her own performance of the messenger-role points up the appeal which the part had for her. The messenger is lithe and androgynous: elusive, always in motion, resisting characterization. He represents a marginal figure, darting between worlds and groups, always keeping himself, as Smith described her own ex-centric existence in an interview with Kay Dick, 'well on the edge' of life.[23] Yet he is a hugely significant character: in Greek tragedy, it is the messenger who brings the news of the play's catastrophic turning-point. The messenger couples marginal status with immense importance, and draws serious and sustained attention from all the characters as he expounds in vivid, writerly detail on what has happened, and passes objective judgement.

Novel on Yellow Paper opens, therefore, with an invocation to the messenger-god Hermes, claiming his mythic messenger-role as well as his powerful, fugitively marginal speech:

> Casmilus, whose great name I steal,
> Whose name a greater doth conceal,
> Indulgence, pray,
> And, if I may,
> The winged tuft from either heel.
>
> (*Novel*, 1)

Hermes/Mercury/Camilus becomes the novel's mascot, its 'tutelary deity ... double-facing, looking two ways ... ' (*Novel*, 164).[24] Smith positions him as a kind of army standard for the text, describing him in a 1936 letter to Denis Johnston as 'a dark name to fight under' (MA, 255). His 'winged tufts' promise her and her protagonist Pompey a kind of narrative agility. Smith wrote the novel in a darting, round-the-edges way: she typed it quickly out at work, in spare moments, on

---

[22] Stevie Smith, interview with Patrick Garland, Series 3, 1:24A, Stevie Smith papers, University of Tulsa.

[23] Kay Dick, *Ivy and Stevie* (London: Allison & Busby, 1983), 70.

[24] The misspelling of Camilus as Casmilus is Smith's. On Hermes' recurrence in her work, see Demmy Verbeke, 'On Knowing Greek (And Latin): Classical Elements in the Poetry of Stevie Smith', *International Journal of the Classical Tradition* 16, no. 3/4 (2009): 470; on Hermes' offer of both concealment and visibility, see William May, *Stevie Smith and Authorship* (Oxford: Oxford University Press, 2010), 69; on the riddling nature of Smith's poem 'The Ambassador', see Stephen James, 'Stevie Smith, "A Most Awful Twister"', *Essays in Criticism* 66, no. 2 (2016): 242–259.

62   STEVIE SMITH AND THE APHORISM

the yellow typewriter paper which gave the book its title. *Novel on Yellow Paper* flaunts, in its run-on style, this precarious marginality of its production, emerging at the borders of other parts of life. Moving quickly from anecdote to anecdote, it embodies the ambivalent, to-and-fro movement of Hermes. In this, the text raises the question of how one might speak ambivalently, in a way that keeps one, like Hermes, on the edge of things, without committing lastingly to one stance.

The novel is autobiographical. Smith describes Pompey's life at home with her aunt, with her friends, and her engagement (eventually broken) to 'Freddy', a thinly-disguised version of Smith's real-life fiancé Eric Armitage. In the centre of the text, Pompey remembers the zealous Miss Hogmanimy, who visited her school to educate the girls about sex and spread her message of temperance. Listening to Miss Hogmanimy condemn alcohol, Pompey remembers her school production of the *Bacchae*, in which she too played the second messenger. Her speech, she recalled, closed with the cry: 'Take away wine and there is no Cyprian, No other joy, nothing left to man' (*Novel*, 103).

The messenger, Michael Halleran notes, performs a set function within Greek tragedies. He delivers a long speech in which he describes, in immense and often graphic detail, and with epic diction, the events which he has witnessed.[25] While the chorus states how things are, commenting on the status quo and what the audience has watched unfold, the messenger primarily testifies to the unseen. Though the audience does not see the horrifying events, the messenger gives these events reality by bearing witness to them. It is within the message that the most destructive and impactful parts of the play's action can happen for the spectators.

The epic diction of messenger speeches, particularly those in plays by Euripides, often culminates in aphorism.[26] In *Herakles*, the messenger concludes his long description of Herakles' murder of his wife and sons in madness with 'No human being could be more miserable'; the messenger speech of *Phoenician Women* ends with a summing-up: 'Some of this day's struggles / ended in joy for our city, others in bitter sorrow'.[27] The messenger in *The Children of Heracles* concludes even more succinctly—'Fortune may vanish in one day'—and the messenger in *Iphigenia in Aulis* prefigures *King Lear:* 'The ways of gods are never such as men expect; / They save those who are dear to them'.[28] In all these messenger-speeches, detail accumulates and accumulates, only to be smelted down to a nugget: the core of the message, all that can survive. Only the hard, sealed aphorism is small and contained enough to be conveyed, finally, across the timeline of the play and into history.

[25] Michael R. Halleran, 'Episodes', in *A Companion to Greek Tragedy*, ed. Justina Gregory (Malden, MA and Oxford: Blackwell, 2005), 174.

[26] '[G]nomic conclusion ... is typical of a messenger speech': Michael Lloyd, *The Agon in Euripides* (Oxford and New York: Oxford University Press, 1992), 97.

[27] Euripides, *The Complete Euripides, Volume IV: Bacchae and Other Plays*, ed. Peter Burian and Alan Shapiro (Oxford: Oxford University Press, 2009), 73, 177.

[28] Euripides, *Orestes and Other Plays*, ed. and trans. Philip Vellacott (Harmondsworth: Penguin, 1972), 133, 426.

The *Bacchae* is unusual among Euripides' tragedies in having not one but two messengers, who each conclude their messages with an epigrammatic nugget. The plot runs thus: King Pentheus of Thebes orders the arrest of anyone caught engaging in Dionysian worship. His guards arrest Dionysos himself. As Pentheus confronts the god, the first messenger arrives to describe the bacchanalian revels of Dionysos's worshippers, demonstrating the god's awe-inspiring power, and to urge Pentheus to receive him into the city:

> And so, O master,
> Receive this god, whoever he may be,
> Into our city, because his power is great—
> Both in other matters and also, as I
> Have heard them say, in this: it's he who gave
> To mortals the vine that stops all suffering.
> And if wine were to exist no longer, then
> Neither would the goddess Aphrodite,
> Nor anything of pleasure for us mortals.[29]

Pentheus ignores the first messenger's contained, pithy conclusion. But Dionysos—working on him with divine powers—persuades him, gradually, not to kill the revellers; he sends Pentheus off, instead, to spy on them.

The second messenger then returns with his report: Dionysos had driven the wild Maenads to tear Pentheus limb from limb. The messenger concludes his description with a sombre, aphoristic reflection on the events of the play:

> Wise moderation and a reverence
> For what is of the gods—this is what's best.
> And this, I think, of all possessions owned
> By mortals, is the wisest one to use.[30]

What Pompey likes in Greek tragedy, she says in *Novel on Yellow Paper*, is its 'bright lovely hard and religious formalism': something 'very strong and very inevitable and impersonal' (*Novel*, 96, 98). The distilled, stark, and absolute moment appeals to her, one which possesses the hardness and the emotional indifference (her language suggests) of the aphorism: 'very strong', 'very inevitable', 'bright lovely hard'. Even Euripides himself does not quite live up to her standards for the 'representative Greeks'; Pompey describes his work as a 'dark shadow of emotion', in comparison with which the ideal outlines of Greek writing stand out in 'hard relief' (*Novel*, 96). To be properly Greek, in other words, is to be engraved like an epigram on a monument.

---

[29] Euripides, *The Complete Euripides*, 272–273.
[30] Euripides, *The Complete Euripides*, 288.

Despite feeling that Euripides might ideally be harder and drier, Smith dedicates several pages in the published version of *Novel on Yellow Paper* to a description of the *Bacchae*'s plot. In the original manuscript, Pompey's description extends even further. After the sentence 'And Pentheus is never seen again alive', Pompey allows herself, in her role as messenger, to enter the narrative in a passage scored out in the manuscript, presenting her lines with the dramatic staginess of her speakers in 'Oh stubborn race of Cadmus' seed ... ' and 'Persephone':

And then at the end of my speech I am talking to the King{,} I am talking to Pentheus and explaining as messengers in Greek plays always do{,} what has been happening{,} I am giving Pentheus stop press news I have brought straight from the ~~horses mouth~~ {front.} I have come running over the mountains straight from Citaeron 'where the snow never melts'{.} I am telling him all that is happening{,} with the women running mad on the mountain{,} and how I have spied upon them{,} and Agave the Queen has known that I was there{,} and how I have barely escaped and so at the end I plead with this obstinate King and I say:

{//} This God, whatever he is, receive him into the city, for he is not only great but also as I have heard he has given the pain-killing wine to man{. A}nd then I finish up with the other two lines: Take away wine and there is no joy left{.} No Cyprian{,} nothing at all left for man.[31]

Here, Pompey misattributes the first messenger's lines to herself as second messenger: a point to which I shall return shortly. Ironically, in line with Shirley A. Barlow's argument that Euripides designs his messenger's imagery 'to convey a rational account of objective fact',[32] Pompey underscores the accurate, eyewitness status of her report in a jumble of mixed metaphors ('stop press news', 'straight from the horses mouth'), highlighting its comprehensiveness ('telling him all that is happening') in a present-continuous stream. Pompey scrupulously includes every part of the narrative in her rendition, up until the moral core of her speech: an epigrammatic finale which reflects on the wonder of alcohol.

And these particular lines, the close of the speech, do survive, very tangibly, in and beyond Smith's canon. Smith reprints them in *Nimbus* in 1955, in a gesture which emphasizes their aphoristic portability:

---

[31] Stevie Smith, typescript of *Novel on Yellow Paper*, U DP-156-1, 81, Stevie Smith Papers 1935–1969, Hull History Centre. Braces indicate sections which have been added to the typescript by hand; parts scored out have been crossed out in the typescript by hand. Over these initial edits, indicated in the text, the whole passage has been scored out in the typescript.

[32] Shirley A. Barlow, *The Imagery of Euripides* (London: Methuen & Co, 1971), 61. Compare with Malcolm Heath, who views the messenger's reports as 'obvious set-pieces' (Malcolm Heath, *The Poetics of Greek Tragedy* (Stanford, CA: Stanford University Press, 1987), 132), and Simon R. Perris, who suggests that Euripides' messengers are 'metatheatrically aware self-parodies' (Perris, 'What Maketh The Messenger? Reportage in Greek Tragedy', in ASCS 32 *Proceedings* (2011), ed. Anne Mackay, 2, available at http://www.ascs.org.au/news/ascs32/Perris.pdf (accessed January 28, 2021)).

APHORISTIC MESSAGES, TOO LATE   65

O Lord!
From 2nd Messenger's Speech To King Pentheus, Bacchae

This god then, O lord whoever he is do receive into the city
For not only is he great but also as I have heard
He gave the pain-killing vine to men.
Take away drink, where's Love?
Any pleasure come to that, O lord there is nothing left. (MA, 242)[33]

More immediately, they survive into the published version of *Novel on Yellow Paper*. Smith transfers them into an imagined confrontation with the fastidious Miss Hogmanimy:

> The last four lines of my speech, there were four of them in the Greek, and they went like this and meant just this, that I always wanted to get up and shout at Miss Hogmanimy because it was what she was saying, what she could not avoid saying, with all the weight of Education behind them. The words were, these were the words: Take away wine and there is no Cyprian, No other joy, nothing left to man.
> Three cheers for Euripides and Miss Hogmanimy.
>
> (*Novel*, 103)

The eventual delivery of this aphorism seems to be all that is argumentatively necessary. Pompey imagines that they conclude the argument, trump everything Miss Hogmanimy has said, culminating in a triumphant 'three cheers' as the field is, instantly, won. The message, Pompey signals, has been delivered: no more needs to be said or done.

The Undelivered Message

Yet, of course, Pompey never delivers her aphoristic message to Miss Hogmanimy. This aphorism might secure something: stabilize the situation, induce a revelation. But in the end, she says nothing. The message is considered, then discarded, without reaching its recipient.

If Pompey is a bad messenger—jettisoning her messages before they reach their intended recipient—so is Miss Hogmanimy. The sex educator's tone and bearing imply that she brings all-powerful truth to her schoolgirl audience: 'to listen to Miss Hogmanimy you'd think just knowing straight out how babies was born was to solve all the problems of adolescence right off' (*Novel*, 94). Miss Hogmanimy casts herself not simply as messenger but as evangelist-prophet, whose message

---

[33] Note that Smith also, here, misattributes these lines to the second messenger.

66 STEVIE SMITH AND THE APHORISM

can have a tangible impact, and save its hearers from a terrible fate. Yet the revelation which Miss Hogmanimy actually engenders is a non-revelation:

> ... we waited and waited, and hoped some time we would get the facts, but no it was all this funny breathless whisper.
>
> (*Novel*, 95)

Revelation hovers around the edges of Miss Hogmanimy's speech, but never materializes. Miss Hogmanimy and Pompey reflect each other in their failure as messengers. And that failure of the message to appear becomes its own revelation, of the nothingness at the centre of the messenger-act.

The *Bacchae* offers a model for *Novel on Yellow Paper* in its loss of a singular, powerful message. By splitting its messenger-function across two separate figures—one bringing a warning, the other a description of the catastrophe which ensued when the first warning went unheeded—the *Bacchae* spreads messages out across the text. The doubling of the messenger, Anne Pippin Burnett suggests, allows the second messenger to '[repeat] the movements of the first, and [bring] a new meaning to them.'[34] This doubling blurs any singular centre, and dissipates the force of the discrete message. Revelation diffuses over the course of the text, reinforcing Charles Segal's observation that anagnorisis happens very gradually in the *Bacchae*. First the maenads return, then Pentheus realizes (too late) that he will die, then Agave realizes what she has done, then Kadmos realizes his age and impotence.[35] No single moment of realization can be located or delivered in this play.

Accordingly, when Smith translates the role into her novel, she makes Pompey a deeply unreliable messenger. She abandons messages undelivered; she buries them under a deluge of information whose significance we cannot locate. *Novel on Yellow Paper* is a book characterized by the unlocatable revelation buried under detail. Her reviewers sense this: Rodney Ackland calls the book a 'stream of confidences, anecdotes, reminiscences, character sketches, asides, digressions, rhymes, poems, printed idiocies ... '[36] A reviewer in the *Times Literary Supplement* describes the text in terms of interruption: the book contains 'evidences of a cultivated and thoughtful mind, interrupted by and often expressed in the language of a devotee of lower-class American films'. She 'dash[es] wildly from one subject to another.'[37] Writing in the *Spectator*, Peter Burra characterized her novel as a mishmash with 'features assembled from many faces.'[38]

Smith's style derives from Pompey's aversion to thinking a thought through: her tendency to avoid a fully-delivered explanation or message:

---

[34] Anne Pippin Burnett, *Catastrophe Survived: Euripides' Plays of Mixed Reversal* (Oxford: Clarendon Press, 1971), 61.

[35] Charles Segal, 'Introduction [to Bacchae]', in *The Complete Euripides*, 228.

[36] Rodney Ackland, 'Bear up Chaps', *Spectator* 223, 30 August 1969, 271.

[37] 'Without Title', *Times Literary Supplement*, 12 September 1936, 727.

[38] Peter Burra, 'Fiction', *Spectator* 157, 18 September 1936, 474.

Well, partly it is like this. You see, they run cheap rides in the Row. On cheap horses? Well, no, not that either so much. Well, here goes my horse.

(*Novel*, 1)

Smith showcases, here, her real aptitude for the dismissive conjunction. 'Well' operates like Seamus Heaney's 'So', in his introduction to his translation of Beowulf: '"so" operates as an expression that obliterates all previous discourse and narrative, and at the same time functions as an exclamation calling for immediate attention.'[39] It implies that an explanation is forthcoming, but simultaneously works to dismiss, and dissociate itself from, what has previously been said. In fact, the original manuscript of *Novel on Yellow Paper* revolves around just such a Heaneyesque 'So' in its retelling of Euripides' *Bacchae*. To cite just one instance:

So he is the son of Zeus and Semele{. S}o Pentheus is ruler of this Theban land{. S}o Pentheus is the ~~brother~~ {nephew} of Semele that died ...[40]

The published version softens the impact of that drumming, relentless 'so' by replacing most of the 'so's with 'and's (*Novel*, 98). The conjunction 'and' is expansive and accommodating; it stabilizes what has already been said in the same gesture as inviting in more. In contrast, Smith's original 'so's cause the account to buckle under the weight of a ponderous implied causality (one statement as following naturally from what preceded it) which also collapses that causality in the same gesture: it constantly begins anew. Each remark is immediately scribbled over by the sentence that follows: each presenting itself as the most important, revelatory element, but immediately deleted by the next. So Smith's dismissive conjunctions promise revelation but in the same gesture veer away from it. The question of revelation is constantly made central even as it is perpetually withheld.

On one level, this is Smith playing with the fragmentary potential of classical writing in reception: suggestively missing crucial parts, leaving gaps for the reader to fill in. 'Professor Snooks Does His Worst with a Grecian Fragment' stages this same loss of the longed-for message:

> CHORUS: I am certain he will come again
> And lighten our remarks with a religious strain
> Or else he'll say
> ... (here a line is missing and the chorus finishes)
> Ah ah ah ah ah. (CP, 708)

Smith's confected manuscript suffers the loss of a line, conveniently, at just the moment when 'his' words are about to be revealed; instead, the chorus fades away

---

[39] Seamus Heaney, 'Introduction', in *Beowulf: A New Translation* (London: Faber & Faber, 1999), xxvii.

[40] Stevie Smith, annotated typescript of *Novel on Yellow Paper*, U DP-156-1, 76, Stevie Smith Papers 1935–1969, Hull History Centre.

68 STEVIE SMITH AND THE APHORISM

in sound, 'Ah ah ah ah ah'. The loss of the central message strips the whole sequence of its communicative function: it becomes a marking of time.

All that exists, in these models, is the buildup to revelation. Smith surrounds Pompey's aphorism from her messenger speech, in *Novel on Yellow Paper*, with phrases which promise immediate revelation while acting to defer it. '[T]hey went like this' and 'The words were' keep Smith's readers on tenterhooks, awaiting this seemingly-imminent revelation. Yet they also mark time, delaying that revelation. When it finally appears, it turns out to be nothing at all. What, then, is at stake in Stevie Smith's revelations of nothing?

In a way, Pompey does not deliver her aphoristic message to Miss Hogman-imy because she does not need to. Even as Pompey stresses the significance of her message, she deflates its localized, urgent value. It is what Miss Hogmanimy 'was saying, what she could not avoid saying' (*Novel*, 103). Its heart is beating through the educator's words, unavoidable, inevitable, and palpable. The aphorism has already been said. It cannot be avoided, and makes itself known even through words which express its contrary. In a sense, it comes too late; it is superfluous to narrative.

This superfluity, this belatedness, is fundamental to the messenger role in Greek tragedy. Firstly, what the messenger brings back is already known in the sense that the audience would have prior awareness of the broad outlines of the tragedy's story. Alan Sommerstein reminds us that even a Greek audience seeing the play for the first time would have a basic knowledge of the plot.[41] The women will always go mad; Pentheus will always be ripped apart. The overall structure was fairly fixed; the appeal for the Greek audience was to see which secondary elements of the familiar story would be altered and how.

Secondly, revelation may reveal something which the characters already know. This is perhaps a more significant trope in reception than in the plays themselves; *Oedipus the King*, in conjunction with Aristotle's *Poetics*, has positioned *anagnorisis* as more central to the workings of tragedy than the texts themselves actually suggest. In Sophocles' play, however, the already-known revelation is the hinge on which the drama turns.

OEDIPUS:
   I have a terrible fear the blind seer can see.
   I'll know in a moment.[42]

Oedipus knows, at this point, of the terrible act he has inadvertently performed, but must summon messengers and shepherds to testify, one after the other, until

---

[41] Alan H. Sommerstein, 'Tragedy and Myth', in *A Companion to Tragedy*, ed. Rebecca Bushnell (Oxford: Blackwell, 2005), 169.

[42] Sophocles, *The Three Theban Plays: Antigone, Oedipus the King, Oedipus at Colonus*, trans. Robert Fagles (London: Penguin, 1984), 203. For evidence of Smith's interest in this mode of resisted knowledge, see 'Angel Boley', CP, 610–614: 'I know now, she said, and all the time I have known / What I did not want to know ... ' (CP, 611).

what is already-known becomes unignorable. He holds full knowledge at arms' length, assembling all the possible evidence before he can admit what he already knew. Euripides reworks Aeschylus' *The Libation Bearers* in his *Electra*, to emphasize the same process. Whereas in Aeschylus's tragedy Electra receives the lock of hair and footprints as evidence for Orestes' being alive (which she is already primed to believe), Euripides has Electra reject sign after sign until the full knowledge of Orestes cannot be denied.[43]

More subtly, the messenger's role necessitates that he carries a report of events which are, in most cases, already over. The most climactic events of Greek tragedy take place offstage, and are attested to after the moment, by the messenger. The important events of Greek tragedy can seldom, therefore, exist in the present. Occasionally, we are cued into the moment of their happening by, for example, a scream offstage.[44] More often, however, events are relegated either to the past or to the future, slipping in their actual moment of occurrence. A truly on-time messenger is a spatial impossibility. Though his narrative style partakes of the epic, he lacks the omniscience of an epic narrator: he can only describe what he has witnessed, as Smith puts it in her draft of *Novel on Yellow Paper*, 'straight from the front'. The messenger reports events after they have already happened. His role necessarily bears witness to the belated.

Such belatedness-unto-itself characterizes the *Bacchae* in particular. The first word of the play, ἥκω, means 'I am here' or 'I have come'.[45] The instantaneousness of this appearance—precisely what gives it the quality of stunning, immediate revelation—in fact removes its immediacy. 'I have come' announces an action already completed. Similarly, by the time Dionysos steps on to the stage to speak, the events he describes have occurred: 'I *have* stung these sisters / To a frenzy' (my emphasis).[46] This slippage of the moment is intrinsic to the story of the *Bacchae*, occurring also in Ovid's version of the tale: 'Liber adest, festisque fremunt ululatibus agri'.[47] Liber or Dionysos *is present*, Ovid declares. The moment of Dionysos's appearance vanishes: what remains is a message, a declaration of something which has already happened.

The *Bacchae*'s final revelation, conveyed by its second messenger, is already known. It is known because the substance of the news had already been communicated ('Pentheus, Ekhíon's child, is dead') in a terse single line; further, however, it is already known to the audience as a familiar story. The content of the message

---

[43] For another interpretation of Euripides' reworking of Aeschylus, see Diana Culbertson, *The Poetics of Revelation: Recognition and the Narrative Tradition* (Macon GA: Mercer University Press, 1989), 39–40.

[44] For instance, in *Electra*, the chorus wonders, 'Do you hear a shout from the house?' (Euripides, *Medea and Other Plays*, trans. James Morwood (Oxford: Oxford World's Classics, 1998), 113), signalling Clytemnestra's murder.

[45] Charles Segal, 'Introduction [to Bacchae]', in *The Complete Euripides*, 215.

[46] Euripides, *The Complete Euripides*, 246.

[47] Ovid, *Metamorphoses: Volume I*, trans. Frank Justus Miller (London: William Heinemann, 1960), 160.

70 STEVIE SMITH AND THE APHORISM

is perfunctory, for the purposes of dramatic continuity. The tragedy's outcome, its climax, is known. The narration of the prolonged message serves only to reinforce its pastness, its already-knownness.

In his later discussion of Dionysiac *anagnorisis*, Segal implicitly recognizes this belated quality to the *Bacchae*'s epiphanies, as he traces the play's series of grim revelations. In all situations, these realizations involve events which have already occurred. Segal further acknowledges the difference between the *Bacchae*'s anagnorisis and that of Oedipus in Sophocles' *Oedipus Tyrannos*. Though Oedipus's too-late realization led to a deeper understanding of himself—and therefore had some broader purpose—the belated revelations in the *Bacchae* engender only 'shock and horror', occluding any 'deeper moral understanding'.[48] Not only, then, are Euripides' revelations or messages belated, they are also useless in comparison to those of contemporary dramatists. They cause no good, only horror.

Stevie Smith's reworking of Greek tragedy explores this mode of speech and action which has no effect at all. An unease about what is necessary, what should be said and what should not need to be said—either because it is already known or because it comes too late to have an effect—runs throughout *Novel on Yellow Paper*, and illuminates much of Smith's juggling with the messenger-role, as she wavers between inclusion and omission. Pompey inserts herself into the manuscript as messenger, then Smith cuts her out for publication. More crucially, as observed earlier, Pompey/Smith misattributes her own lines. In Euripides' *Bacchae*, Pompey's speech (about the power of wine) belongs to the First Messenger; the Second Messenger brings the news of the horrifying climax. Yet Smith claims that Pompey is not the First but the Second Messenger. So she changes her role as First Messenger (who, unusually for Greek tragedy, delivers a message at a point where it might have had an effect, if only Pentheus had listened) to the role of Second Messenger, who brings news too late to be acted upon. In other words, Smith puts the First Messenger's warning (pointing to the future) in the place of the Second Messenger's lament (pointing to the past). She places her messenger-speech—which urges Pentheus to learn from it and take heed, and which might have had an impact—in a decidedly terminal, too-late position. Even an aphorism which could, theoretically, have an effect on the narrative action is stripped of agency through this repositioning, rendered literally too late.

Pompey, as messenger to her reader, is always running late. By the time she reveals the inflection or significance of a narrative, it is already too late to do anything about it:

> ... though the war stayed the advance, the armistice already saw the builders at busy work, and the streets of houses going up, and the paving stones going down. And presently it was already a suburb.
>
> (*Novel*, 128)

---

[48] Segal, 'Introduction [to Bacchae]', 228.

APHORISTIC MESSAGES, TOO LATE   71

The word 'presently', a favourite of Smith's,[49] in itself designates a sedately linear passage of time, in which events succeed in an orderly and calm fashion, to take the stage of the 'present'. Here, by coupling 'presently' with 'already', Smith undoes the 'present' in 'presently'. It ceases to imply a gently succeeding future, or even a present moment; it becomes the epitaph, the surviving aphoristic trace, of something already past. We are already post-suburb before the moment of suburbization has tangibly occurred; the houses and paving-stones have failed to add up to that moment until after the fact.

This approach roots in a sense that things happen too early: that they take an irrevocable form before characters receive enough warning of change to enable them to intercede. In this loss of interventionary power, Smith's digressions often originate, particularly at the beginning of the novel, in a conviction that finishing her thought is actually superfluous. 'Didn't I say all to say had been said?' she asks (*Novel*, 3). Repeatedly she couches her anecdotes in terms of the self-evident: 'Well this girl was christened Gladys, but of course that wouldn't do' (*Novel*, 10).

This circumspection derives, at least in part, from the embarrassment of spelling out the self-evident. In agony over her broken engagement, Pompey manages at last to articulate something which is true to her:

> For me but one significant fact that stands out, and for which I would live or die. But this fact. That is this fact. That is. That is what I cannot bring myself to write. It has been written so many times and soiled with every falseness and base stupidity. Can you not see it?
>
> > Oh little creature form'd of joy and mirth,
> > Go, love without the help of anything on earth.
>
> Indeed we have done this.
>
> (Novel, 194–195)

Pompey circles Blake's aphorism with the wariness Smith described in an interview with Jonathan Williams: she stays away from Blake, she explains, because she finds his echoes 'easy ... to catch'.[50] Blake invites Smith to fall into easy, well-worn rhythms whose familiarity is alluring. So Pompey prevaricates before revealing Blake's aphorism from his Notebooks. She stutters: 'That is. That is ... ' The line is overwritten, she protests, self-evident ('Can you not see it?'), 'soiled' with overuse and triteness.

The aphorism therefore discloses something which is simultaneously formally marked as thunderously revelatory and contextualized as entirely obvious, always

---

[49] 'And presently the trees give way and there is nothing but the road, and presently the road gives way and there is nothing but a track ... ' (*Novel*, 58).

[50] Jonathan Williams, 'Much Further Out Than You Thought', in *In Search of Stevie Smith*, ed. Sanford Sternlicht (Syracuse: Syracuse University Press, 1991), 43.

72 STEVIE SMITH AND THE APHORISM

already known. Smith couches the revelation as at once unexpected and expected, surprising and inevitable. Aphoristic revelation is deferred because it is taken for granted: a given which problematizes its own necessity and urgency.

Viewing revelation as both thunderous and unnecessary in this way allows Smith's opening salvo in *Novel on Yellow Paper* to resolve into a kind of sense:

> Beginning this book ... I should like if I may, I should like, if I may (that is the way Sir Phoebus writes), I should like then to say: Good-bye to all my friends, my beautiful and lovely friends.
>
> (*Novel*, 1)

An over-prolonged beginning is maintained through a build-up of opening phrases, mounting to a climax (a 'message', some content for the sentence) without quite reaching it. Then the colon which should present that climactic message instead closes it off: Pompey wishes her friends goodbye, closing off her narrative before it has even begun. The implication is that everything that follows in the novel, its entire substance, is instead after-the-fact, belated. The whole book is the aphoristic remnant, the problematic message of the *Bacchae's* messenger which bears witness only to the loss of events to a devouring past before they have even been apprehended. The event has not occurred, and then it has already happened.

> Now, Reader, I am going on my holiday to Germany. This is already several years ago.
>
> (*Novel*, 60)

As soon as we have absorbed the information which claims grammatically—in its use of the present-continuous tense, as so often in *Novel on Yellow Paper*—to be the present moment ('I am going'), Pompey informs us that we are already too late to engage with it. So when Pompey eventually laments 'My sweet boy Freddy has left me' (*Novel*, 159), it has of course already happened, and neither Pompey nor the reader, we feel, had any control over it. *Novel on Yellow Paper's* present-continuousness has given Smith's book its reputation as stream-of-consciousness real-time chatter. Yet it conceals the fact that, for Pompey, the climactic present is always (already) past. Over and over again, the text is trapped in bearing witness to its own belatedness.

Epitaph as Belated Aphorism

The form of aphorism builds in a particular kind of embarrassment: a sense that the known or obvious is being restated. Often it literally is: proverbs are well-used

APHORISTIC MESSAGES, TOO LATE   73

and well-known, for instance, and Karl Kraus's aphorisms adapt clichés into a new signification.[51] More obliquely, though, the aphorism's elegant phrasing establishes it as something which could not be expressed any other way: which has surely always existed. As a result, the appearance of aphorisms can seem belated. The brevity of the form reinforces this sense: brevity allows the aphorism to discharge its force then withdraw quickly from the ring, managing its sense of its own superfluity through a performative frugality.

In 'Aphorism Countertime', Derrida associates the aphorism with survival against the grain of a literary text and its narrative: 'One aphorism in the series can come before or after the other, before *and* after the other, each can survive the other ... '[52] In Greek tragedy, a messenger comes to deliver the news of deaths, to explain that survival has not occurred. Instead of making the deaths visible to us onstage, directly experienced by the audience, the playwright instead gives the tragic messenger an aphorism to deliver.

Here, tentatively, we can locate the use-value of the aphorism in the messenger speech. The messenger in Greek tragedy performs an essential consolatory function. Christopher Cannon notes that, at the end of Chaucer's *Nun's Priest's Tale*, for instance, the fox reproves himself with a proverb after he has already let Chauntecleer go. Here, Cannon notes, the 'cited wisdom is apt, but it comes too late'.[53] Cannon argues that the belatedly-offered proverb did at least offer the comfort of community, of knowing that others had made the same mistakes before.

The delivery of the too-late aphoristic message remains essential, therefore, despite (and perhaps because of) its belatedness. Jennifer Wallace notes that the 'story of pain' which Greek tragedy's messenger-figures recount both forces the listener to experience horror vicariously, and is the first stage in the reconstruction of a ruptured world.[54] This reparative function of the messenger reflects Richard Seaford's belief that the messenger's function is 'to control and stage the experience so that it is assimilable to the spectator bit by bit in an ordered way', distancing the story so that it can be digested by the viewers.[55] The messenger speech's closing aphorism performs part of this useful function. As a textual survivor, it acts as epitaph; it confers a form of survival on the dead. They are immortalized, granted longevity.

---

[51] See, for instance, Karl Kraus, *Half Truths and One-and-a-Half Truths: Karl Kraus: Selected Aphorisms,* ed. and trans. Harry Zohn (Manchester: Carcanet, 1986), 124.

[52] Jacques Derrida, 'Aphorism Countertime', trans. Nicholas Royle, in *Psyche: Inventions of the Other,* ed. Peggy Kamuf and Elizabeth Rottenberg (Stanford: Stanford University Press, 2008), 2: 128.

[53] Christopher Cannon, 'Proverbs and the Wisdom of Literature: *The Proverbs of Alfred* and Chaucer's *Tale of Melibee*', *Textual Practice* 24, no. 3 (2010): 411.

[54] Jennifer Wallace, *The Cambridge Introduction to Tragedy* (Cambridge: Cambridge University Press, 2007), 111.

[55] Richard Seaford, *Euripides: Bacchae* (Warminster: Aris & Phillips, 1996), 14.

Smith is interested in this idea of the surviving remnant, the ruined residue from what has occurred. Pompey's own name, she notes in passing, gives her the status of a kind of ruin:

> There's something meretricious and decayed and I'll say, I dare say, elegant about Pompey. A broken Roman statue.
>
> (Novel, 10)

The focus is on what has survived from this decay, which acts as an epitaph for what has passed. Smith is fascinated by the epitaph: its bid to encapsulate and preserve the salient elements of the deceased. Readable or unreadable, it recurs in her poetry. Individual poems often present themselves as mysteriously decontextualised epitaphs; for instance, 'Suicide's Epitaph':

> Oh Lord have mercy on my soul
> As I had none upon my body.
> And you who stand and read this rhyme
> How do you do, Tomnoddy? (CP, 172)

However, the memorialization they enact or describe is seldom fully successful. Smith's illustration to 'Suicide's Epitaph', in May's edition, shows an angel holding a sword, and a man kneeling by a grave with a cross at its head and flowers upon it. What isn't marked, anywhere in the image, is an epitaph. The cross is blank; the epitaph is missing. In 'Death Bereaves our Common Mother / Nature Grieves for my Dead Brother', moreover, the speaker struggles to assemble a suitable epitaph for a dead lamb:

> Lamb dead, dead lamb,
> He was, I am ... (CP, 41)

The speaker experiments: she tries it both ways, chiastically. But she finds that the text is equally meaningless regardless of its arrangement. She cannot talk the death, or indeed the lamb, into importance:

> Can I see lamb dead as mutton
> And not care a solitary button? (CP, 41)

This epitaph is evacuated, already belated. Smith takes it one step further, forcing it to bear witness only to its own lack of significance. Her poem memorializes emptiness and absence just one degree of separation beyond an epitaph's standard efforts: like ancient Greek epigram, epitaph is engraved at sites where something happened (a life, an event) which has now come to an end.[56]

---

[56] On the easy companionship of death and the lapidary (concise, epitaphic) style, see Denise Riley, 'On the Lapidary Style', *d i f f e r e n c e s* 28, no. 1 (2017): 33.

At the close of his message, the messenger in Greek tragedy leaves us with an aphorism: to mark a place where something has happened, give us the meaning to carry away. The epigram becomes a monument in Derrida's terms: not only portentously sizeable, but standing in for an absence. The aphorism becomes a circumscribed memory, an authoritatively-delimited memorialization which carries mythology in seed form. It exists only for the benefit of those who will come after.

In a Bit

The failure of revelation to materialize fully is, as Franco Moretti notes, visible in High Modernist texts. In *Ulysses*, for example, he describes how 'the great novelty of the stream of consciousness consists in its proceeding for pages and pages *without the slightest revelation*'.[57] Here, the amazement of revelation's disappearance derives from the sheer bulk of text: how can so much be said and so little revealed? *Novel on Yellow Paper* mimics that bulk through a polyvocality which hides, overwrites, and over-promises revelation. Aphorism is available to Pompey in hindsight. It is in looking back that she can make out a single aphoristic surviving idea from what has passed. '[O]ne significant fact ... stands out' against the digressive chaos of her writing, in the form of Blake's aphorism. She can pick out the hard musculature under her excess of distracting detail, and carries that message to the reader. This is not revelation which can be used or heeded: it comes too late, for us and for her, but crucially is no less essential to say.

This faithful deferring of reading and identification to a point in the future, where truth, we hope, might be seen entire, underpins Stevie Smith's 'Magna est Veritas' (published in her 1957 collection, *Not Waving but Drowning*):

> And I do not deceive because I am rather simple too
> And although I collect facts I do not always know what they
> amount to.
> I regard them as a contribution to almighty Truth, magna est veritas et praevalebit,
> Agreeing with that Latin writer, Great is Truth and will prevail in
> a bit. (CP, 427)

The speaker participates in the fact-gathering which represents such a familiar trope in Smith's work. In *Novel on Yellow Paper*, Pompey amasses 'FAVOURITE QUOTATIONS' into a list, which interrupts her narrative at two points:

From the *East African Courier*: No more popular figure in Holy Orders ever motor-bicycled in Mombasa.

---

[57] Franco Moretti, *Modern Epic: The World System from Goethe to García Márquez*, trans. Quintin Hoare (London and New York: Verso, 1996), 153.

76 STEVIE SMITH AND THE APHORISM

Venus ... *quae quoniam rerum naturam sola gubernas.*
Pompey is an arrogant high hollow fateful rider, In noisy triumph to the trumpet's
mouth ...

(*Novel*, 27–28)

These lines are pleasurable in their own right because of this gap between Pompey's presentation of them as epiphanic and the reality of these lines as already-known and utterly familiar. This gap overlaps with the gap between the drama of their delivery and the banality of their content. Coyle's aphoristic boundary-effects surround only emptiness. As a result, the collection of these grand-but-empty statements compounds that satisfaction, since the act of collection is also a kind of boundary-effect, promising a significance which may never materialize.

When collected, as in Smith's lists of 'nice little quotations', they remain aphoristically separate, refusing to 'amount to' or build up into a larger coherent structure. Smith's speaker in 'Magna est Veritas' admits frankly to the same problem. Her collection of facts is disparate; she does not 'know what they amount to'. She displaces interpretative responsibility on to 'almighty Truth', allowing her to be philosophical about her own invisibility.

With streaming long hair, Smith's unnamed speaker in this poem presents herself as an unusually placid Cassandra. She is unbelieved by those around her, like the Hellenic prophetess; the facts she accumulates cannot be used or understood, and—we suspect—they never will be.[58] Smith's nod to the 'temple' of the tall hat strengthens this link with the classics, which the final lines clinch. Smith has her speaker quote an aphorism from a 'Latin writer': 'magna est veritas et praevalebit'. Her unique mistranslation of the Latin line builds in delay: truth will prevail, she promises, 'in a bit'. Her phrasing allows these processes to take as much time as they need. It acknowledges that their duration can't be predicted, that an ending can't be enforced. In short, this phrasing renounces responsibility for the prevailing of almighty Truth.[59] Collecting the poorly understood involves a leap of faith: it demonstrates a (very probably vain) belief that, with the passage of 'a bit' of time, the meaning and significance of the items collected will be revealed. The sentiment reflects Isaac D'Israeli's defence of the apparently-trifling in his *Dissertation on Anecdotes* (1793):

It is certainly safest, for *some* writers, to give us all they know, than to permit themselves the power of rejection; because, for this, there requires a certain degree of taste and discernment, which many biographers are not so fortunate as to possess

---

[58] On the capacity of tragic figures to disbelieve or dismiss messengers, see Simon Goldhill, *Reading Greek Tragedy* (Cambridge: Cambridge University Press, 1986), 8–9).

[59] For a reading of this poem which emphasizes the speaker's lofty grandeur rather than her surrendering of interpretative responsibility, see James Najarian, 'Contributions to Almighty Truth: Stevie Smith's Seditious Romanticism', *Twentieth-Century Literature* 49, no. 4 (2003): 478.

... an anecdote, or a circumstance, which may appear inconsequential to a reader, may bear some remote or latent connection, which a mature reflection often discovers. It is certain, that a biographer, who has long contemplated the character he records, sees many relations which escape an ordinary reader.[60]

Preserved for posterity, the final two lines of 'Magna est Veritas' justify themselves, self-legitimizing through the cast of classical authority conferred on them by Latin. Smith plays on the double meaning of 'bit': this 'bit' or scrap of language, the overheard and preserved nugget redeemed from waste, is also, she believes, the place in which truth will prevail. Aphorism-like, these are enough in themselves, representing or signalling truth without necessarily being successful at expounding it, deferring the revelation of their own meaning. In Stevie Smith's classically-framed texts, revelation disappears from the tiny aphoristic compasses, the knife-edges between before and after, which promise to contain them. Aphorisms can only be read and received when it is too late. They freeze instead into epitaph: a memorial for what might have happened. Positioning itself within this schema, *Novel on Yellow Paper* rushes on, turning abundance of content into a refusal of intimacy, rejecting readerly engagement by embalming itself instantly within a past that cannot be accessed. Its prattling overflow becomes a double sort of hardness: the difficulty of language made monumental too soon.

Even the most innovative aphorism signals—in its self-sufficient form, withdrawing almost physically from the situation on which it comments—that it is already dated, of only marginal relevance to the matter at hand. And it takes only a little time for maxim to become cliché: to be absorbed, once its origin is defaced, and its past life blurred into vagueness, into the sphere of 'proverb'. If aphorisms which signal their own flattened novelty always come too late, that lateness, in the case of proverb—that sense that this is age-old wisdom, handed down from history's collective voices—offers the form its rhetorical power, conveying comfortingly (as the next chapter suggests) what we already know.

---

[60] Isaac D'Israeli, *A Dissertation on Anecdotes; by the Author of Curiosities of Literature* (London: Kearsley and Murray, 1793), 78–79.

3

Proverbs through Fairytale

Cool as a cucumber calm as a mill pond sound as a bell
Was Mary
When she went to the Wishing Well.

But a fairy came up out of the well
And cursed her up hill and down dale
And cursed her from midnight to morning hail.

And now she gets worse and worse
Ever since she listened to the fairy's curse
She is nervy grim and bold
Looks over her left shoulder and does not do as she is told.
(CP, 275)

If aphorisms in the tradition of Nietzsche and Karl Kraus are cutting, alienating, and witty, then their flip side seems to be the proverb or platitude: the well-thumbed phrase, offering comfort in its familiarity.[1] The opening line of 'Cool as a Cucumber' offers three proverbial idioms in quick succession, situating us immediately in an imagined rural English environment where standards for both behaviour (cool, calm, sound) and modes of language (traditional, nothing fancy) are thoroughly known. Smith explored proverb forms in her collection *Mother, What is Man?* (1942), with brief poems offering nuggets of familiar, folky 'wisdom':

---

[1] See John Fagg, *On the Cusp: Stephen Crane, George Bellows, and Modernism* (Tuscaloosa: The University of Alabama Press, 2009), 129; John Dominic Crossan, *In Fragments: The Aphorisms of Jesus* (San Francisco: Harper & Row, 1983), 20. Compare this contemporary usage to the model of the proverb offered by Erasmus in his *Adagia*. In practice, Erasmus includes a wide range of phrases in his collection: from full sentences such as 'Seven make a feast, nine make a fray' to brief metaphorical phrases like 'swan-song'. He suggests in his introduction: 'a complete definition ... may be reached by saying: "A proverb is a saying in popular use, remarkable for some shrewd and novel turn"'. Far from being well-worn and clichéd, Erasmus sees the proverb as possessing originality and difficulty of the sort we might now associate with, for instance, Nietzschean aphorisms. 'The difficulty of proverbs', he remarks, 'calls for respect'. Erasmus's proverbs abandon dutiful work in favour of undertaking the tasks of the audacious twentieth-century aphorism. Erasmus, *Collected Works of Erasmus, Adages [i] to Iv100*, trans. Margaret Mann Phillips (Toronto: University of Toronto Press, 1982), 315, 195, 4, 19.

Stevie Smith and the Aphorism. Noreen Masud, Oxford University Press.
© Noreen Masud (2022). DOI: 10.1093/oso/9780192895899.003.0004

A couple of women is one too many,
Oh, how I wish I could do without any!

> ('The Fool', CP, 240)

My child, my child, watch how he goes,
The man in Party coloured clothes.

> ('Hast Du dich verirrt?', CP, 244)

Proverbs issue from a place of wisdom, or at least (in the case of 'The Fool') experience. With its paternal tone, 'Hast Du dich verirrt?' offers guidance which promises to be reliable if gnomic. So, in 'Cool as a Cucumber', Mary was, previously, neatly subject to the proverbial phrases issued by her elders. In the poem's first line, the speaker (channelling the tone of a stern aunt) remembers fondly how Mary managed to exemplify three clichéd idioms of sedateness at once. Since then, however, Mary has moved, in classic fairytale fashion, from her ordinary home into an enchanted space: a fairy emerges from a wishing well, and curses her, and her behaviour changes. She is now, the elders tut, 'nervy grim and bold'. The newly disobedient Mary does not behave as she ought.

'Nervy grim and bold' is a three-part summary which carries, or attempts to carry, the controlling effect of the three proverbial similes which opened the poem. 'Cool as a cucumber calm as a mill pond sound as a bell' stylized Mary into a stereotype and put her in her (quiet, cool, sound) place. '[N]ervy grim and bold', similarly three-part, makes the same disciplinary bid.

In Smith's final novel *The Holiday* (1949), the wise and paternal Uncle Heber trades particularly in these managerial three-word utterances. Celia, Caz, and Tiny stay with Heber in Lincolnshire for a holiday, longing, in the limbo of the post-war, for the old, safe, predictable world he represents, and for the security of his certainties. Heber is an Anglican priest, and a fountain of wisdom, and Celia lingers on the authoritative, proverbial guidance that he offers, hoping to find comfort by submitting to it. Early in the novel, Celia recounts Heber's remarks after a disruptive party had ended: 'He said: "Solitude, reform and silence"' (*Holiday*, 23).

Heber's summative, economical language defines a whole matter in three words, after which no more needs to be said. Later in the novel, Celia will come under this three-word fire, and counter it with her own:

My uncle now began to storm and rave at me: You are blasphemous, spoilt and evasive.
No, Uncle, I am nervy, bold and grim.

> (*Holiday*, 192)

In 'Cool as a Cucumber', the same phrase came as a line of condemnation from Mary's disapproving elders, seeking to keep her in her place; in Celia's hands, it becomes an act of defiance. Yet it follows the same rhetorical rules as her uncle's

80   STEVIE SMITH AND THE APHORISM

line. Celia contradicts Heber's three-word summary, but keeps herself within its world. Her proud self-definition is, at the same time, an act of judgement on herself, as she steals the pre-made phrase from another text.

In their familiarity or survival across texts, their authoritative three-part structure which refuses argument, and their espousal of conservative and submissive values, Celia's and Heber's remarks occupy the same textual space as the proverb. This space, as 'Cool as a Cucumber' makes clear, is also the territory of the fairytale. This poem features many of the fairytale's greatest hits (the wishing well, the fairy, the curse) as well as a string of proverbs. The 1857 edition of *Grimms' Fairy Tales* is full of proverbs.[2] Fairytale often appears to be an elongated version of proverb, or proverb an abbreviated version of fairytale. Both often centre on, or originate in, a 'folk' atmosphere—smallholdings, forests, the activity of the farmyard and the dairy, observations of everyday animals—presenting clear visual images which are striking if not startlingly novel. And the tripartite structure which often underpins proverbs, especially the Biblical proverbs which a Western audience tends to associate with the form, also spearheads climax and change in the Western fairytale: transformation occurs at the third attempt, say, or is effected by the third child.[3]

This close connection between fairytale and proverb bolsters a sense of cosy recognition. In its secure childhood space, fairytale's disciplinary pattern (the good are rewarded, the bad punished) is already known, anticipated, and enjoyed. Proverb and fairytale enjoin us to behave as we know we must. Fairytale passes between the generations; like proverb, it is anonymous and evolving, a familiar narrative shaped by a collective. Just as 'nervy grim and bold' moved through the fairytale territory of 'Cool as a Cucumber' to pop up again in *The Holiday*, Smith's final novel actually depicts the shaping of quasi-proverbial wisdom through repetition and recycling. Caz, Heber, and Heber's son Tom repeat the same preachy, slightly irritating line, apparently without reference to one another:

> And Tom said it was different with boys, this classical idea, and it was a burden and a misery and an outrage, and that twice was he flogged through Homer ...
>
> (*Holiday*, 117)
>
> I was flogged twice through Homer, said Caz with another malicious look in my direction.
>
> (*Holiday*, 126)
>
> Pronouncing simply in his lovable sober manner, our uncle said:

---

[2] See, for instance, 'The Cat and the Mouse in Partnership' ('All good things come in threes', 5), 'The Woodcutter's Child' ('Whoever will repent and confess their sins, they shall be forgiven', 11), and 'The Wonderful Musician' ('Who wishes to attack must take care of himself', 33), in Jacob and Wilhelm Grimm, *Household Stories*, trans. E. H. Wehnert (London: David Bogue, 1857).

[3] See, for instance, 'Puss in Boots', 'Rumpelstiltskin', 'Snow White', 'East of the Sun and West of the Moon'.

I hold with discipline, control, sobriety and diligence. I was myself twice flogged through Homer.

(Holiday, 196)

Celia detects the melancholy, dogged pride in this act of formalized selective memory. The men collectively organize a distressing childhood experience into a recurring phrase; it cycles around the novel, until it is unclear who invented it, or indeed whether it originates from a past beyond any of them. The line moves laterally, rebuffing interrogation or questioning as it recurs and recurs. For the proverbial edict to seem credible, the hearer must experience it as absolute and foreordained. Rules issuing from an individual, as maxims do, are tyrannical, or at best bullying and open to dispute. Rules shaped anonymously by a collective, in contrast, undermine our capacity to protest, or to see them as other than self-evidently true. Unlike other variants of aphorism, the proverb has become separated from its original speaker, repeated over generations until it assumes a stable form. Its anonymity allows its speaker to redirect responsibility and guilt for didactic instruction on to a nameless, past source.[4] Since no one person can be said to have composed the proverb (shaped into its final version, as Wolfgang Mieder notes, by a cross-generational collective), no one can dispute it.[5] Proverb's status on the margins of cliché means that we experience the proverb as a reminder, rather than the startling novelty which other kinds of aphorism claim to offer.

Earlier chapters have suggested that aphorism is less useful than it seems; that it suggests a mode of transformative revelation which it nevertheless stops short of offering. Aphorism originating from a particular individual gets away with this failure because of its arresting form and promise of novelty. Proverbs, in contrast, represent an exception among aphorisms in that they are the opposite of arresting: their status as already-known means that it is necessary that they should never surprise us. A proverb seems only to derive value from being useful: 'practical' wisdom, or '*strategies* for dealing with *situations*', in Kenneth Burke's phrase.[6]

In *The Holiday*, Smith strips proverbs and quasi-proverbial modes of use, ensuring that they fail to enable the practical action which they advise. Instead, I will suggest, Smith trains her reader to read the proverb differently: through the phenomenon of fairytale survival. Our attention is drawn away from the proverb's didactic content, and towards the sensational images which exist just adjacent to these disciplinary messages: the cores of these forms, which survive most strongly.

---

[4] E. Ojo Arewa and Alan Dundes, 'Proverbs and the Ethnography of Speaking Folklore', *American Anthropologist* 66, no. 6, pt.2 (1964): 70.

[5] Wolfgang Mieder, *American Proverbs: A Study of Texts and Contexts* (Bern: Peter Lang, 1989), 23.

[6] Kenneth Burke, 'Literature as Equipment for Living', in *The Philosophy of Literary Form: Studies in Symbolic Action* (Baton Rouge: Louisiana State University Press, 1967), 296.

82 STEVIE SMITH AND THE APHORISM

By framing proverbs towards the image, and away from powerful literary and moral authority, Smith attenuates their power to collude in abuse, such as the anti-Semitism with which she engages particularly strongly in her second novel, *Over the Frontier* (1938). Instead of agents of didactic power, proverbs become instead a means of tuning into the experience of possessing knowledge which one cannot use: of the failure of clear and striking understanding to translate into tangible impact.

Circling the Fairytale

Stevie Smith relished fairytales, and kept a copy of *Grimms' Fairy Tales* by her bed.[7] Fairytales form a crucial part of Pompey's visit to Germany in *Novel on Yellow Paper*; the Schloss in *Over the Frontier* is a fairytale space as much as a reference to Kafka's *Das Schloss* (1926), and countless of Smith's poems centre on or rework fairytale narratives.[8] Smith's archives hold one completed fairytale, 'The Poet and the Pussycat', one half-finished in typescript, and one half-finished in a notebook. In the completed story 'The Poet and the Pussycat', the perfect cat Sukeina leaves Pussy-cat Land to find out who she is and where she comes from. Eventually she meets a poet, who explains to her that she is looking for love. Poet and pussycat fall in love, and when the poet confesses to Sukeina, she transforms into a beautiful girl.[9] Smith's story centres rhetorically on a feigned assumption of shared common knowledge, into which she casually institutes the reader:

> *As everyone knows*, the job of pussycats in the world is to look after People.
>
> ...
>
> But *of course* they must rest. So back they go to Pussy-cat Land ... they know a very special language, a language of their own. If you watch a cat while it is in the ordinary world, looking after people, you will see them try and teach them the same language. But *of course* it is very difficult and only a few learn it.[10]
>
> (My emphasis)

---

[7] Though Smith's interest in fairytale is broad ('The Castle', for instance, riffs on the Norwegian 'East of the Sun and West of the Moon') she returns most often, in her broadcasts and poem introductions, to the Grimms. This chapter focuses, therefore, on this particular tradition.

[8] See, for instance, 'I rode with my darling ... ' (CP, 296), 'The Fairy Bell' (CP, 351), 'The Frog Prince' (CP, 471), 'The Forlorn Sea' (CP, 608).

[9] Stevie Smith, 'The Poet and the Pussycat', Series 2, Box 5, Folder 5, Stevie Smith papers, 1924–1970. Coll. No. 1976.012. McFarlin Library. Department of Special Collections and University Archives. The University of Tulsa.

[10] Stevie Smith, 'The Poet and the Pussycat', Series 2, Box 5, Folder 5, Stevie Smith papers, 1924–1970. Coll. No. 1976.012. McFarlin Library. Department of Special Collections and University Archives. The University of Tulsa.

PROVERBS THROUGH FAIRYTALE 83

This collusion between storyteller and listener is key to the fairytale: the sense that even the most outrageous claims spring out of, or are corollaries to, what one already knows. Jack Barbera and William McBrien connect Smith's interest in fairytales with a fascination with myth and its capacity to 'universalise common experiences.'[11] Even when told or written for the first time, the fairytale still presents itself as a retelling, a recalling of shared knowledge which brings the circle of teller and hearers closer together. In 'The Poet and the Pussycat', Smith deflates her stranger claims (such as her suggestion that cats shoulder the responsibility of caring for human beings) into statements of familiar, everyday experience. So when Jan Montefiore suggests that Smith's interest in fairytales springs out of her plain and quotidian idiom,[12] one might add that Smith's fairytales are also invested in establishing and defining what counts as plain and quotidian: marking out a territory of assumed familiarity within the space of the fantastic.

Smith establishes this familiarity—often belatedly, in the sense of making something new appear instantly well-known and established—in part through her use of refrains in her fairytale poems. Fairytales, as already suggested, accrete around repetition: things often need to happen three times. This is part of their pleasure (as in Chapter 1, centring on the need to have an experience of the short text again and again), but repetition is also as key to their legitimacy as it is to the authority of proverbs. 'I rode with my darling ... ' and 'The Forlorn Sea' centre around a line whose repetition establishes and justifies its power, giving it weight to convince. In 'I rode with my darling ... ' the girl remains in the wood, outside the social systems which the repeated line, warning her not to stay in the dark wood at night, shored up (CP, 296–267). 'The Forlorn Sea', meanwhile, circles around a refrain of 'forlorn sea' as it describes a visit to a palace shared by a princess and fairy king, who are waited on by white cats (CP, 608–609). This refrain pulls the poem's centre of gravity towards its otherworldly setting, its strangeness emphasized by the shifted accent in the word 'forlorn'. 'Forlorn sea' assumes the status of a set phrase, a known quantity which carries weight, a shorthand for all manner of fairytale implications. Like 'nervy, bold and grim', or 'flogged twice through Homer', its repetition pushes it back towards the status of an unquestionable truth, establishing it retrospectively as somehow prior to the text in which it was coined.

Romana Huk's nuanced examination of Smith's use of fairytale involves a consideration of the genre's familiar language. Smith's poem 'Cool as a Cucumber', for Huk, merges fairytale diction with colloquial language to dramatize how discursive codes collude in the formation of identity.[13] This question of identity formation

---

[11] Jack Barbera and William McBrien, *Stevie: A Biography of Stevie Smith* (London: Macmillan, 1986), 96.

[12] Jan Montefiore, *Feminism and Poetry: Language, Experience, Identity in Women's Writing* (London and New York: Pandora, 1987), 39.

[13] Romana Huk, 'Eccentric Concentrism: Traditional Poetic Forms and Refracted Discourse in Stevie Smith's Poetry', *Contemporary Literature* 34, no. 2 (1993): 255.

84 STEVIE SMITH AND THE APHORISM

establishes the basis for Huk's later arguments, that for Smith fairytale involves its own kind of entrapping circumscription, transmitting stories of female experience as discourses which shape Smith against her will, even as she probes them.[14] Huk suggests that ambiguity and clashes of 'cultural-textual trajectories' are fundamental to the fairytale; Smith has her characters get lost in that nexus rather than escape it neatly.[15] For Huk, therefore, fairytale does not permit Smith's characters to escape from entrapping social discourses; rather, it reasserts those discourses. Smith resists the fairytale (or stages the consequences of her failure to) because it threatens to entrap: to tie up or elide loose ends in ways which subsume dissent within comforting quasi-religious sop narratives. Fairytale and proverb seem to invite us into a too-sweet childhood space, which nevertheless derives its cosiness from a repressive disciplinary function. The good are rewarded and the bad (the immoderate, the imprudent) are punished; Tiny's nasty brother Clem is ejected from Uncle Heber's house. It is no surprise, therefore, that *The Fairchild Family*, that infamous Victorian children's book describing punishments for small childhood sins, forms a recurring motif in *The Holiday* (*Holiday*, 69, 195), as well as the men's reminiscence of being 'flogged twice through Homer'.

Because of their aggressively authoritative ethos, proverbs have a particular capacity to gloss over situations, or cover up the unpleasant. Towards the end of the book, Celia's cousin Caz also parodies Heber's three-part rhetorical style:

> Observation, discipline and company, said my cousin, as if he were offering a plate of sandwiches, with the flag stuck on them to say what they were.
>
> (*Holiday*, 194)

Caz's proverbial parody redirects the attention forcibly away from all but these virtues. Like the sandwich-flag to which Celia compares it, the line signifies respectability and social participation in a set of niceties. In the unpublished, unnamed fairytale which Smith left unfinished in a notebook, proverbs perform this social glossing-over. King and queen, classic fairytale protagonists, muse on how to raise their sons:

> As to the children—well boys would be boys—young people must learn to fend for themselves—no school like that of experience—let them carve out their

---

[14] Romana Huk, 'On "the Beat Inevitable": The Ballad', in *A Companion to Poetic Genre*, ed. Erik Martiny (Oxford: Wiley Blackwell, 2012), 127. See also Romana Huk, 'Poetic Subject and Voice as Sites of Struggle: Toward a "Postrevisionist" Reading of Stevie Smith's Fairy-Tale Poems', in *Dwelling in Possibility: Women Poets and Critics on Poetry*, ed. Yopie Prins and Maeera Shreiber (Ithaca and London: Cornell University Press, 1997), 149, on Smith's casting of traditional fairytale narratives into dialogue with 'oppositional others'.

[15] Romana Huk, *Stevie Smith: Between the Lines* (Basingstoke: Palgrave Macmillan, 2005), 286.

own destinies—and with these comforting platitudes they turned their sons out to graze.[16]

Here, proverb works parodically within the fairytale to smooth over social rupture, its soothing clichés securing and reinforcing societal norms. Jack Zipes points out that the fairytale, like the proverb, had a didactic socializing function, training its listeners in proper behaviours.[17] As Gill Plain notes in her analysis of Smith's *Over the Frontier*, fairytale narratives 'teach us to accept the consequences of our actions'.[18] The sense, in both proverb and fairytale, is of reasserting rather than disrupting (as other kinds of aphorism do) the natural order of things, maintaining rather than re-evaluating the status quo.

Although Frances Spalding suggests that fairytale attracted Smith because of its model of Fate as 'simple and peremptory',[19] Smith shows suspicion of this aspect of fairytale and proverb: clear answers and comforting authority. In her radio broadcast 'World of Books', as she dismisses the solace often found in religion, she balances between confessing a love of fairytales and rejecting them:

> ... [if man is lonely he] must just be lonely ... It's better than making up fairy stories, though nobody loves fairy stories more than I do, provided they're recognised as being fairy stories.[20]

For Smith, fairytales and religion both reassure, but ultimately lie; they should be avoided, unless they can be held at a critical distance. Smith's performance introduction to 'The Castle' reflects this ambivalence towards the form. Her edits minimize the poem's alliance with fairytale, instead slipping it in casually, and subordinating the text primarily to a classical narrative:

> Here is a happy love poem. ~~But of course it is a fairy story, really~~. It is based on the {fairy story} 'East of the Sun and West of the Moon' ~~story~~, which is also {of course} the Cupid and Psyche one.[21]

---

[16] Stevie Smith, unfinished fairytale, Series 5, Box 1, Folder 7, Stevie Smith papers, University of Tulsa.

[17] Jack Zipes, *Fairy Tales and the Art of Subversion* (London and New York: Routledge, 2012), 7.

[18] Gill Plain, *Women's Fiction of the Second World War: Gender, Power and Resistance* (Edinburgh: Edinburgh University Press, 1996), 84.

[19] Frances Spalding, *Stevie Smith: A Critical Biography* (London: Faber and Faber, 1988), 21.

[20] Stevie Smith, TS of 'World of Books', Series 2, Box 6, Folder 20, Stevie Smith papers, University of Tulsa.

[21] Stevie Smith, TS of 'The Castle', Series 2, Box 2, Folder 9, Stevie Smith papers, University of Tulsa. Braces indicate sections which have been added to the typescript by hand; parts scored out have been crossed out in the typescript by hand.

86 STEVIE SMITH AND THE APHORISM

Amended introductions to 'I rode with my darling ... ' conceal the fairytale connection even more vigorously:

> ~~I will now read some of the lost and fearful poems, where things have gone {go} awry and shapes have been {are} changed, it may be through magic and witchcraft, they are fairy stories often.~~ Of course, some people choose to be lost. The girl in this poem had a lover and kind friends and relations, but she rode away from them, she chose to be lost.[22]

In these narratives of escape—of 'cho[o]s[ing] to be lost'—fairytale itself becomes something to be escaped, either because its childish associations mean that it lacks credibility, because the tightly-controlled narrative of fairytale is limiting, or because fairytale promises an idealized response to human behaviour which Smith's writing refuses to deliver. The question then becomes why, despite her suspiciousness of fairytale neatness, fairytales and proverbial turns of phrase still recur so often in Smith's writing.

Smith's use of proverbs, I argue, activates a particular historical disjunction between fairytale narrative and its proverbial moments. The critical view of fairytale as bolstering disciplinary social narratives derives, to a large extent, from tales which had undergone significant revision. As the Grimms went through their editions the tales became more sanitized and ornamented, adding, as Lüthi describes, more detail and psychological explanation.[23] Also added, Wolfgang Mieder notes, are many of the proverbs with which the tales have become so closely identified. Mieder describes how Wilhelm Grimm's fascination with proverbs led him to incorporate newly-identified proverbial texts into later editions of the *Kinder- und Hausmärchen*, justifying his additions on the grounds that he was preserving the folk speech which belonged to fairytales.[24]

Maria Tatar outlines the consequence of this addition of proverbial moral lessons to tales to which they are not fundamental. Though the father in 'The Frog King' lectures his daughter on the importance of keeping promises, the spell on the frog is not broken until the princess acts cruelly towards him, throwing him against the wall. Ethical codes, she suggests, are not intrinsically relevant to fairytale narrative.[25] The proverb which we expect to comprise the tale's moral is not

---

[22] Stevie Smith, TS of 'I rode with my darling ... ', Series 2, Box 2, Folder 10, Stevie Smith papers, University of Tulsa.

[23] Max Lüthi, *The European Folktale: Form and Nature*, trans. John D. Niles (Philadelphia: Institute for the Study of Human Issues, 1982), 103.

[24] Wolfgang Mieder, '"Ever Eager to Incorporate Folk Proverbs": Wilhelm Grimm's Proverbial Additions in the Fairy Tales', in *The Brothers Grimm and Folktale*, ed. James M. McGlathery, with Larry W. Danielson, Ruth E. Lorbe, and Selma K. Richardson (Urbana and Chicago: University of Illinois Press, 1988), 112, 116.

[25] Maria M. Tatar, 'Beauties vs. Beasts in the Grimms' *Nursery and Household Tales*', in *The Brothers Grimm and Folktale*, ed. James M. McGlathery et al., 143.

reflected by the story: is not, in fact, an abbreviated version of the overall tale. It may instead be belatedly added, reframing a fairytale's reception.

Smith can position her use of proverb, therefore, in the juncture where fairytale and proverb fall out of sync: where the historical contingency of their relationship becomes visible. In her writing, fairytale represents neither a space of freedom, as Ruth Baumert and Ingrid Hotz-Davies imply,[26] nor yet entirely a space of entrapment, as Huk argues. Smith is drawn to fairytale's capacity to be a haunting form: however, she repurposes its historical trauma, offering it a different way to haunt and survive. Fairytale pervades her writing, visible but unacknowledged, frequently restrained from entering the foreground. This is the relationship of proverb to fairytale. Fairytale presents a proverb (often added late in its history), but strips it of narrative power, allowing it to fade from memory when other, more cryptic images survive.[27] Proverb's moral message, its particular instruction for action, appears clearly and visibly (for instance, the king's admonition to the princess in 'The Frog King') but it remains outside authorial and readerly focus. *The Holiday* models the same draining away of the proverb's use-value.

Repositioning the Proverb

Uncle, I say, I was reading the Proverbs last night, what I just quoted, they are very practical, but in some fashion also they make an unpleasant picture of a too practical, too self-advantageous virtue. The ones that are repeated so often, you know? Don't waste time talking to fools, don't chatter, don't go after strange women, don't stay in bed. Be a squirrel, be an ant, the improvident person shall have nothing to eat in the winter. Don't spare the rod, beat your children, beat sense into your little ones, etc. And above all, don't back bills for strangers. There is, of course, this real noble love of wisdom, this is very strong, but it is so often the wisdom of Polonius, 'looking out for Number One'. Uncle, a lot of gay and generous people ... chatter an awful lot, and borrow money, and are not ants or squirrels. It is necessary to be practical. But it is not the whole of wisdom, it is not, it is only a part. Everything in this world is in fits and splinters, like after an air raid when the glass is on the pavements; one picks one's way and is happy in parts.

(Holiday, 142–143)

---

[26] Ruth Baumert, 'Fear, Melancholy, and Loss in the Poetry of Stevie Smith', in *The Abject of Desire: The Aestheticization of the Unaesthetic in Contemporary Literature and Culture*, ed. Monika Mueller and Konstanze Kutzbach (Amsterdam and New York: Rodopi, 2007), 205; Ingrid Hotz-Davies, '"My Name is Finis": The Lonely Voice of Stevie Smith', in *In Black and Gold: Contiguous Traditions in Post-War British and Irish Poetry*, ed. C. C. Barfoot (Amsterdam and Atlanta, GA: Rodopi, 1994), 226.

[27] This fairytale capacity for the cryptic, argues H. J. Blackham, differentiates it from the fable. While the fairytale contains hidden, ambiguously symbolic content, the inventions of fable 'have a different orientation and source, openly explicable' (H. J. Blackham, *The Fable as Literature* (London and New York: Bloomsbury, 2013), 189).

88 STEVIE SMITH AND THE APHORISM

As Celia digs potatoes with Heber, she finds herself protesting against Biblical Proverbs: the model of wisdom, recommending prudence in sententious terms, in which Uncle Heber participates. She criticizes Biblical Proverbs because they are 'too practical', excluding the unnecessary or the frivolous in favour of direct, useful observations.

This focus on the moral status of usefulness and practicality emerges in another text which Smith published, like *The Holiday*, in 1949. In 'Beside the Seaside: A Holiday with Children', the childless Helen goes on holiday with gentle Margaret and her family. Smith based Helen on herself (Helen recites part of Smith's 'Advice to Young Children', describing it as 'the moral poem I wrote') (MA, 13), and Margaret on her friend Betty Miller, whose novel *Farewell Leicester Square* (1941) explored the struggles of a young Jewish film-maker against anti-Semitic attitudes.[28] Smith's short story estranged her from Miller, in part because of her unsympathetic portrayal of Miller's children, but also because of the anti-Semitism which Helen expresses in the story:

> 'I do not hold with the theory that the Jewish people is an appeasing, accommodating people, knowing, as some say, on which side their bread is buttered, and prepared to make accommodations with conscience for their own advantage. No, I think that they are an obstinate and unreasonable people, short-sighted about their true interests, fanatical ... ' (MA, 19)

Helen objects to the Jews because she thinks they are (to adopt Celia's terms in *The Holiday*) not 'practical', not 'self-advantageous'; they cannot or will not act in their 'true interests'. Prejudice and practicality become doubly linked. Helen expresses an anti-Semitic prejudice that Jews are not practical; equally, practicality (as Celia imagines it in *The Holiday*) involves acting on prejudice. One stays away from fools, strange women, strangers. Prejudice, like proverb, operates through shorthand: its 'shrewdness', Christopher Ricks argues, in part 'consists in its not going out on the limb of insisting that it will be proved right'.[29]

Prejudice restrains itself from explanation or justification. It positions itself prior to the possibility of interrogation, operating immediately and automatically. The protagonist Pompey notices this tendency in herself in Smith's *Over the Frontier* (1938), when the subject of the Jews arises: 'I am in despair for the racial hatred that is running in me in a sudden swift current, in a swift tide of hatred, and Out out damned tooth, damned aching tooth, rotten to the root' (*Frontier*, 158). What does the clichéd phrase 'rotten to the root' refer to here? To the racist tendencies in Pompey herself, which she wishes to drive out of herself? Or to the Jews themselves, framed as a decay in society? These dangerous opposing feelings collapse

---

[28] Betty Miller, *Farewell Leicester Square* (London: Robert Hale, 1941).
[29] Christopher Ricks, *T. S. Eliot and Prejudice* (London: Faber and Faber, 1988), 11.

together; the proverbial language smooths over the ambiguity. This is the dark side of the aphoristic line's capacity to contain and display socially unacceptable feelings. Not all sentiments which issue from those on society's margins are heroic.

The shorthand of prejudice and proverb enables quick decisive action, based on what is peremptorily assumed to be true. In that sense, both may share a destructive 'practical[ity]'. Set in the shadow of rising European fascism, the dreamlike plot of *Over the Frontier* follows the depressed and pining Pompey first through a round of London parties, then to Schloss Tilssen for rest and recuperation, then—suddenly—into uniform, as she rides across the landscape as a soldier in an unknown war. Challenged on whether she would fight on the side of the Jews, two clichéd set-phrases occur to Pompey: 'None but the Jews would have survived their persecutions' and 'But I have had some very dear Jewish friends' (*Frontier*, 158). She cannot move past these received anti-Semitic platitudes. They become, very explicitly, the engine which transforms prejudice smoothly into oppression: Pompey observes, of the second line, 'Do not all our persecutions of Israel follow upon this smiling sentence?' (*Frontier*, 158). *Over the Frontier* focuses on the question— thoroughly explored by Romana Huk—of how rhetoric can become a means of concealing abominations.[30] Prejudice, in this novel, is practical; it makes life easier and (monstrously) convenient for Pompey. But in Smith's next novel, *The Holiday*, she has Celia place herself on the side of the impractical: the chattering, the borrowing, the unwisely happy.

This nexus of terms does not neutralize the anti-Semitic prejudice expressed by the characters in 'Beside the Seaside' and *Over the Frontier*. It does accommodate a reversal of connotation: prejudice is practical, but practicality can derive, in a way disturbing to Celia in *The Holiday*, from prejudice. Proverb, for Celia, uses partial or skewed knowledge as a convenient shorthand. '[R]epeated too often', positioned as pre-existing wisdom which demands to be used and acted upon, proverb excludes other ways of thinking and acting from the world.

In *The Holiday*, therefore, Celia evacuates usefulness from the proverb. She plays with it, makes it light: sound and flashes, rather than something which can be listened to or put into action. A world in 'fits and splinters' demands not certainty but free experiment; not usefulness but precisely that 'gay and generous' frivolity which, Celia feels, the proverb risks excluding. So her handling of the proverb in *The Holiday* repositions the form as a site of pleasure. When Caz quotes a proverb, Celia swiftly steers the line away from any potential use-value by countering with a quotation of her own:

> Care killed the cat, said Caz.
> The foolish reader bites the man of genius.
> The dog it was that died.

---

[30] Huk, *Between the Lines*, 173.

90   STEVIE SMITH AND THE APHORISM

> I laughed: I like best, Who bites the Pope dies of it.
> We fell asleep in the sun.
>
> (*Holiday*, 159)

The typescript shows that this exchange of proverbs was inserted into the first draft on a separate page. Since Smith edited comparatively lightly, the change demonstrates that the proverb game is part of a deliberate narrative strategy, rather than a writer simply running on. Caz's quotation of a proverb immediately gives way to a game of 'capping quotations'. In manuscript, the text is explicit that this game is being played: instead of 'I like best', the original reads 'I'll cap that with my favourite, I said'.[31] Capping quotations is an aristocratic performance of learning held lightly, with a line seen as valuable not in itself but as a swappable cipher. We see one performance in Dorothy L. Sayers' *Gaudy Night* (1935):

> 'You look', said the Dean, 'like a nervous parent whose little boy is about to recite *The Wreck of the Hesperus* at a School Concert'.
> 'I feel', said Harriet, 'more like the mother of Daniel.
>
> > King Darius said to the lions:–
> > Bite Daniel. Bite Daniel.
> > Bite him. Bite him. Bite him.'
>
> 'G'rrrr!' said the Dean ...
> ... 'Miss Shaw's got a new frock', said Harriet.
> 'So she has! How posh of her!
>
> > And she was as fine as a melon in the corn-field,
> > Gliding and lovely as a ship upon the sea.
>
> That, my dear, is meant for Daniel.'[32]

Quotation—and specifically, in *The Holiday*, proverb—is made useless but enjoyable. The lines exchanged are toys to be played with and then left, their use-value reduced to strengthening friendships and temporarily winning tiny amounts of power. Celia's proverb-swapping performs a reclamative function because it makes the individual proverb just one in a network of proverbs, which may, as proverbs do, contradict or disrupt each other. It is a way of disempowering the proverb, instituting instead significance of a different sort, to do with what is immediately visible rather than what is euphemistically implied.

Editing the manuscript line 'I'll cap that with my favourite' to the less-competitive, pleasure-oriented 'I like best' reduces that minimal power struggle still further, foregrounding instead an enjoyment of sound and semantic absurdity. Smith emphasizes how this game allows its constituent lines to be unnecessary

---

[31] Stevie Smith, TS of *The Holiday*, Series 2, Box 2, Folders 15–17, Stevie Smith papers, University of Tulsa.
[32] Dorothy L Sayers, *Gaudy Night* (London: Hodder & Stoughton, 1970), 390–1.

PROVERBS THROUGH FAIRYTALE   91

in any practical sense. Instead, it opens them up to desertion: before the game between Celia and Caz has fairly got going, they 'fell asleep in the sun'. The proverbs die away, unused. All they have done is to lull the characters to sleep, like a story before bed.

Smith continues to position proverb as a space for pleasure in her selections for *The Batsford Book of Children's Verse* (1970). In this anthology, alongside poems by Byron, Edward Thomas, Shakespeare, and herself, she presents two separate passages from Proverbs in the Bible. She evidently values this genre, despite Celia's ambivalence in *The Holiday*. However, her choice of passages prompts her readers to shift their focus: from seeing the proverb as guide to action, to seeing it as a much less determined form:

> There be three things which are too wonderful for me, yea, four which I know not:
> The way of an eagle in the air; the way of a serpent upon a rock; the way of a ship in the midst of the sea; and the way of a man with a maid.
>
> [Proverbs 30:18–19]

> There be four things which are little upon the earth, but they are exceeding wise:
> The ants are a people not strong, yet they prepare their meat in the summer;
> The conies are but a feeble folk, yet make they their houses in the rocks;
> The locusts have no king, yet go they forth all of them by bands;
> The spider taketh hold with her hands, and is in kings' palaces.[33]
>
> [Proverbs 30:24–28]

Each of these numerical proverbs is structured in terms of a riddle and its answer. The second implicitly challenges the reader to think up four animals which meet a set of miraculous or contradictory conditions.[34] The pleasure and game-playing on show in the proverb, here and in *The Holiday*, demonstrate that Celia's remarks to Heber cannot be taken as Smith's wholesale rejection of the mode. Smith signals the scale of her attraction to the proverb's poetics by including these selections in the *Batsford Book*. Importantly, however, she is attracted to the cryptic and the

[33] Stevie Smith, ed., *The Batsford Book of Children's Verse* (London: Batsford, 1970), 31, 75.
[34] On the debate surrounding the historical relationship between riddle and biblical proverb, see R. B. Y. Scott, *The Way of Wisdom in the Old Testament* (London and New York: Macmillan, 1971), 71; Philip Johannes Nel, *The Structure and Ethos of the Wisdom Admonitions in Proverbs* (Berlin and New York: Walter de Gruyter, 1982), 11; and Wolfgang Roth, *Numerical Sayings in the Old Testament: A Form-Critical Study* (Leiden: Brill, 1965), 96.

92 STEVIE SMITH AND THE APHORISM

riddling; proverbs which hold open a space of doubt, which elicit play and intellectual experiment from their readers, rather than providing guides to action or use-value.

The Proverb as Fairytale Core

These riddling, playful proverbs reflect the structures of fairytale: another form which centres its narrative patterns on verbal and numerical formulas of threes, and which survives in a manner which resists utility.[35] Both fairytales and proverbs are shaped by the collective: passed down between generations, their origins lost, changing slightly in each set of hands until, as Mieder notes, a generally-accepted wording is hit upon.[36] In 'The Storyteller', Walter Benjamin calls a proverb 'an ideogram of a story', comparing it to 'a ruin which stands on the site of an old story and in which a moral twines about a happening like ivy around a wall'.[37] We are reminded of Derrida's description of an aphorism as 'ruin and monument', discussed in Chapter 2. Though time strips away superfluous or culturally-specific content from both, proverb appears as a reduced or pared-down version of fairytale (Benjamin associates storytelling specifically with the teller of fairytales).[38] Fairytale is already worn down to archetypal, self-sufficient essentials: proverb, in this model, is then the bone of fairytale.

This sense of fairytale as surviving primarily in hard, memorable cores characterizes Stevie Smith's response to the genre. Smith's enjoyment of the fairytale hinges on key, haunting images, which bear repetition. In 'The Ironing-Board of Widow Twanky' (1961), an essay about stage adaptations of fairytales, she dwells with clear enjoyment on iconic moments in the stories:

> I like the poems in the fairy stories ... (as an editor said once, 'Yes, by all means put some poems in your article, it will help to break the text up').
>
> I should like to see our fairy-play text broken up by such verses as the Cinderella one, after the Ugly Sister has cut her toe off so as to get the shoe on and is riding away with the prince, and the grass cries out 'Look behind, look behind, there's blood upon the shoe. The shoe's too small, the one behind, is not the bride for you' ... Or the Talking Head story, where the dead horse's head hangs on the wall, and passing underneath the goose-girl princess cries: 'Fallada, Fallada, there

---

[35] See, for instance, Lüthi, *The European Folktale*, 32–33, on the structural function of pairs and triads in the fairytale. See also Andrew Teverson, *Fairy Tale* (Abingdon: Routledge, 2013), 24, on how fairytale operates through the repetition of verbal formulae.

[36] Mieder, *American Proverbs*, 23.

[37] Walter Benjamin, 'The Storyteller', in *Illuminations*, trans. Harry Zorn (London: Pimlico, 1999), 107.

[38] Benjamin, 101.

PROVERBS THROUGH FAIRYTALE   93

thou are, hanging', so the horse replies: 'Child, child, there thou art ganging. Alas, alas, if thy mother knew it, Sadly, sadly, her heart would rue it'.[39]

The level of detail in these examples implies that these episodes represent the emotional centres of the tales: the striking moments which linger in Smith's mind, more than the stories' endings, narrative strategies or individual characters.[40] The songs—repetitive when presented in this format—are given in full, a rhythmic space in which Smith can fully inhabit the fairytale in her retelling.

This shifted focus, away from narrative detail of cause and effect on to individual, core moments, manifests in Smith's manuscript revisions of *Novel on Yellow Paper*. She describes her German holiday, where the child of her hosts is constantly being punished for small misdemeanours, and then consoled with a fairy story.

> ... and all the time it was just the one fairy story that I got nearly by heart. Reader, it was The Wolf and the Seven Little Kids, and when it ended up *Der Wolf ist tot Der Wolf ist Tot*. Hurra, hurra, hurra, the blood lust and ferocity on the infant face of the infant neurotic was something more than I could stand.
>
> And there was another one she would allow sometimes to be told. It is the one about Snowdrop and her cruel stepmother ... by and by of course the little Snowdrop grows right up and marries her prince. And the wicked stepmother? Ah well, this is what happens to her. She falls in with the happy wedding-party and they take her by force and make her dance in red-hot shoes until she is dead ...
>
> (*Novel*, 74–75)

Smith's language here emphasizes the predictability of fairytale: in phrases like 'of course', and in the satisfyingly bloody endings for which Trudi listens out avidly. Narrative, plot, and causality are shrunk right down in her summary, so that what stands out is the image of the stepmother dancing in red hot shoes. The experience of fairytale, with its vivid core moments, is one which Trudi wishes to have again and again: one which cannot be spent or fulfilled in a single rendition. This is, as Chapter 1 suggested, the rhythm of aphorism, where the sealed inaccessibility of the textual nugget incites a desire for a repeated experience. Pompey disapproves of Trudi's bloodthirsty love of gory images; that she recounts the tale in the same terms, however, indicates a similar line of interest.

Strikingly, Stevie Smith chooses a different fairy story in her manuscript version of *Novel on Yellow Paper*: a botched and confused version of 'The Goose Girl', referred to also in 'The Ironing-Board of Widow Twanky'. Instead of 'Snow White':

---

[39] Stevie Smith, 'The Ironing-Board of Widow Twanky', *Queen* 219 (20 December 1961): 11.
[40] On the adult tendency to remember only single, striking images from fairytales, see Max Lüthi, *Once Upon A Time: On the Nature of Fairy Tales*, trans. Lee Chadeayne and Paul Gottwald (New York: Frederick Ungar, 1970), 67.

94   STEVIE SMITH AND THE APHORISM

... it was the one about the princess that is going to the court of a neighbouring king to get fixed up with the King {,} and she goes along with her maid{. N}ow the maid is a strapping big girl{,} and presently she makes the princess take her place and be the servant{,} and she is the princess{. W}ell what they did about the clothes{,} ~~like~~ how they certainly wouldnt fit that strapping big girl{,} I dont just remember{,} but it was all o.k. and no questions asked{,} until by and by it all came out ~~how I foget~~ and the wicked girl was made to dance in red hot shoes until she was dead{: Da musste sie in die rotglühenden Schuhe treten und so lange tanzen, bis sie tot zur Erde fiel.}[41]

Here, the ending is emphasized—but it is the wrong ending, imported, as we see above, from Snow White.[42] Someone, Smith or Pompey or perhaps the original storyteller, has forgotten quite how the story goes. Pompey has certainly forgotten how the story proceeds from the initial premise to the ending; she tacks it on, abruptly. She slides quickly over inconvenient details, like the fit of the clothes and the mechanics of the eventual revelation, dismissing the fact that she cannot remember them, and declaring instead 'it was all o.k. and no questions asked'. In stripping the fairytale of shape and narrative linkage, Smith flattens the fairytale's passage from crime to solution to punishment, foregrounding instead the key images of clothes being swapped and dancing in red hot shoes. These images survive not only in the retelling; they survive into other stories, where they do not belong. Snow White's ending lasts into 'The Goose Girl': it haunts and repeats.

Turning, then, to the question of *The Holiday*'s interaction with the fairytale mode, one of the major ways it echoes the genre (or at least that aspect of it which drew Smith) is in its repetition of key images beyond its own textual boundaries. Though *The Holiday* was not published until 1949, Smith published a short story 'Is There a Life Beyond the Gravy?' in 1947, with Celia, Cas (here with an 's', short for Casivalaunus), and Tiny still going to visit their uncle Heber (MA, 60–73). Ten years after *The Holiday* was published, moreover, Smith would repurpose portions of the text directly in her radio play 'A Turn Outside' (1959):

S.S.: ... The flowers that you will not let me pick. 'Do you want to raise the devil?' you say.

INTERLOCUTOR: I would not let you pluck the flowers?

S.S.: No, *then*, on that occasion, you would not.

('A Turn Outside', MA, 352)

---

[41] Stevie Smith, annotated typescript of *Novel on Yellow Paper*, U DP-156-1, 56, Stevie Smith Papers 1935–1969, Hull History Centre. Braces indicate sections which have been added to the typescript by hand; parts scored out have been crossed out in the typescript by hand.
[42] The Grimms' first edition of 'The Goose Girl' punishes the servant by rolling her in a barrel full of internal spikes.

This is just one example of an occasion in this play which recycles passages from 'Is There a Life Beyond the Gravy?' and *The Holiday*:

> 'Don't pick the flowers, Celia,' said Cas. 'Do you wish to raise the devil?' ('Is There a Life Beyond the Gravy?', MA, 71)

> ... the soft grass on top of the cliff is speckled with flowers, the flowers that my cousin will not let me pick.
> Do you want to raise the devil? he says.
>
> (*The Holiday*, 149)

Like the fairytale, these scenarios and snatches of language are repeatable, passing through a series of retellings and being subtly shaped in the process. This is not even a crucial narrative moment (nor is the singing horse's head in 'The Goose Girl'), but it becomes the core which survives, passing from one text into another. This image (like those remembered in 'Twanky') has the fairytale motif's resistance to explanation. In all the texts, the moment comes from nowhere and leads to nothing: no devil is ever raised. The image is haunting precisely because of its excess. It is superfluous to each of Smith's narratives. Because it remains undigested—resistant to interpretation and assimilation—it lasts and lasts across her writing.

Tatar comments on the 'notorious flatness' of fairytale characters, which discourages critics from analysing their motivations even as the 'boldness of their deeds invites careful scrutiny'.[43] Fairytale refuses to answer our questions (like aphorism) even as it makes it clear that there are many questions to be asked. Its frugality of description compounds this effect: not only are fairytale characters presented with minimal psychological depth, but landscapes are barely described, and in fact description in general is basic. Elements arise only as required by the action of the story, against a near-blank background: they appear from darkness, and then vanish again.[44] Like the proverb, the fairytale image presents itself without explanation, justification, or apology. The impossible (for instance, the horse-head speaking in 'The Goose-Girl') occurs with absolute nonchalance. Unable to interpret, we simply pass it on.

A Lion is in the Street

> ... with my sin of sloth there runs also the sin of fear; the sluggard saith: There is a lion in the way, a lion is in the street. It is fear and mistrust, fear of action and

---

[43] Maria Tatar, *The Hard Facts of the Grimms' Fairy Tales* (Princeton: Princeton University Press, 2003), 56.
[44] Lüthi, *The European Folktale*, 17.

96 STEVIE SMITH AND THE APHORISM

so inaction. I could never marry because of fear, I should like to have one-third of a man, to be the third wife, perhaps, with her own house...but to be the one wife, that is the dear one and the comfort, to be the dear one and the comfort of one man, that I admire, that I could not dare to be, I should be afraid there was a lion in the street.

(*Holiday*, 142)

Just before Celia criticizes proverbs to Uncle Heber in the garden, she uses Proverbs 26:13 to explain why she resists marriage. This arresting proverb describes a sluggard's protest that he cannot go out because a lion is in the street. The image is sensational: the wild erupts into the urban space, escaping concretizable explanation. It would slide straight into one of Hilaire Belloc's poems (the lion poised to gobble up an ungrateful child) or a Grimms' fairytale. And yet, appearing in the Bible as part of a sequence about sloth and foolishness, the sluggard's extraordinary claim vanishes under the weight of the moral message.

In this passage in *The Holiday*, Smith reverses the dynamic of the sluggard and lion. The Book of Proverbs steers us to focus on the sluggard, whose behaviour we should avoid. Yet it is the lion which survives into Smith's text. She chooses to focus on the sensational image rather than the moral purpose: that inexplicable lion in the street, clear and disconnected as the speaking horse-head in 'The Goose Girl'.

Here, the refusal of fairytale to explain or justify its narrative vagaries becomes central to Smith's use of this proverb.[45] She allows the figure of the lion in the street to survive, as an emblem of the absurd. The lion in the street is paralysing because it cannot be understood or properly reacted to: it becomes a symbol of excessive, unusable knowledge.

In Smith's hands, the proverbial lion embodies both interpretative and ethical paralysis. Celia associates intimacy with a nameless fear which is too close and prevents action. Marriage brings her right up against an apocalyptic conception of reality: a perception of events no less horrifying for being objectively absurd, barely understood. No one else sees the lion which the sluggard perceives in the street. The Bible urges us to conclude that there is no lion there, no reason not to act, and that the sluggard is making excuses. Celia raises the unsettling question: what if there is a lion there, a real reason not to act, which only I can sense, but cannot explain or justify? In the Bible, this proverb urges action by minimizing its own rhetorical power. Stevie Smith reactivates its poetics, reconfiguring the line as a space between action and inaction by allowing its central image to stand free of interpretative baggage.

---

[45] Lüthi, *The European Folktale*, 84.

PROVERBS THROUGH FAIRYTALE   97

Smith establishes the unusability of this image, later in the novel, as its main point of interest by re-versioning it: by allowing Celia and Caz, indirectly, to meet the lion in the street:

> In the middle of the white road that crosses the esplanade there is a baby crawling fiercely. How reckless the creature is, I pick him up, he is very heavy, his hair is bleached white by the sun, his romper suit bulges over his fat back. He begins to roar and stiffen. As he cries out a tall thin pale girl comes running out of the shelter. 'Oh, he is so naughty', she says, 'I can never leave him for a moment, I must have fallen asleep'. Well, there is not much traffic about, I said, looking at the empty miles before us and behind. How swiftly he crawls, he is bold and forceful. The mother sighs and takes him from me. The child has sucked the strength quite out of her, she is pale and shadowy, he is a lion in the road.
>
> (*Holiday*, 166–167)

Smith presents the baby starkly: our central focus, positioned in a white road, empty of distractions. The reader is cued to receive him as significant: partly because he echoes Celia's earlier 'lion in the street' monologue, and partly because he recalls a particular baby image in *Novel on Yellow Paper*:

> There is a vast flooded prairie, a rushing mud-yellow foam-curded rain-lashed torrent, as if all the dams in the world were burst ... not Christian at all, but just the old element at its savagery ... And riding ... on top of that brown flood was A little child shall ride it, in a cradle with a cat on top.
>
> (*Novel*, 5)

Are we to read this as the same baby who resurfaces in *The Holiday?* Did the baby leave the cat riding over the sea, for later in *The Holiday* Celia and Caz encounter a cat floating on a spar? No interpretative clarity is possible here. The baby's 'romper suit bulges', and we are inclined to feel that he is bulging with meaning. Yet this is meaning which can never be activated. The baby is dense with an oversignification which he cannot carry and which we cannot begin to mine. It is impossible to engage with him, literally or interpretatively ('I pick him up ... He begins to roar and stiffen'). He is a 'lion in the road' precisely because of his paralysing resistance to interpretative utility. The only option available, to Smith or to us as readers, is to pass him by: to allow him simply to vanish:

> Where is the girl and her baby? I said, for the tide was now flowing swiftly over the flat beach.
>
> We sat on the empty terrace beneath a bright torn awning. There was no sign of them ...
>
> (*Holiday*, 171)

Both the cat, floating on its spar, and the baby escape. They escape Celia and Caz, and they escape any attempt at interpretation or use. When Caz and Celia try to rescue the cat, to 'get it in', it tears Caz's hand open, and the spar sails 'far away upon the current' (*Holiday*, 169). The two sense the consolatory possibilities of this escape. Celia remarks, 'it does not wish to be rescued' (*Holiday*, 170). The two then clap and dance, celebrating this freedom.

It would be easy to read this performance of exuberance as a celebration of strictures escaped: the confining proverb as wiped away or subverted. The novel does detail a resistance of the Biblical proverb's command to act, in the characters' unproductive dancing. Yet Smith's use of the Biblical proverb is not subversive, partly because granting the proverb its own different use-value fulfils its demands by another road, but more because she does not deploy anything which was not clearly already available for attention in the proverb. She simply hinges her usage on the arresting central image—which is already fundamental to how fairytale and proverb work and survive—rather than the moral lesson the Biblical framing demands that we glean from it. If we witness an escape from the proverb, it is an escape which occurs within the proverb space and according to its own poetic rules. The lion in the street persists: Smith simply recasts it. Instead of a moral guiding us towards action, it becomes a symbol of suspended action: the product of fear, bewilderment, and self-distrust. What Smith's shifted focus enables, in fact, is a contemplation of the experience of possessing knowledge which one does not know how to use: didactic meaning, embedded metaphorically, which she overlooks in favour of the compelling surface image.

Three and Four

Returning to Smith's selections of proverbs in *The Batsford Book*, it becomes clear that this sense of problematized or unusable knowledge is intrinsic to the Book of Proverbs, rather than a subversion of it. We are called on to find an interpretative path through conflicting sets of information.

> There be three things which are too wonderful for me, yea, four which I know not:
>
> The way of an eagle in the air; the way of a serpent upon a rock; the way of a ship in the midst of the sea; and the way of a man with a maid.[46]
>
> [Proverbs 30:18–19]

---

[46] Smith, *Batsford Book*, 31.

The list format promises knowledge which, as Roth argues, is clearly delineated and organized.[47] However, it delivers no neat model of clearly usable knowledge. The reader's overt challenge is to discover what connects the movement of an eagle, a serpent and a ship, and a man's treatment of a maid: any answer can only be provisional.[48] Even more perplexing, however, is the intellectual dilemma implicit in this proverb's numerical slippage. An announcement of three things is quickly replaced by an announcement, and listing, of four: 'There be three things ... yea, four which I know not.'[49] The distinction between three and four is significant, and yet the proverb carries us rhetorically across this split, with the indifference to strangeness which Lüthi sees as characteristic of fairytale.[50] We are not allowed to perceive a difference between three and four.

The technique is not unique to Proverbs. 'Graded numerical sayings' recur, as Roth notes, across Psalms, Amos, Job, and others.[51] Smith's quoted sentence, however, most closely mirrors other structures in Proverbs 30:

> There are three things that are never satisfied, yea, four things say not, It is enough ...
>
> [Proverbs 30:15]
>
> For three things the earth is disquieted, and for four which it cannot bear ...
>
> [Proverbs 30:21]

These proverbs navigate the experience and fear of unnecessary excess: the earth which crumbles under the weight, the things which should (but do not) cry out 'It is enough.'[52] Their use of three and four lines up with this focus: D. H. Lawrence's interpretation of the Book of Revelation, *Apocalypse* (1931), presents three as the number of the divine (the Trinity) and four as the number of creation

---

[47] Roth, *Numerical Sayings in the Old Testament*, 100.

[48] For a summary of possible connections between these items, see Michael V. Fox, *Proverbs 10–31: A New Translation with Introduction and Commentary* (New Haven and London: Yale University Press, 2009), 870–871.

[49] For arguments that the Biblical three and four signify vague quantities rather than precise numbers, see Fox, *Proverbs 10–31*, 863; and W. O. E. Oesterley, *The Book of Proverbs: With Introduction and Notes* (London: Methuen, 1929), 272). However, Smith would have encountered the graded numerical proverb in a particular, minimally-glossed translation (King James): she would have taken it 'whole', with form emphasized over content.

[50] Lüthi, *The European Folktale*, 6.

[51] Wolfgang M. W. Roth, 'The Numerical Sequence x/x + 1 in the Old Testament', *Vetus Testamentum* 12, no. 3 (1962): 302–303.

[52] This is not universal across graded numerical sayings in the Bible, but it is common: the graded numerical sayings in Amos suggest the magnitude of punishment for transgressions. However, this negotiation with excess witnessed in the quotations above is particularly appropriate to Proverbs: one feeds enemies who have not deserved it, one withdraws from the houses of one's friends. Enemies are given more than they have deserved, and friends are granted less than they have earned.

100 STEVIE SMITH AND THE APHORISM

(the four-cornered Earth).[53] Both are motifs of wholeness and perfection: of boundaries precisely defined and inhabited.

So in this proverb, the perfect is established (three), and then compromised (four). Excess is added. And yet, crucially, this extra addition is accommodated. Four replaces three without acknowledgement; a new model of perfection seamlessly replaces the old. The reader's capacity to register and protest against the overflow (to cry out, perhaps, 'It is enough') is deactivated. These proverbs showcase the process in which perfection is compromised by excess, *and yet* in which that experience of overflow is contained: to quote Karl Kraus on the aphorism, as described in Chapter 1, they embody the phenomenon of being at once half and one-and-a-half. Boundaries are breached and redefined in a single gesture. They lose their power to exclude: to identify and declare what is unnecessary.

The publication history of *The Holiday* reinforced just such a poker-faced elision of temporal boundaries, and explores the experience of that elision. Delays meant that though the novel was written during the Second World War, it was not published until 1949. Undaunted, Smith simply changed all instances of 'war' in the manuscript to 'post-war'.[54] Like the graded numerical proverb, in which an already-complete three tips over into an impossibly equally-perfect four, this is a text which exceeds its own temporal borderlines; which is positioned, in a sense, after itself. This dynamic, and the phenomenon described in the proverb above, underpins Celia's repeated cry in the novel: 'Now it is over, now it will soon be over' (*Holiday*, 35, 118). The borders crumble between past and future; the perfected is collapsed into the contingent. Proverbs, as Celia points out, are best known for telling their listeners to tread a line which holds short of excess: 'Don't waste time talking to fools, don't chatter, don't go after strange women' (*Holiday*, 142). They reject superfluity, presenting themselves (ready-known, ready-formulated wisdom) as all that is needed. And yet, reading *The Holiday* against the *Batsford* proverbs, our very sense of 'enough'—what it is, where it begins and ends—becomes unstable. Under these circumstances, it becomes almost impossible to respond in practical ways to the proverb's demand for frugal behaviour.

Selected and deployed by Smith, the proverbial mode preaches a frugality—of thought, of engagement, of behaviour—which does not bear out into moral action. Her characters embody that frugality, therefore, by withdrawing themselves from the narrative stage. In the vegetable garden, Celia confesses to Heber that she could

---

[53] D. H. Lawrence, *Apocalypse and the Writings on Revelation*, ed. Mara Kalnins (Cambridge: Cambridge University Press, 1980), 133. Stevie Smith read *Apocalypse* early in her career; she transcribes a passage (63) into her reading journals (Series 5, Box 1, Folder 6, Stevie Smith papers, University of Tulsa), and incorporates some of the same text, modified, into *Novel on Yellow Paper* (172).

[54] Stevie Smith, TS of *The Holiday*, Series 2, Box 2, Folders 15–17, Stevie Smith papers, University of Tulsa.

be the third wife but not the 'one wife'. She needs a contingent position, one from which she can always extract herself or avoid the spotlight of scrutiny and intimacy. The remark echoes Smith's own comment to Kay Dick, that she loved life precisely because she always kept herself 'on the edge'.[55] One remains poised on the margins, ready to leave before friendship or love can warp into resentment; before one might tip, horribly and irreversibly, into the state of having had enough.

The Holiday ends, in fact, on a departure. The characters have been fighting and crying throughout, but suddenly decide to go away from the situation: to lie down and sleep:

> When Caz came back we spread the blankets on the hearthrug and lay down together.
> God bless you, Celia, said our uncle, and you too Caz, and my son Tom, God bless him.
> God bless us all, sir, said Caz, and took my hand in his.
> Amen, I said, and fell asleep.
>
> (*Holiday*, 202)

Exchanging affectionate platitudes, lulled by pious set-phrases, the characters go to sleep abruptly, like good children, with nothing solved or answered. What saves this ending from easy obeisance to the proverbial mode is the fact that Smith's proverbial world, as we have discussed, hinges not on the contemptible laziness of sluggards, but on lions in the street; not on the possibility of moral action, but on the crisis-point in which the paralysing absurdity of action, the failure of vivid apprehension to have a real-world impact, bears in upon one. In refraining from action, the characters enter a proverbial space of reticence, uniting into a collective where surprise becomes impossible. Prudently refraining from excess, withdrawing from the situation, the characters are in fact obedient to the proverbial—albeit a particularly Smithian version.

Proverb, for Smith, is valuable only via a fairytale reading. The fairytale both is and is not its proverbial moral; its images survive independent of any moral content. What remains in the ending to *The Holiday* is a tableau of submission to the proverbial, an aestheticized response which play-acts at obedience. Celia protested to Heber that the proverb is 'not the whole of wisdom, it is not, only a part'. Proverbs enjoin us to be obedient, call us to act appropriately. But when Smith uses the proverb, she reduces that command to incoherence, by refusing to attend to the part of it which we expect. Its moral message remains in peripheral vision: haunting the foregrounded image, but restrained from coming fully into view and, more importantly, use. Read through this lens, *The Holiday* explores a third relationship to contained, epiphanic knowledge-claims. *Novel on Yellow*

---

[55] Kay Dick, *Ivy and Stevie* (London: Allison & Busby, 1983), 70.

Paper's aphoristic revelations about love and intimacy skittered instantly out of a reader's reach; *Over the Frontier* explored a catastrophic choice to act on the prejudice of proverb in the run-up to war. *The Holiday*, in contrast, becomes a novel about the experience—in the stunned ethical paralysis of the post-war period—of staying in a holding-space with knowledge: in proximity to epiphany without seeking to sound it out or use it.

For Smith's proverbs, the moral message is a false promise: palpable but unnecessary, a red herring beside the paramount image. Her use of the proverb strips it of power. She does not use proverb 'appropriately', according to the demands of the social. In her hands, it becomes a too-literal form, stickling to letter rather than spirit; it adheres to its own imagery too closely to be a successful call for appropriate conduct. And in this shift in focus, she interrogates, as the next chapter will suggest, what it means to be, and to behave in ways that are, appropriate.

4

Captions and the 'Appropriate'

On 4 January 1955, Mervyn Horder wrote to Stevie Smith, regretfully declining to publish her poems. He suggested an alternative: 'I don't see why you can't fit some of those drawings with little captions and send them in to Punch'.[1] Three years later, Smith did 'fit' some of her drawings with 'little captions' for publication. Frances Spalding describes how, invited to compile a collection of her drawings, Smith spent a day selecting and arranging pictures and writing captions, 'laughing a great deal as she did so'.[2] The Gaberbocchus Press published the result as *Some Are More Human Than Others* (1958).

Smith's archives show that preparing the book took much longer than a day. The texts of the captions went through several drafts: more drafts, in fact, than many of her poems seem to have received. Smith, we know, loved the one-liner, the compactly witty or enigmatic sentence. Her archive contains at least three lists entitled 'Beyond Words', composed entirely of one- or two-line mini-texts.[3] The one-liners cross over between lists, changing slightly in the process, drafted and redrafted. 'Beyond Words', and the care its mini-texts receive, demonstrates Smith's pleasure, as I have argued, in the punchy aphoristic unit.

And these lists certainly served, even if they were not designed, as preliminary work for *Some Are More Human Than Others*. Smith eventually selected a great many of these lines, and married them to meticulously-selected drawings. In the process, the self-contained aphoristic line shifts identity slightly: it becomes a caption. Whereas the aphorism trades on its self-sufficient air of absolute truth, a caption depends for its success on context: its relationship to the image it accompanies. The funny captioned picture stands or falls on that interaction between text and image: the question of whether they are socially suited, appropriate to each other.

Presented in isolation, on a page, the aphorism creates its own imagined context in which it might be quipped or retorted; existing only *in potentia*, its wit is maximized. Put to practical use, however, quoted or thrown off in response to a social situation, the aphorism's worth depends entirely on its appropriateness to

---

[1] Mervyn Horder to Stevie Smith, Series 1, Box 3, Folder 2, Stevie Smith papers, 1924–1970. Coll. No. 1976.012. McFarlin Library. Department of Special Collections and University Archives. The University of Tulsa.
[2] Frances Spalding, *Stevie Smith: A Critical Biography* (London: Faber and Faber, 1988), 227.
[3] Stevie Smith, 'Beyond Words', Series 2, Box 1, Folder 7, Stevie Smith papers, University of Tulsa.

Stevie Smith and the Aphorism. Noreen Masud, Oxford University Press.
© Noreen Masud (2022). DOI: 10.1093/oso/9780192895899.003.0005

104 STEVIE SMITH AND THE APHORISM

the situation which called it forth. The captioned drawing represents just such a social environment: the aphorism in practice, applied to a context. What we witness in the captioned drawing, therefore, is the aphorism under social trial. The image is the situation; the caption is the quipped aphorism, framing what has happened and casting it into humour. Or perhaps, if the caption-aphorism is not appropriate enough, failing to do so, and falling flat.

If a caption works well, it produces the reader-response which E. H. Gombrich describes in his work on the caption-cartoon:

> most readers, including myself, will let their eyes rest on it for a few seconds, take it in and say to themselves, 'Clever, that's how it is', and turn to the book reviews, the sports reports, or the financial page.[4]

Gombrich's remarks could equally have been applied to the aphorism: one takes it in, agrees that it is true and clever, and passes on. Both the aphorism and the caption of a drawing induce the same pattern of behaviour in a reader. The aphorism is a general remark whose suitability to a situation must be thought through; the caption's interaction with the image should be just opaque enough to demand a small portion of consideration from the reader. Achieved, one mentally moves on.

So both the caption and the aphorism participate in this sense of the 'appropriate', a word which is both emphatic and understated. For something to be appropriate, it is barely worth remarking on: you are basically remarking that it needs no further remark. The appropriate statement assumes the right size for a situation, taking up the right amount of space. The caption—brief, potted, summarizing—becomes a signal that the viewer has permission to move on, just as in Wilde's plays (as Chapter 1 described) his charming, witty aphorisms are immediately abandoned as the story continues.

This chapter investigates Smith's aphoristic lines as they socialize with images in the role of captions. Coming through a wider tradition of captioned images which revolve around social behaviour—where the caption either instructs the reader in how to behave properly or pretends to gloss over improper behaviour which is still clearly visible in the image—Smith's captioned pictures feel out the potential on both sides of this social spectrum. Either Smith's captions seem not to match at all, or, more often, they match the image too exactly, reiterating without any twist what is self-evident in the picture. They are too appropriate, in other words; too fitting to be funny. And in this they are inappropriate, because our reading strategies (which expect the caption to introduce new information or angles to the image) fail. We laugh not because we are charmed, but because we are confused, unsure of how to

---

[4] E. H. Gombrich, 'The Cartoonist's Armoury', in *Meditations on a Hobby Horse and Other Essays on the Theory of Art* (London: Phaidon Press, 1963), 131.

CAPTIONS AND THE 'APPROPRIATE' 105

react. When caption and picture fit exactly, both vanish from view: they resist reading and critical intervention. Stevie Smith's caption-drawing dyads are particularly difficult and compelling, I argue, where they sabotage the rules of their social intercourse. Describing these captions offers a language for Smith's taxonomy of failed social encounters: where overtures are not responded to, where communication dissipates, where wit trails off into the faux pas and joyless interactions are spun out with platitudes.

Smith's Drawings

Stevie Smith's texts are in constant dialogue with the appropriate: appropriate behaviour, appropriate rhymes and language, the questions of propriety which circle the institution of small talk. She satirizes social platitudes, the gestures designed to smooth over horrors and neuroses and maintain harmony at any cost. 'Everything is Swimming' and '"The Persian"', for instance, skewer gossipy, judgemental voices which undermine vulnerable women:

> She said everything was swimming in a wonderful wisdom
> Silly ass
> What a silly woman
> Perhaps she is drunk
>
> ('Everything is Swimming', CP, 498)
>
> Now Agnes, pull yourself together.
> You and your friends.
>
> ('"The Persian"', CP, 499)

At other times, however, Smith's relationship to propriety and the 'appropriate' is less clearly subversive. 'Dear Little Sirmio' sees Smith translate Catullus with a chatty society diction: 'Dear little Sirmio / Of all capes and islands / Wherever Neptune rides the coastal waters and the open sea / You really are the nicest' (CP, 400). 'The nicest': Smith keeps up this warm prattling tone so perfectly, without cessation, that she does not quite allow the poem's satirical point to sharpen. Ultimately, Sirmio's socially-appropriate praise stands as valid.

Her often-jarring images, published alongside her poems at her own tenacious insistence, compound these questions of the appropriate. Smith's sense of responsibility towards the drawings, refusing to exclude them from their partnerships with the poems, echoes W. S. Gilbert's approach in his 'Bab' Ballads. In his preface, he explained his decision to include illustrations alongside the poems:

I have ventured to publish the illustrations with them because, while they are certainly quite as bad as the Ballads, I suppose they are not much worse. If, therefore,

106   STEVIE SMITH AND THE APHORISM

the Ballads are worthy of publication in a collected form, the little pictures would have a right to complain if they were omitted.[5]

Pictures and text become a social milieu in absurd miniature: if the texts are invited to the publication party, the pictures will expect to be invited too, and it will be a faux pas, Gilbert signals, to omit them from the gathering.[6] Gilbert's language positions ballads and illustrations as matching or equivalent: they are 'quite as bad' as each other, birds of a feather which therefore flock together. So he underlines the intrinsic social relationship between his texts and his images to appease his readers, who do tend to expect a clear connection between the words and the pictures in a book. For the same reason, studies of Smith's art have focused primarily on how (or whether) the doodles accompanying the poems in her published volumes illustrate or illuminate the poems. Though the placement of the images on the page can encourage readers, wisely or otherwise, to view them as illustrations,[7] Laura Severin finds that the poems and drawings are most often 'decidedly out of sync'.[8] Kristen Marangoni suggests that the deliberate confusion surrounding the mismatching picture accompanying 'Not Waving But Drowning' (a woman standing in the water and smiling, next to a poem about a man drowning) underlines the poem's point about failed communication.[9] Unsurprisingly, then, destabilization and subversion arise as common critical tropes in studies of Smith's art. The images deliberately disrupt gendered perspectives,[10] resist definitive readings,[11] or help Smith punctuate her difference from her predecessors,[12] especially in a context, post-T. S. Eliot, where good poetry was thought to be impersonal.[13]

Largely omitted from these discussions, however, are Smith's captions. Smith created and enjoyed captions within her published work (aside from her caption-books, *The Frog Prince* (1966) contains four drawings with captions) as well as beyond it, such as the captioned picture which she stuck into Hamish Miles's copy

---

[5] W. S. Gilbert, 'Preface', in *The 'Bab' Ballads: Much Sound and Little Sense* (London: John Camden Hotten, 1869), vi.

[6] On etiquette's role in regulating the 'frequent, parodistic violence' of the 'Bab' Ballads into laughter, see Jane W. Stedman, *W. S. Gilbert: A Classic Victorian and his Theatre* (Oxford: Oxford University Press, 1996), 26.

[7] Marsha Bryant, *Women's Poetry and Popular Culture* (New York: Palgrave Macmillan, 2011), 63–68.

[8] Laura Severin, *Stevie Smith's Resistant Antics* (Madison: University of Wisconsin Press, 1997), 51.

[9] Kristen Marangoni, '"Not Waving": Miscommunication Between Stevie Smith's Poems and Drawings', in *Picturing the Language of Images*, ed. Nancy Pedri and Laurence Petit (Newcastle upon Tyne: Cambridge Scholars Publishing, 2013), 168.

[10] Kristin Bluemel, 'The Dangers of Eccentricity: Stevie Smith's Doodles and Poetry', *Mosaic: An Interdisciplinary Critical Journal* 31, no. 3 (1998): 113.

[11] Will May, 'Verbal and Visual Art in Twentieth-Century British Women's Poetry', in *The Cambridge Companion to Twentieth-Century British and Irish Women's Poetry*, ed. Jane Dowson (Cambridge: Cambridge University Press, 2011), 49–51.

[12] Julie Sims Steward, 'Pandora's Playbox: Stevie Smith's Drawings and the Construction of Gender', *Journal of Modern Literature* 22, no. 1 (1998): 76.

[13] Jack Barbera, 'The Relevance of Stevie Smith's Drawings', *Journal of Modern Languages* 12, no. 2 (1985): 236.

CAPTIONS AND THE 'APPROPRIATE' 107

of *A Good Time Was Had By All*.[14] In a 1961 interview with Peter Orr, she describes her pleasure in writing what she calls 'underline[s]' for pictures. A drawing of a child with 'a terrible look on its face', for instance, 'does not have a poem. I just wrote as an underline for it: "Eighteen months old and already odious"'.[15]

In these instances, pictures come first and suggest poems, or perhaps just captions. In a letter to Helen Fowler, Smith laments the tendency of the drawings to outstrip her writing: 'I love drawing and am nearly off my head with all the new drawings and nothing to put to them'.[16] Smith, as matchmaker between drawing and text, pretends to be driven to distraction by a proliferation of lonely singletons calling out for partners. We know, however, that the relationship of her images to captions was sometimes reversed. Spalding describes how, in January 1942, Smith wrote to Hayward asking for his opinion on a selection of one-liners. These included 'my left arm turned blue', 'I dreamed I was dressed in cellophane; was I to blame?' 'Think it Over', and 'From the maniac life of Blessed Mary Agatha'.[17] Smith's approach suggests that her captions are aphoristically detachable.

In *Some Are More Human Than Others*, however, Smith finds one-liner partners for many of her images. She adds humorous or enigmatic captions to her pen-and-ink sketches of dogs, cats, bulls, and humans. A fat, cross-eyed canine, for instance, is captioned 'Such an animal is not responsive to love' (see Figure 4.1).[18]

This caption turns on ideas of the appropriate. In its stern put-down, we sense a bid for control over what constitutes acceptable behaviour: the dog is given a disciplinary frame by the brief line. The dog is scolded for not being 'responsive', for not returning love obligingly for the love offered to him. In her introduction to *Cats in Colour* (1959), her second caption-book which appended remarks to photographs of prize-winning cats, Smith underlines our love-demands as a vital reason why we choose to caption animals:

How nice ... to turn to the indifferent cat who can be made to mean so many things—and think them—being as it were a blank page on which to scrawl the hieroglyphics of our own grievance, bad temper and unhappiness, and scrawl also, of course, the desired sweet responses to these uncomfortable feelings.[19]

Here, captions are part of an economy of love and emotion. Images of cats are inscrutable: the captioner can project their own emotions on to the animals, and experience them returned in a sweeter, more manageable form. In the case of the

[14] Will May, *Stevie Smith and Authorship* (Oxford: Oxford University Press, 2010), 215 .
[15] Peter Orr, 'Stevie Smith', in *In Search of Stevie Smith*, ed. Sanford Sternlicht (Syracuse: Syracuse University Press, 1991), 36.
[16] Letter to Helen Fowler, 30 May 1952, Series 1, Box 3, Folder 7, Stevie Smith papers, University of Tulsa.
[17] Spalding, 161.
[18] Stevie Smith, *Some Are More Human Than Others* (London: Peter Owen, 1990), n. pag.
[19] Stevie Smith, *Cats in Colour* (London: Batsford, 1959), 11.

Figure 4.1 'Such an animal is not responsive to love'. Stevie Smith, *Some Are More Human Than Others* (London: Peter Owen, 1990). © Stevie Smith 1958. Copyright © James MacGibbon 1989. Reprinted by permission of Faber and Faber Ltd and New Directions Publishing Corp.

dog, however, he is perceived as disrupting this call and response. He is not, we infer, behaving appropriately.

The failures of correct and timely social-emotional responses, as earlier chapters have suggested, are fundamental to Smith's rhetoric and aesthetics. They centre on a world which cannot respond adequately to a speaker's pain, or on speakers who cannot sustain legible responses to their own pain. The remedy, in Smith's aphoristic hands, is a mode of speech which contains and disciplines its own appeal for a hearing. In *Some Are More Human Than Others*, we witness the mocking side of this preoccupation. The caption performs a parodic bid to make this animal appropriate; to make it respond obediently, in ways that are absurd to expect. If, in *Cats in Colour*, captions reframe 'uncomfortable' or inappropriate emotions into something 'sweet', here we sense a sterner act of dialing-down, of controlling. The speaker's repressive language puts the dog firmly in his place: it reframes a not-very-objectionable-looking animal to foreground one viewpoint. As readers, we laugh at that severity, but laughter disciplines, as Henri Bergson knew: '[b]y the fear which [laughter] inspires, it restrains eccentricity'.[20] Laughter shames its subjects into behaving in socially appropriate ways. Both captioner and reader are enmeshed in a pattern of interpretative and social control, a reinscribing of the 'appropriate'.

---

[20] Henri Bergson, *Laughter: An Essay on the Meaning of the Comic*, trans. Cloudesley Brereton and Fred Rothwell (London: Macmillan, 1921), 20.

CAPTIONS AND THE 'APPROPRIATE' 109

Ideas of the 'appropriate' haunt reviews of captioned books at this time. Praise of *Cats in Colour* in a *Times Literary Supplement* review describes Smith's captions as 'appropriate remarks'.[21] John Betjeman's review *of Some Are More Human Than Others* discusses a number of illustrated, captioned cartoon-books as well as Smith's drawing-book; one, he finds, has 'careful old-fashioned drawings', another has 'singularly appropriate and meticulous drawings'.[22] It is striking that the captioned sketch, a genre associated with humour—often, with the slapstick or surreal—should be praised in these finicky terms of the 'careful' and 'appropriate'. Another reviewer in the *Spectator* noted, in the same vein, that *Some Are More Human Than Others* was 'fastidiously presented'.[23] This is approving establishment language, used to praise a genre which often seems subversive.

From this perspective, Horder's advice to Smith to 'fit some of those drawings with little captions' participates in the same trope of disciplinary management. Horder's language implies a scaling-down, from full-length poems to 'little captions'. The idea of captions which 'fit' the drawings, slotting neatly and tidily in, bolsters this sense of the 'fitting', the appropriate or correct thing to say.

Smith published both *Some Are More Human Than Others* and *Cats in Colour* at a time when these social norms of the caption-cartoon—a genre with which Smith's books are aligned if not identical—were well-defined: towards the end of the heyday of magazine cartooning.[24] The *Esquire Cartoon Album*, published in the same year as *Some Are More Human Than Others* and also reviewed by Betjeman, notes as a point of pride that its captions use as little text as possible.[25] Humour and value, it is suggested, issue from brevity: a frugal, snappy understanding of when to stop and let the picture speak instead. This strategy deliberately maximizes the interplay between words and pictures. Starved of textual information—given only a contained nugget of a captioning phrase or sentence—the reader scours the picture for details which would fill in the gaps and help them decode the 'message' of the piece.

We are trained, therefore, to treat the contemporary caption as a route, a treasure-map, into the picture. Roland Barthes suggests in 'The Photographic Message' that 'the text loads the image, burdening it with a culture, a moral,

---

[21] 'Cats', *Times Literary Supplement*, 18 September 1959, 535.

[22] John Betjeman, 'Something Funny', *Daily Telegraph and Morning Post*, 12 December 1958, 15. While Smith's captioned drawings are not exactly cartoons, they establish a close relationship to the mode, and—as Betjeman's grouping suggests—were received as within the same broad genre.

[23] 'Picture Books', *Spectator* 201, 21 November 1958, 730.

[24] Robert C. Harvey locates this 'heyday' from the mid-1930s to the 1960s. Robert C. Harvey, 'How Comics Came to Be', in *A Comics Studies Reader*, ed. Jeet Heer and Kent Worcester (Jackson: University Press of Mississippi, 2009), 34.

[25] Arnold Gingrich, introduction to *Esquire Cartoon Album* (London: Heinemann, 1958), n. pag.

an imagination'.[26] It assigns an interpretative scheme, demands that the reader view it on a certain level of understanding: 'the text *directs* the reader through the signifieds of the image, causing him to avoid some and receive others' ('Rhetoric of the Image').[27] The caption becomes, as Norman Bryson puts its, 'a handle on the image';[28] it tells an audience what to look for in a picture.[29]

Captions prescribe our reading framework. They tell us what to see, and, implicitly, what to ignore. Smith plays, in *Some Are More Human Than Others* and *Cats in Colour*, with the capacity of the caption to steer the interpretative encounter. A kitten with its eyes shut is cast as a pompous snob:

> 'I think this tabby cat is a Perfectly Common Thing. So I shall shut my eyes. Do you like my white waistcoat? I give a good deal of thought to it'.[30]

We are encouraged to see, and therefore read, the cats in a particular way: to reframe a white kitten tummy as central to the point of the picture, as a pernickety point of pride. The kitten ignores the tabby and foregrounds his waistcoat; in doing so, he mirrors the work of the caption, which guides us through the social situation represented by our encounter with the image.

Smith's caption in *Cats in Colour* plays with the two sides of etiquette that we see acted out between her kittens in the caption above: the rules about what not to notice, and what to acknowledge, which underpin socially tactful behaviour. During the time that Smith worked for Pearson's, the publisher churned out magazines and books which issued specific, strict instructions to women about how they ought to behave. *Etiquette for Women* (1928) lays down clear rules about whom to notice and whom not to notice:

> Greet your hostess before you pay any attention to anybody else, and then your host.
> [when leaving a party] there is no need to shake hands with any of the guests, or to give more than a bow and smile to those nearest you.[31]
> Refrain ... from rushing across the lobby to greet your host when he does arrive

---

[26] Roland Barthes, 'The Photographic Message', in *Image Music Text*, trans. Stephen Heath (London: Fontana Press, 1977), 26.

[27] Roland Barthes, 'Rhetoric of the Image', in *Image Music Text*, 40.

[28] Norman Bryson, *Word and Image: French Painting of the Ancien Régime* (Cambridge: Cambridge University Press, 1981), 5.

[29] David Novitz, *Pictures and their Use in Communication: A Philosophical Essay* (The Hague: Martinus Nijhoff, 1977), 49. See also Ruth Bernard Yeazell, *Picture Titles: How and Why Western Paintings Acquired Their Names* (Princeton and Oxford: Princeton University Press, 2015), 81, 9.

[30] Smith, *Cats in Colour*, 46.

[31] Irene Davison, *Etiquette for Women: A Book of Modern Manners and Customs* (London: C. Arthur Pearson Ltd, 1928), 46–48.

CAPTIONS AND THE 'APPROPRIATE'   111

... never linger at your escort's elbow while he settles a bill, takes theatre tickets, and so on.[32]

According to this how-to guide, success depends on attention to what is necessary, and studious inattention to what must be ignored. Like the caption-cartoon, a social situation can thus be navigated efficiently.

This association of the caption with the etiquette guide was more than metaphorical. French maxims, such as La Rochefoucauld's, staged (or seemed to) an offering of concise guides to moral and social behaviour:

The glory of great men should always be measured against the means they used to acquire it ...
It is not enough to have great merits; you must also know how to employ them.[33]

If one were to add an image to these epigrammatic guides to correct behaviour, they would become—startlingly—caption-cartoons. While Smith was working for Pearson's, their magazine *Home Notes* included a series called 'How To Be Happy', offering slangy but earnest advice on how to behave in various situations, accompanied by captioned cartoons which illustrated particular points in the article. The installment in the issue of 12 July 1930 focused on how to behave 'when you're in love'. A cartoon of a crying woman and a grave-looking man is captioned 'Don't quarrel just for the niceness of making up—or you'll do it once too often!' A caption to a cartoon of a man looking at his watch, as a woman hurries towards him, tuts, 'She's always late for appointments and makes neither excuse nor apology ... '[34] The caption-cartoon, in the magazines published by Smith's own employer, becomes a cautionary tale about the consequences of slack etiquette.

This capacity in the caption to steer appropriate behaviour lays wide open to satire. Dorothy Parker, a fan of La Rochefoucauld's combination of pithy observation and wryness, collaborated with George Chappell and Frank Crowninshield to produce a tongue-in-cheek captioning to proper etiquette: *High Society* (1920), a large book of captioned illustrations which claimed to offer 'Advice as to Social Campaigning, and Hints on the Management of Dowagers, Dinners, Debutantes, Dances ... '. Parker's book offers a satirical shorthand to allow (she promises, straight-faced) her readers to navigate through the social minefield of high society: once they can recognize the 'Seven Deadly Temperaments' of women and the 'Six Brands of Week-End Hostesses' (lavishly illustrated, with pointed captions),

---

[32] Davison, 73.
[33] François de la Rochefoucauld, *Collected Maxims and Other Reflections*, trans. E. H. and A. M. Blackmore and Francine Giguère (Oxford: Oxford University Press, 2007), 45.
[34] 'How to Be Happy', *Home Notes*, 12 July 1930.

112 STEVIE SMITH AND THE APHORISM

readers can respond to the exigencies of society not with awe but with cynical knowingness.[35]

Such an established focus on the caption-cartoon's relationship to social life—its capacity to manage it, to demonstrate the unsound consequences of poor etiquette—underpins Betjeman's review of *Some Are More Human Than Others* and other picture books, which praises texts and images for being 'appropriate' with all the word's weight of social approval and acceptance. He celebrates 'those few, those happy few, where drawing and text are well matched'.[36] The happy couple of image and caption have, after careful consideration, been successfully paired by their friends and benefactors.

Caption and Euphemism

For Horder and Betjeman, the comedy which captions offer is not anarchic but social: the right interjection, the remark which the situation demands. The word 'etiquette', etymologically, implies a tag or label.[37] This same sense of courtesy animates the labelling caption. Faced with an image of a person or an animal, or a pen-and-ink tableau, the captioner must respond in a way that lifts the mood, that lightens the tension, and allows (to quote the title of Smith's first poetry collection) a good time to be had by all. This is the territory of the *bon mot*, the witty aphoristic rejoinder. Wilde puts one-liners into his characters' mouths to allow them to gloss a ridiculous social situation—to annotate it, pointing out its absurdity—and simultaneously to gloss over it, to provoke the laughter which permits the evening to go with a swing. The caption, similarly, is a one-liner elicited in response to visual absurdity—we recall Smith laughing as she wrote captions to her drawings—which both unmasks and validates a social idiosyncrasy. It bandies with the appropriate, managing to be socially conservative even as it points out that the emperor has no clothes.

Our cultural and historical expectations of the caption dictate that it 'should' be appropriate to the picture in often a clear and well-defined way. Fulfilling that requirement, in fact, demands a big splash of the inappropriate, operating just under the surface, visible to view but unacknowledged by the caption, which very often glosses over an unruly social situation (in other words, renders it socially appropriate once more). To be 'appropriate' or fitting therefore involves being anarchic or unfitting, but only to a particular, culturally legible extent. The captioner must know when to go on—when to push the envelope a little bit further,

---

[35] Dorothy Parker, George S. Chappell and Frank Crowninshield, *High Society: Advice as to Social Campaigning, and Hints on the Management of Dowagers, Dinners, Debutantes, Dances, and the Thousand and One Diversions of Persons of Quality* (New York and London: The Knickerbocker Press, 1920), 34, 36.

[36] Betjeman, 'Something Funny'.

[37] 'etiquette, n', OED Online, June 2017, Oxford University Press, http://www.oed.com/view/Entry/64853?redirectedFrom=etiquette (accessed 17 February 2021).

be a little wilder—and when to stop, before the social moment turns sour. Any more unfitting and the caption becomes inappropriate; it ceases to fit the image it accompanies. We still have expectations of propriety, a certain defined kind of behaviour, from this rebellious art form.

These socially-sanctioned (indeed, demanded) mild transgressions identify, therefore, expectations of the caption-cartoon at this time. Contemporary cartoons both portray social transgressions, and enact them, in the failure of captions to be entirely appropriate to their image. In Sheila Dunn's 1957 cartoon, the year before *Some Are More Human Than Others* was published, guests have gathered in the living room, where the host suavely observes that his new roof garden 'was perhaps a mistake'.[38] A glance up at the image throws the understatement of the remark into relief: the plants' roots are poking through the ceiling. Juxtaposing a caption with an image allows the artist to reveal the chaos which underlies the pleasantest of society remarks. The cartoon depicts a measured attempt to calibrate a bizarre situation, absurdly, against a known standard of propriety, and smooth the moment over. Yet the image-caption dyad allows the cartoonist to say something without saying it. Bizarre, troubling reality bursts through the smooth surface, like roots poking through the paint: euphemism has managed this trauma, but it is still clearly visible.

Captions from the 1950s very often work like this: a social platitude, undercut by the accompanying visual. The dyad works around tact and understatement: more is meant than is said, and we are trusted to pick up on the subtext without being cued. Brockbank's *Manifold Pressures*, about the adventures of a hapless and violent driver, functions through captions which are euphemistic. Brockbank subsumes the appalling road behaviour depicted in the images under text such as 'Courteous to Womankind – – and other Road Users – '. Truth can only be reached, then, when the captioner withdraws (as he quickly does) and the reader is left to 'judge for himself' from the images.[39] This is a model where the caption glosses over and the picture illustrates what is 'really' happening or true: the impropriety that flows beneath the flaunting of the proper. In *The Dog's Ear Book*, captions parrot over-fond owners ('He's just like one of the family', 'He understands every word we say') while the pictures reveal the truth about the hostile or uncomprehending hound in question.[40]

The caption therefore exists in two states at once. On one hand, it is an etiquette guide: filtering the picture in front of us, advising us about what aspects it is suitable or acceptable to notice. On the other hand, however, the cartoon caption's functioning depends, on another level, on our ignoring it. For the joke to

---

[38] Helen Walasek, *The Best of Punch Cartoons* (London: Prion, 2008), 323.

[39] Russell Brockbank, *Manifold Pressures: Motoring Misadventures of Major Upsett* (London: Temple Press, 1958), n. pag.

[40] Geoffrey Willans and Ronald Searle, *The Dog's Ear Book* (London: Max Parrish, 1958), 37, 82.

work, we must allow the picture to cast the caption into doubt. We must invariably take the caption with a pinch of salt: look to the picture for confirmation and, often, complication. By its nature the image exceeds the caption within the caption-cartoon. And this means that the very act of reading a captioned sketch is socially transgressive: it embodies a performance of disbelief in the euphemism, the social smoothing-over, which the caption almost always offers up to us. We put the euphemism to one side, and seek for more.

Nevertheless, this misbehaviour by image and by reader represents only a very limited transgression, contained within a socially-accepted dynamic. Even a cartoon where the image vastly exceeds the text can be seen as 'appropriate' to it. Revelation is achieved, it elicits a laugh, and the viewer moves on. It is in meeting these contemporary expectations so well, ironically, that Frances Spalding considered *Cats in Colour* one of Smith's weakest productions. She describes the 'arch chatty captions, inferring human intent from the cat's look or pose' in audibly critical terms.[41] The sense is of meagre scope and attenuated ambition. Here, we are to understand, the captions are throwaway remarks, pointing out a basic, mildly surprising similarity which is amusing but ultimately forgettable. Smith's language, in framing these images, is filled with false jeopardy and exaggerated concern:

> This little deb cat left her key behind and has 'broken in' to a *very* peculiar part of Daddy's grand house. Shall she try soft smiles on the butler who has come to see what the noise is about? Or promise him a bribe tomorrow? O lord, what *shall* she do?[42]

The point is of course that there is no social crisis: the cat looks far more anxious than its pampered life should require it to. *Some Are More Human Than Others* offers, often, the same familiar and unchallenging experience. Certain of its captioned-images echo other contemporary books of cartoons. A haughty cat announcing 'So what!', for instance, evokes a number of cartoon-books published in the same year (see Figure 4.2). For instance, Siné's drawings of cats literalize their captions, with words like 'catnap' acted out by solemn looking cats sitting in human chairs, books unheeded, having a rest.[43] *Dog's Best Friend* by Loriot illustrates its premise that dogs keep humans rather than vice versa,[44] while *The Dog's Ear Book* presents itself as a deadpan guide to life with dogs, which the pictures undercut and subvert.[45]

---

[41] Spalding, 251.
[42] Smith, *Cats in Colour*, 30.
[43] Siné, *Scatty: British Cats, French Cats and Cosmopolitan Cats* (London: Max Reinhardt, 1958), n. pag.
[44] Loriot, *Dog's Best Friend* (London: Hammond Hammond, 1958), n. pag.
[45] Willans and Searle.

Figure 4.2 'So what!' Stevie Smith, *Some Are More Human Than Others* (London: Peter Owen, 1990). © Stevie Smith 1958. Copyright © James MacGibbon 1989. Reprinted by permission of Faber and Faber Ltd and New Directions Publishing Corp.

Within this broader context, Smith's disdainful cat is amusing but not unusual. The captioned image is appropriate to the rules of its genre, anthropomorphizing an animal in a way whose gentle humour is immediately and widely acceptable. Against Smith's tendency to produce disconcerting or misleading images as accompaniments to her poetry, these captioned images seem extremely conventional. There is nothing more to discover, we feel: the joke is immediately visible and instantly digested. We experience the same sensation as when, in another of the book's captioned drawings, one animal snuggles confidingly up to another. The caption below reads, 'I will tell you everything'. Everything necessary for interpretation has been supplied; the reader can relax into their jaunt through this comedic middlebrow experience.

The Caption's Social Life

Yet it is precisely in these terms of the social that Smith's less digestible captions come into focus. The frequently-made comparison of Smith to James Thurber (1894–1961), who contributed drawings and stories to the *New Yorker* from 1930 to the 1950s, helps to bring out the fact that Smith's captions are best understood in terms of an exploration of social-textual propriety. A 1970 review of Smith's collection *The Best Beast* noted her 'Thurberish drawings';[46] this represents, incidentally, a promotion from John Gross's 1966 assessment of the 'sub-Thurberish

---

[46] Daniel Hoffman, 'Two Cases of Double Vision', *New York Times*, 6 December 1970.

*"If you can keep a secret,
I'll tell you how my husband died."*

Figure 4.3 'If you can keep a secret, I'll tell you how my husband died'. By permission of Cartoon Collections www.CartoonCollections.com. First published *New Yorker* 10, 9 June 1934, 26.

drawings which festoon her pages'.[47] Not only is Smith a version of Thurber in these assessments, but she is a pale or derivative version: Thurberish or sub-Thurberish. Smith herself resented these comparisons: she thought that Thurber's humour was only 'the blunt fun of the comic picture postcard, slightly up-graded'.[48]

Smith's tart dismissal of Thurber nevertheless highlights his role as a social cartoonist, interested in the comedy of situations. The encounters in his captioned cartoons, usually between timid men and vast, monstrous women, take place in living rooms, bedrooms, pubs, and parties. Furniture clearly defines geographical settings, and there are almost inevitably two or more figures in play. Here the viewer is voyeur, peering into a social space whose rules they have to deduce (but without much difficulty). In the cartoons, the viewer receives in that moment—from a single captioning line—an unsettling snapshot of these figures' interaction (see Figure 4.3).

This significance of the social is, in fact, the basis on which Spalding defends Smith against the charge of similarity to Thurber. Not only does 'the anarchy of her humour [run] deep' (deeper than Thurber, Spalding argues),[49] but 'whereas Thurber deals with social comedy and situations, [Smith] pinpoints states of mind'.[50] And in fact, for every well-located scene by Smith which captures social dynamics (in, for instance, her illustration to 'The Castle'), there are numerous single figures: awkwardly posed in a sea of white space, relating to no one and nobody. Thurber's characters are always doing something, holding themselves in dynamic curved lines, rather than Smith's stiff, static angles; Smith's drawn characters might answer, when asked what they are doing—like the little girls in one poem—that

---

[47] John Gross, 'Ruthless Rhymes', *Observer*, 11 December 1966.
[48] Stevie Smith, 'Party Views', *Listener* 77, 25 May 1967, 690.
[49] Spalding, 167.
[50] Spalding, 227.

CAPTIONS AND THE 'APPROPRIATE'   117

Figure 4.4 'These girls are full of love'. Stevie Smith, *Some Are More Human Than Others* (London: Peter Owen, 1990). © Stevie Smith 1958. Copyright © James MacGibbon 1989. Reprinted by permission of Faber and Faber Ltd and New Directions Publishing Corp.

they are 'not looking for [or doing] anything at all' (CP, 314). Unlike Thurber's fleshed-out social scenes, only a few of Smith's drawings in *Some Are More Human Than Others* have a physical background: chairs, gardens, living rooms.[51]

While Thurber's cartoons revolve around social humour and the bizarre undertone of seemingly-affable exchanges, most images in *Some Are More Human Than Others* do not depict social situations. Solitary animals or people pronounce, or are pronounced upon. And even when Smith does couple her creatures, they contrast with the social lives depicted in Thurber's work. However anarchic their details, Thurber's social worlds obey the laws of physics. His characters may be mad, but we do not doubt that they are occupying the same physical spaces. In contrast, Smith's social situations (such as they are) are flagrantly contingent. Even when they are drawn on the same page, her characters never seem to be inhabiting the same mutual world. So in the image captioned 'These girls are full of love', the girls tilt at odd angles, smiling to themselves, inclining away from one another (see Figure 4.4). This is a social situation which failed wholly to happen: its players passed each other in the night, without quite connecting.

'Think!'—where the creatures look past each other, their eyes never meeting—has this same sense of a missed or ghostly social opportunity. While Thurber is sociable, Smith's sketchbook is full of characters retreating from life—'The Countess of Egremont does not wish for visitors'—or failing to carry off a social

---

[51] For instance, 'Athalie and Hypatia chose to be lost', 'This does not break down any barriers', and 'Wag, wag!' Smith, *Some Are More Human*, n. pag.

Figure 4.5 'I will tell you everything!' Stevie Smith, *Some Are More Human Than Others* (London: Peter Owen, 1990). © Stevie Smith 1958. Copyright © James MacGibbon 1989. Reprinted by permission of Faber and Faber Ltd and New Directions Publishing Corp.

situation.[52] It is a parody of social interaction, a puppeteered illusion in which no communication is possible.

Some Are More Human Than Others overflows with creatures yearning to speak who never quite manage to 'tell [us] everything' (see Figure 4.5). Marangoni has written well on how the disjunction between image and text in Smith's poem 'Not Waving But Drowning' is highly appropriate (to use this word again) in the context of a poem which is itself about miscommunication.[53] In *Some Are More Human Than Others*, failed communication becomes a central theme. Smith's sketchbook opens with a picture of an angry-looking human-headed dog, and the caption 'Someone should speak'. We tend to assume that the dog is the speaker here, becoming impatient at a prolonged silence. But as the book goes on, we are unsure that anyone is speaking at all. Smith repurposes her poem 'Lord Say-and-Seal', another epigrammatic injunction to speak or initiate revelation, as caption to an image of an animal (see Figure 4.6). The poem urges its addressee to 'speak and reveal' his thoughts; here, appended to a picture of an animal, we feel that if Lord Say-and-Seal is a cat then the poem's mission is futile.

More broadly, speech is impossible to locate in this book. Voices exist in vexed relation to the creatures portrayed. A further comparison of Smith and Thurber makes this clear. Thurber's captions are single lines, which follow convention scrupulously: they are almost always spoken by one character in the drawings to another, and we know which character is speaking because their mouth is drawn

[52] Smith, *Some Are More Human*.
[53] Marangoni, 167.

Figure 4.6 'Lord Say-and-Seal'. Stevie Smith, *Some Are More Human Than Others* (London: Peter Owen, 1990). © Stevie Smith 1958. Copyright © James MacGibbon 1989. Reprinted by permission of Faber and Faber Ltd and New Directions Publishing Corp.

open. Thurber steers us, in other words, through the image: we know what we are looking at, and who is speaking, and by moving between the text and the image we can work out the joke. It may not be the only part of the picture worth noticing and contemplating—Dorothy Parker declares that one could 'while away eternity' pondering the tiny details in his cartoons, and the full backgrounds of the characters—but it at least comprises a single, cogent reading, which Thurber encourages us to reach.[54]

In contrast, Smith does not support her reader's interpretative strategies in *Some Are More Human Than Others* at all. It is almost always unclear who is speaking: whether it is the animal or person depicted, or an external narrative voice. The cat in 'My mother was a fox' sits turned away from the viewer, and the girl's smiling mouth is shut (see Figure 4.7).

Where two or more creatures are depicted, we have no way of knowing who is speaking. The source of speech is hinted at but seldom confirmed: Smith's captions float in the space between reader, writer, and character. No one fully takes responsibility, or commits posturally (with clearly-open mouth) to the statements which they seem to have made. Vocalization does not line up with speaker: the word is out, but no one will confess it was them. The speaker has withdrawn from the situation before they can be identified.

Yet a review in the *Spectator* confidently paraphrased some of the images in the book in phrasing which elides this ambiguity:

---

[54] Dorothy Parker, 'Preface [to Men, Women and Dogs]', in *Vintage Thurber: Volume I*, ed. James Thurber (Harmondsworth: Penguin, 1983), 245.

Figure 4.7 'My mother was a fox'. Stevie Smith, *Some Are More Human Than Others* (London: Peter Owen, 1990). © Stevie Smith 1958. Copyright © James MacGibbon 1989. Reprinted by permission of Faber and Faber Ltd and New Directions Publishing Corp.

'I could eat you', says a girl, hugging a spread-eagled owl to her bosom.
'I am not without friends in high places', says an immensely supercilious cat.
'I loved [sic] and am loved', says some sort of gargoyle, crouching.[55]

Focusing on the first example, as seen in Figure 4.8: we cannot know who is speaking here. It might be the girl—but it could be the animal, fantasizing about devouring his tormentor. If there is a joke or a punchline here, if the image was indeed paraphrasable, it might revolve around the fact that we do not and cannot know who could eat whom.

In *Some Are More Human Than Others*, then, we do not understand our social role, or what is being said and why. Often, the captions are entirely inappropriate to the images they accompany, bearing little relation to what is seen. Returning to 'My mother was a fox'—how do we parse that caption? Whose mother is a fox? It does not seem likely to be either girl or cat. More disconcerting still is the picture's near-miss: the girl appears to be bringing flowers to the cat (and if the cat was her mother we might accept this as credible) but the animal sitting on the ground is clearly a cat, not a fox, showing no interest in the girl. The girl herself stares into the distance, a sinister smile on her face, tilting back at an impossible angle. The sense is of a wider story which cannot be accessed—perhaps even three stories, for fox, girl and cat—and absolutely resists easy decoding. The idea of a mother-fox is

---

[55] 'Picture Books', *Spectator* 201, 21 November 1958, 730.

CAPTIONS AND THE 'APPROPRIATE'   121

Figure 4.8 'I could eat you'. Stevie Smith, *Some Are More Human Than Others* (London: Peter Owen, 1990). © Stevie Smith 1958. Copyright © James MacGibbon 1989. Reprinted by permission of Faber and Faber Ltd and New Directions Publishing Corp.

unsettling enough; coupled with the internally incomprehensible and eerie illustrations, the result is uncomfortable. This caption is troublesomely inappropriate to its image.

Resisting the images they accompany, these captions call upon us to react—to laugh, to agree—without the information or detail we need to formulate a complete response. For all Thurber's surreality, he does guide us through his social situations. His cartoons follow a similar pattern: the speaking character (usually) transgresses appropriate standards of behaviour (apparently unaware that they are doing so) and the other characters' horror or confusion cues us in to how we should respond. As a result, Thurber's cartoons offer the sense of community which Bergson identifies as essential to successful humour:[56] like the etiquette cartoons in *Home Notes*, they reinscribe the norms of a social situation in portraying their transgression. In Smith, however, there are often no other characters visible to react to the speaker. Instead of behaving as voyeurs, safely watching characters communicating with each other, we find that the speaker is addressing us. We become participants, stimulated and unnerved by our complete lack of understanding of how to participate.

If captions are, as Smith hints elsewhere, an etiquette guide for reading, these captions promise a clarity of exposition which they largely withhold. The deictic quality of the caption breaks down; it loses both its origin and target. The line floats ambiguously, like an aphorism gnomically stated, leaving it to us to hypothesize

[56] Bergson, 7.

how it might be applied. With no guidance on how to receive it, we must pass on, uneasily.

The Too-Appropriate Caption

Pivoting right round from this very visible transgression of standards for humorous captioned images in *Some Are More Human Than Others*, a brief return to *Cats in Colour* demonstrates that its text is less invisibly submissive to caption-norms than it initially appears. Alongside sickly anthropomorphic moments sit several instances of the performatively banal caption: the caption which displays information which is so redundant, so resistant to use or value, that it startles the inquiring reader into laughter. If 'My mother was a fox' was disconcertingly inappropriate, these captions are bewilderingly appropriate. They are entirely right (responding in plainly predictable or self-evident terms to their subject) and also essentially useless.

> Oh how much I love this one! His wild dark beauty is made for movement. He has been caught in a flash and will be off before you can touch him. Oh how beautiful he is![57]

Nothing can be done with this 'spontaneous' exclamation of pleasure. It derives from the image without providing us with the interpretative paradigm which we expect a caption to present. It is vacuous, banal, but also irrefutable. In another caption in the same book, Smith notes of a Siamese cat, 'His eyes are blue': a fact difficult, in the original, to overlook (see Figure 4.9).[58]

Why does Smith use these eerily empty captions, which state little which is not already clearly visible? Her essay 'Art' (1938), on visiting an art gallery and

Figure 4.9 'His eyes are blue'. Stevie Smith, *Cats in Colour* (London: Batsford, 1959), 24.

---

[57] Smith, *Cats in Colour*, 52.
[58] Smith, *Cats in Colour*, 24.

enjoys the 'terse' weeding out of the assumed-irrelevant: the detail which is precisely the point of the painting (who are these figures? What is their religious significance?), but which can be omitted because the viewer is expected to know already. Predicated on the assumption that its viewer is religiously literate, the catalogue-caption can therefore restrict itself, contentedly, to pointing out rose orange collars and hedges of herbs. This caption's banality is an act of limitation of the reader's perception, but it also graciously makes space for something: something taken-for-granted, over which it can have no control. Smith laughs because the caption's shifted focus is audacious, but it also curates a generous, merciful space—one which is 'evocative'—in or beyond the burdensomely numinous. This is etiquette: making no trouble, not being obtrusive, taking up no more physical or mental space than has been allotted to you. It is about gracefully ending an interaction as much as perpetuating it.

Smith is often seen as a transgressor of etiquette (buying a hat from a jumble sale to wear when she received her Gold Medal for Poetry, being rude at lunch-parties),[62] but etiquette fascinated her. The Lion Aunt as 'shining gold' (*Novel*, 174), salt-of-the-earth figurehead is part of this stylized enjoyment of etiquette. And in her essay 'Art', she fetishizes it. Susan Sontag points out that a visit to a museum or gallery is primarily 'a social situation, riddled with distractions, in the course of which art is seen and commented on'.[63] A gallery-space and its inhabitants train a visitor, subtly, in proper social behaviour: how to look, how to stand, how to experience and demonstrate good taste. The gallery's architecture encourages each visitor to take pleasure in art without evincing inappropriately intense attachment to any one piece: they must murmur approvingly, and move on. In her emphasis on the gallery's social function and distractions from the business of art itself, Sontag could have been summarizing Smith's 'Art'. Seeing a nun leading a school party around the National Gallery, Smith's speaker follows them secretly, listening with agonized ardency. The nun groups the children and hurries them along; she wishes her charges to behave appropriately, to be socially cooperative. Smith has '[some] quarrel' with this approach; she does not think this is the right way to look at pictures.[64] In part because of this, however, she is also undeniably fascinated by the hurry and scolding which she hopes will overlay the experience:

I followed the nun, on a lazy familiar impulse. Almost again I expected to hear: 'Don't loiter; tie up your shoe-lace; your hair-ribbon is undone ...' And all this would be followed, I thought, by the special *bon mot* of one of my own forgotten schoolmistresses: 'You are too slow to catch a cold.'[65]

---

[62] Jack Barbera and William McBrien, *Stevie: A Biography of Stevie Smith* (London: Macmillan, 1986), 3–5.

[63] Susan Sontag, *Regarding the Pain of Others* (London: Penguin, 2003), 108–109.

[64] Smith, 'Art', 155.

[65] Smith, 'Art', 154–155.

CAPTIONS AND THE 'APPROPRIATE' 123

musing over the captions in the catalogue, offers some indications. In the catalogue caption, we have an analogue to the entirely 'appropriate' caption. It makes a claim to factual accuracy, promising to provide all the information which the gallery viewer needs to know. Its form and positioning present it as measured: simply describing what is necessary, precisely, without providing new information. These are exactly the functions which W. J. T. Mitchell lists for texts which exist in relation to images: they may 'explain, narrate, describe, label, speak for (or to)' the image.[59] These texts present themselves as entirely subordinate to the image: simply supporting it or translating it into textual form. They supply nothing new; they simply mark time.

In 'Art', Smith's speaker relaxes, with a not-unironical pleasure, into the catalogue entries. Her remarks on the entry for Fra Filippo Lippi's 'Seven Saints', *c.*1450–1453 show her giving into the unhurried, untroubling curation which the catalogue offers:

> Catalogues, as you see, have a language of their own, terse and evocative: 'S. John, centre, facing right, wearing a lavender-grey dress. Left: S. Francis, profile right, S. Lawrence, in grey, with rose orange collar ... All seated full-length on a marble seat ... along the bottom of the picture a little hedge of herbs ... '[60]

Smith carefully selects an entry which focuses on absolute minutiae. These small details would be of importance to an old-fashioned art historian, each carrying iconographic relevance, but in Smith's hands they lose that charge: the 'little hedge of herbs' being, in its miniature irrelevance, the climactic, humorous moment. The catalogue entry reads like a fashion show, the saints transformed into models whose clothing is their most salient feature. It draws a tactful veil over the question of religious interpretation, and draws our attention instead to the saints' sartorial choices. What is there to say about a rose orange collar and a little hedge of herbs? The catalogue caption in 'Art' shuts up further discussion, steers the viewer away from observing anything but the most banal details.

Smith is of course laughing at these fashion-focused catalogue-captions. They do not merely recount fact: describing a saint's clothing as 'lavender-grey' or 'rose-orange' implies a level of aesthetic observation and judgment. A decision has been made to filter the viewer's perception only in these trivial, rather camp terms. Observing poker-faced how fortunate she is to have access to captions which are not over ten years old (and indeed she lifts this entry verbatim from the 1929 National Gallery catalogue, nine years old when the essay was written in 1938),[61] Smith flags up her recognition of how dated this descriptive approach is. Yet she is not precisely critical of her catalogue. Being dated may be an advantage. She

---

[59] W. J. T. Mitchell, 'Beyond Comparison', in Heer and Worcester, *A Comics Studies Reader*, 117.
[60] Stevie Smith, 'Art', in *London Guyed*, ed. William Kimber (London: Hutchinson, 1938), 159.
[61] *National Gallery Trafalgar Square Catalogue*, 86th edn. (London, 1929), 194.

CAPTIONS AND THE 'APPROPRIATE'   125

There is an erotic charge in this fantasy of prosaic schoolday philistinism, this hoped-for performance of empty society language and etiquette training which is, like the catalogue, beginning to date. Smith's speaker is tantalized by expectation, on tenterhooks to receive 'the special *bon mot*', the climax of this nostalgic experience. She chases after the particular sensuous pleasure of cliché, of banal language which, importantly, fails to hit the fundamental issues in question here. 'How do people see pictures?', she asks near the beginning of the essay.[66]

And this relish of the banal, of the caption or *bon mot* which aims to pinpoint the essence of the picture or situation but misses the point entirely, comes through when Smith turns to her catalogue. Although Smith mocks the catalogue caption, she also enjoys it. When she cites an entry, she is relishing rather than simply mocking it, participating theatrically in the catalogue's ethos. She is drawn, her other work would suggest, by the catalogue's combination of the mundanely precise—'centre, facing right'—and the not-entirely-successfully poetic—'a lavender-grey dress', 'rose-orange collar'. Smith is attracted to this finicky account of facts, carefully presented, but ultimately adding up to nothing at all.

We recognize this taxonomic fashion language from Pompey's description of Leonie in *Novel on Yellow Paper*: 'She has a yellow pullover and fawn jodhpurs and a fawn felt hat. And who cares' (*Novel*, 2). That final 'And' is telling. Indeed, in the typescript, the phrase is not set off in a separate sentence: it reads 'She has a yellow pullover and fawn jodhpurs and a fawn felt hat and who cares.'[67] A full-stop, and a capital 'A' in 'And', are added in blue pen. In the original, then, Pompey's indifference to Leonie's curated outfit becomes one of the parts of the list, one of the items in the outfit. Pompey does not follow her description of Leonie's stylish outfit with 'But who cares', a formulation which would dismiss everything that had come before. What is crucial, in this phrase, is the sense that the banal can be simultaneously attended to and found lacking. Indifference to the banal detail can coexist with a model of description which embraces it.

This confusingly exact descriptive relationship between image and appended-description is, I have suggested, particularly characteristic of *Cats in Colour*. However, Smith compounds the complexity of *Some Are More Human Than Others* by alternating her strikingly-inappropriate captions with ones which are too appropriate in the same way. Some of her captions obligingly match their accompanying image with exact precision—and, in fact, it is in this that they become illegible. Captions like 'Sometimes it holds its head on one side' are excessively appropriate to their image (see Figure 4.10).

With its captioned images alternating between clearly inappropriate and excessively appropriate, contemporary reviewers (of which there were not many) often

[66] Smith, 'Art', 154.
[67] Stevie Smith, typescript of *Novel on Yellow Paper*, U DP-156-1, 2, Stevie Smith Papers 1935–1969, Hull History Centre.

Figure 4.10 'Sometimes it holds its head on one side'. Stevie Smith, *Some Are More Human Than Others* (London: Peter Owen, 1990). © Stevie Smith 1958. Copyright © James MacGibbon 1989. Reprinted by permission of Faber and Faber Ltd and New Directions Publishing Corp.

profess themselves flummoxed by *Some Are More Human Than Others*. One writes, mock-gossipingly, 'I looked and looked at these pictures and most of them didn't make much sense to traditional old me.'[68] These evocations of 'traditional' standards underline the fact that readers do not expect captioned picture-books to stymie them. They are to be interpretable, image and text following established dynamics of similarity and divergence, not demanding more than a few seconds of our attention. Another reviewer declares, 'Frankly, although I always have been able to appreciate the odd, most of these little cartoons ... fail to get through to me.'[69]

The images in *Some Are More Human Than Others* resist critical responses because they do not walk the balance of appropriate inappropriateness which their reviewers sought: of being just inappropriate enough to elicit a satisfying laugh. Their captions are either overly fitting—such as that of the bull with its head on one side, which simply describes the image—or alienatingly unfitting, as in 'My mother is a fox'. These images are social faux pas: the gauche little girl in the art-gallery who stutters out something self-evident, or else blurts out something which shocks the company completely.

No one can win in this situation. Smith's captions veer between the too-appropriate and the too-inappropriate. Even when they are judged to be 'just right', that rightness entails a kind of invisibility, a quick look and nod before being passed by, and lukewarm responses. Faced with this reception, we may sense a

---

[68] Clive Cullerne-Browne, 'Letter from Anywhere', *Hampstead and Highgate Express*, 14 November 1958.
[69] F. M., 'Among the New Books', *Natal Witness Saturday Magazine*, 25 April 1959.

draining away of effort in Smith's caption-books: a rendition of the inanely-factual in place of anything more exciting, because energy has lapsed, or because the project is suddenly no longer felt to be of value. Often, therefore, Smith's captions flag up their own arbitrariness: reveal themselves to be a choice which can be suspended or terminated. *Some Are More Human Than Others* brings together incompatible figures, randomly, from her sketches; Smith makes no effort to position the characters to make them look as though they belong together, and the resulting sense is that they can at any moment be uncoupled, from each other and from the caption. So a caption in *Cats in Colour* shows the writer performing her own loss of interest, her withdrawal from the interpretative enterprise:

'Someone has put us in a basket!' Yes, but you look quite pretty, you know. It's a shame? Very well, it's a shame.[70]

The captioner becomes passive, pliable in the face of the kittens' protest. She allows the meaninglessness of the whole affair—of remarking on situations, acknowledging emotion, expressing solidarity—to show through, and peacefully concedes that the situation is, indeed, 'a shame'. Other *In Colour* books take themselves far more seriously than *Cats in Colour*. Though it allows itself an occasional facetious aside, Barbara Woodhouse's *Dogs in Colour* (1960) quickly subordinates these to outlining the economic and social role of the dog in grave factual captions:

'Alas, no carriage waits for me!' In Victorian days to be really smart at least two Dalmations should have accompanied their owner's carriage. Today these dogs have no real work to do, although with training they are ideal companions for an active owner.[71]

Horses in Colour's captions are longer and even more factual.[72] Images of the animals offer these authors a springboard for sharing appropriate facts, which place the pictures in a broader context of knowledge. *Cats in Colour*, in contrast, flags up the absurdity of the project. It holds its captions at an indifferent angle; it shows its awareness that *Cats in Colour* is a coffee table book, used to mark time while waiting for something to happen, having no real consequence in itself. Captions trail off with a dismissive 'et cetera':

'Angela has passed out. I said Angela has passed out.' 'Somebody will have to tell Lady Catte-Beer.' 'Lady Catte-Beer. Ha ha. Pity Angela doesn't stick to the family brew. I said, Pity Angela doesn't stick ... ' (*et cetera.*)[73]

---

[70] Smith, *Cats in Colour*, 42.
[71] Barbara Woodhouse, *Dogs in Colour* (London: Batsford, 1960), 38.
[72] Dorian Williams, *Horses in Colour* (London: Batsford, 1959).
[73] Smith, *Cats in Colour*, 66.

The sense is that whatever they're discussing has no import: it doesn't matter. The subject is missing. This is phatic conversation; the idea of intense, important interaction is what matters here, rather than any particular content. Smith flags up, here, just the nominal idea of a social situation, offering a selection of verbal gestures without fleshing them out.

Captions become, then, a means by which time is marked. Comment is passed perfunctorily, for the sake of it. Caption books were (and are) not necessarily done out of a sense of an artistic calling. Dashed off quickly, often for financial reasons, these books need only be 'appropriate', a word which demands the most minimal level of readerly engagement and analysis before the viewer passes on to the next. With their associations with cartoons, with the assumption that they perform practical and not aesthetic purposes, captions are already highly dismissible; when they are generated for financial gain, they lose another layer of literary credibility.

This is the caption as social platitude, as unignorably 'et cetera': social life operating at degree zero, knowing and displaying its failure or refusal to do any more than this. It is superfluous; like Smith's early poem 'Spanky Wanky', it is 'unnecessary'. Smith signals that she knows this is the case. She writes excess which knows that it is excess; her captions flag up their own redundancy, their own refusal to lift into literary value. They either flatly restate what is already obvious in the picture, or—in their refusal to adjudicate meaningfully on the picture they accompany— they flatly decline to acknowledge their lack of fittingness. And this mode of writing the unnecessary, having to go on producing text even when everything necessary has already been said, forms the subject of the next chapter.

5

Fragments 'Going On'

To her brief poem 'Flounder', Stevie Smith adds two paratexts, in the form of title and subtitle, which seem wholly inappropriate to the text:

> Flounder
> *(Part of an Acrostic)*
>
> Rather a fishy thing to do—
> And yet this is not wholly true. (CP, 671)

Insisting that the couplet is 'part of an acrostic', the subtitle presents it as a fragment: a piece which is or will become part of a larger whole. But if, as the title hints, this acrostic spells out FLOUNDER, why do these two lines begin with R and A? The situation immediately seems fishy: even Smith's occasionally wobbly spelling would not have fished out a floundra. If the couplet comes from an acrostic, we cannot identify the key to this larger text.

The two initial letters point to what Elizabeth Wanning Harries calls '[t]he fragmentary "method"': 'a strategy for indicating [the whole's] location, its boundaries, and its incalculable dimensions'. Yet, as Harries notes, this flourish towards a totality does not mean that the totality exists or ever has existed.[1] Readers cannot locate the acrostic on which 'Flounder' is supposedly dependent. 'Flounder' may in fact be complete in itself, despite the claims of its paratexts. Its tight little rhyme seals the poem off into a single unit, and, in publishing it, Smith offers up the poem with apparent airy confidence that this scrap of writing is valuable, and ready for public appraisal. Yet, ending on the ambivalent note of 'this is not wholly true', and with its title claiming that it is only a part of something larger, the text claims an identity as fragment.

This may, as so often in Smith's writing, be a case of mistaken identity. Smith warns us, here, to be suspicious of what we assume ('this is not wholly true'), and indeed her poetry continually promises one poetic mode before instituting another. 'The Bereaved Swan' transitions imperceptibly from comedy to tragedy (CP, 35), opening with the flippant comparison of a swan to a 'cake / Of soap', and ending with the bird longing for death; 'In Canaan's Happy Land', designed after the pattern of a joyous hymn, reveals itself to be a cheerful meditation on mass

---

[1] Elizabeth Wanning Harries, *The Unfinished Manner: Essays on the Fragment in the Later Eighteenth Century* (Charlottesville and London: University Press of Virginia, 1994), 163.

Stevie Smith and the Aphorism. Noreen Masud, Oxford University Press.
© Noreen Masud (2022). DOI: 10.1093/oso/9780192895899.003.0006

death (CP, 135). The same indeterminacy governs the length of her texts: single lines turn into poems, poems turn into punchlines. 'Advice to Young Children', leads a double life as a full-length poem and as a single couplet, and, as Chapter 4 described, Smith often excerpted lines from her poems to use as captions for her drawings.

Faced with a slew of titles such as 'From the French', 'From the Coptic', and 'From the Italian', as well as 'From the Greek', discussed in Chapter 1, Smith's readers may wonder if they are mistaking the short, self-contained poem for a fragment, or indeed vice versa:

> From the French (2)
>
> 'We shall never be one mummy only
> Beneath the antique deserts and the happy palms.' (CP, 463)
>
> From the Italian
> *an old superstition*
>
> A woolly dog,
> A red-haired man,
> Better dead
> Than to have met 'em. (CP, 465)

The 'From the' construction in 'From the French', 'From the Coptic', and 'From the Italian' indicates, strictly, only that the poems have been translated. Their brevity and resistance to interpretation, however, activates 'from' into an act of excerpting or lifting: the sense in which extracts in an anthology might announce that they are 'from' longer works. These texts self-present as completed acts of translation; simultaneously, however, they cast themselves as enigmatic scraps pulled out of their indecipherable foreign contexts. As this chapter will argue, Smith's poetic project involves precisely this constantly staged misrecognition of an aphorism (a short text which is complete and self-sufficient, refusing to elaborate or answer questions) as a fragment (a short text or scrap ghosted, in some way, by a longer whole: offering the possibility of its own past or future continuation).

Smith was explicit about the potential tension, in her poems, between these pressures of stopping conclusively, and of going on.[2] She describes, in an interview with Kay Dick, how she thought her poem 'The Stroke' was finished, but ended up writing four more verses.[3] The final poem was not the shape and size she originally thought it would be: it grew, unexpectedly, far beyond its original length, into something wholly new. A poem like 'Yes, I know' (1966) offers conflicting

---

[2] For a different angle on the 'refusal [of Smith's poems] to know when to stop', see Will May, 'The Untimely Stevie Smith', *Women: A Cultural Review* 29, no. 3–4 (2018): 384.
[3] Kay Dick, *Ivy and Stevie* (London: Allison & Busby, 1983), 76.

guidance about whether to view it as stable and finished, or as a text which might suddenly extend further, go on past its original ending:

> The pale face stretches across the centuries
> It is so subtle and yielding; yet innocent,
> Her name is Lucretia Borgia.
>
> Yes, I know. I knew her brother Cesare
> Once. But only for a short time. (CP, 531)

The short, assertive sentences which make up the second stanza signal that the conversation is over; 'Once', at the start of the line, positions the acquaintance between the speaker and Cesare firmly in the past, and the speaker audibly draws a line under this relationship ('But only for a short time'). Yet so many questions remain unanswered. What happened between the speaker and Cesare? Grief or pain is audible, but barely: the brief text manages these emotions expertly, squirrelling them away from further enquiry. The poem reads like the beginning of a story, inviting the continuation which the fragment might allow, and yet also displays the rebuffing stoppage and withdrawal occasioned by the aphorism, as Chapter 1 described. Aphorism may refuse to risk diluting itself by going on. To overexplain, to justify and elaborate on itself, is embarrassing: it suggests an inability to recognize the right moment to withdraw. Texts which present themselves as fragments may turn out to be surprisingly self-contained and complete, pointing in fact to no larger original whole: the writer departs, with aphoristic social grace, although more seems to remain to be said.

For Christopher Ricks, working on Keats, embarrassment derives from witnessing an abandonment to sleep or passion: a too-complete emotional departure from the other person through unselfconscious slumber, or an excessive or too-prolonged emotional presence in the other person's space.[4] So Smith's writing experiments with excess by testing out different responses to embarrassment. Her texts may terminate before they have fleshed themselves out (withdrawing, embarrassed), cutting themselves pithily short. Alternatively, they may grow far longer than expected, embarrassing their reader or listener. Contrasting Smith with W. H. Auden helps to illustrate this variation. Auden excelled at the short pithy text: he published an entire collection of clerihews in *Academic Graffiti* (1971), as well as writing humorously aphoristic short pieces:

> Man would be happy, loving and sage
> If he didn't keep lying about his age.[5]

---

[4] Christopher Ricks, *Keats and Embarrassment* (Oxford: Clarendon Press, 1974), 9, 13.
[5] W. H. Auden, *As I Walked Out One Evening: Songs, Ballads, Lullabies, Limericks and other Light Verse*, ed. Edward Mendelson (London: Faber & Faber, 1995), 12.

132   STEVIE SMITH AND THE APHORISM

Auden also inhabited a more visibly serious aphoristic mode in poems such as 'If I Could Tell You',[6] and his book of aphorisms *The Prolific and the Devourer* (written 1939):[7]

> Our grounds for Faith: the unhappiness of man.
> Our grounds for Scepticism: the same.[8]

Allied within a similar serio-comedic tradition of poetic brevity, then, Smith and Auden were recorded singing together in the pub in 1965, and read one after another at an event in Edinburgh which was broadcast on the BBC Third Programme.[9] Auden is laughing in this recording, but seems embarrassed. As Smith waves her arms and carols 'Amen', Auden buries himself in his glass.[10] Smith later reflected that she didn't think Auden liked her poems very much, adding as explanation: 'he's very Anglican'.[11] More tangible, in Auden's body language, is a sense that Smith was overdoing things (drawing the note out too long, singing too enthusiastically) in a way that he found excessive and embarrassing. Even in his long poems, Auden keeps his form tight, resisting excess. With its short last lines of each stanza, 'Under Which Lyre' has a biting and disconcerting humour:

> Among bewildering appliances
> For mastering the arts and sciences
>   They stroll or run,
> And nerves that steeled themselves to slaughter
> Are shot to pieces by the shorter
>   Poems of Donne.[12]

Like many of Smith's brief, witty poems, Auden here imagines short poems as compact, destructive bullets. The final lines of Auden's stanzas hold themselves, accordingly, short; their prosodic weight, here and through the text, gathers forcefully at the end of the line. In contrast, while Smith's poems are often short and compact, they also often accommodate overlong line endings:

> O happy dogs of England
> Bark well as well you may

---

[6] On this poem's aphoristic tendencies, see Edward Mendelson, *Early Auden, Later Auden: A Critical Biography* (Princeton and Oxford: Princeton University Press, 2017), 478.

[7] W. H. Auden, *The Prolific and the Devourer* (Hopewell: Ecco Press, 1981), vii.

[8] Auden, *Prolific and the Devourer*, 31. Auden called these texts 'my pensées' (Mendelson, 392).

[9] BBC Third Programme, 'Poets in Public: W. H. Auden and Stevie Smith Introducing and Reading Their Own Poems', British Library, NP884.

[10] BBC Arts, 'WH Auden and Stevie Smith in the Pub in 1965', BBC.co.uk, http://www.bbc.co.uk/programmes/p034md2x (accessed 15 February 2021).

[11] Jack Barbera and William McBrien, *Stevie: A Biography of Stevie Smith* (London: Macmillan, 1986), 252.

[12] W. H. Auden, 'Under Which Lyre', in *Collected Poems*, ed. Edward Mendelson (London: Faber and Faber, 1991), 335.

If you lived anywhere else
You would not be so gay.

O happy dogs of England
Bark well at errand boys
If you lived anywhere else
You would not be allowed to make such an infernal noise.
(CP, 100)

Instead of cutting the last line short, Smith lets it run startlingly long. Auden strikes with an economic force which cancels the possibility of embarrassment; Smith's short, humorous poem spends itself before it can strike home. Deryn Rees-Jones writes that Smith's drawing accompanying her poem 'The Songster' (reproduced on the cover of this book) 'embarrass[es] us', showcasing as it does Miss Paunce-fort's 'excessive femininity' and enthusiasm for her own performance.[13] If Auden's poetics avoid embarrassment, Stevie Smith's centre around eliciting embarrassment as part of a consideration of how it might be managed.

Chapter 1 explored the weightiness and lightness of the aphorism: a text both more and less weighty than it appears at face value. This chapter focuses on not weight but length. It investigates what happens to the aphoristic poem when 'more' is demanded of it: when aphorism's flat impenetrability occasions a demand for some kind of repetition or prolonging, a 'going on'. This may take the form of more texts on the page, as in an aphoristic collection. When Smith gathers fragments into collections, in *Novel on Yellow Paper*, she treats them like aphorisms: sealed objects, for display. Their partial status only shores up their gnomic tone. Alternatively, 'more' may involve more of the poem itself, as it is (literally or imaginatively) lengthened on the page, going on past the point at which it might originally have stopped. As I will suggest, longer poems like 'Thoughts about the Person from Porlock' hinge on the effects of failing to recognize when a text has reached its own end: they stretch aphoristic nuggets past the point of their natural closure. A short poem continues out of guilt and a sense of duty: a desire to hold up one's social end, and depart when one has said enough (but not too much). The aphorism-turned fragment goes on when it would rather have 'gone away'.

Fragment and Aphorism

Fragment and aphorism—one supposedly unfinished, the other making a performance of its own finishedness—are not easily differentiated in terms of form. The Jena Romantics described their pithy, self-contained lines as 'fragments' even

[13] Deryn Rees-Jones, *Consorting with Angels: Essays on Modern Women Poets* (Tarset: Bloodaxe, 2005), 76.

134 STEVIE SMITH AND THE APHORISM

though they had access to the term 'aphorism'.[14] Indeed, fragments like Friedrich Schlegel's bear the rhetorical marks of completion, while many aphorisms (such as Nietzsche's) are fragmentary and provisional:

Wit is an explosion of confined spirit.[15] [Schlegel]

Seriousness in play. At sunset in Genoa, I heard from a tower a long chiming of bells: it kept on and on, and over the noise of the backstreets, as if insatiable for itself, it rang out into the evening sky and the sea air, so terrible and so childish at the same time, so melancholy. Then I thought of Plato's words and felt them suddenly in my heart: *all in all, nothing human is worth taking very seriously; nevertheless ...*[16] [Nietzsche]

Schlegel underscores this conflation in his definition of the fragment: 'A fragment, like a miniature work of art, has to be entirely isolated from the surrounding world and be complete in itself like a porcupine'.[17] Schlegel could be describing the aphorism: sealed, self-sufficient, complete, prickly in its insistence on isolation.

Often the question of relationship with the other, with other texts or contexts, comes to underpin differentiations of aphorism and fragment. Christopher A. Strathman focuses on the sociability of the two forms: while the aphorism is isolated and static—avoiding, as Chapter 4 suggested, the possibility of fully fitting, and merging, into a social situation—Strathman builds on Blanchot to identify the fragmentary by its mobility and exposure to otherness.[18] Paul van Tongeren distinguishes between aphorism and fragment on the basis of meaning: the fragment remains from a whole which could theoretically be reconstructed, making the fragment's original context and signification available, while the aphorism was taken from no whole, 'and thus there never is a definite meaning'.[19] Brian Dillon positions fragment and aphorism on a temporal continuum, calling the fragment a 'ruined aphorism': one that has decayed in an inhospitable environment, perhaps, or been attacked by an iconoclast.[20] Either way, it has been interfered with. Ben Grant's definition hinges on how the text is produced, defining a fragment as 'cut short' by 'an interruption from outside'.[21]

---

[14] Ben Grant, *The Aphorism and Other Short Forms* (London and New York: Routledge, 2016), 22.

[15] Friedrich Schlegel, *Lucinde and the Fragments*, trans. Peter Firchow (Minneapolis: University of Minnesota Press, 1971), 153.

[16] Friedrich Nietzsche, *Human, All Too Human*, trans. Marion Faber and Stephen Lehmann (London: Penguin, 1994), 260.

[17] Schlegel, 189.

[18] Christopher A. Strathman, *Romantic Poetry and the Fragmentary Imperative: Schlegel, Byron, Joyce, Blanchot* (Albany: State University of New York Press, 2006), 164.

[19] Paul J. M. van Tongeren, *Reinterpreting Modern Culture: An Introduction to Friedrich Nietzsche's Philosophy* (West Lafayette, Indiana: Purdue University Press, 2000), 65.

[20] Brian Dillon, 'Brief Encounters: The Pleasure of Aphorisms', *Frieze* 74 (2003), online, n. pag.

[21] Grant, 21.

Straddling these varied origin-stories (a remnant of something lost, a seed of a larger text which never fully materialized, a blueprint for a whole which could be reconstructed), the fragment manages a contradictory demand to be at once sealed and open: to a past whole, to future continuation. Often, a particular fragment juggles several origin-myths at once. Helen Maria Williams, for instance, writes her 1786 poem 'Part of an Irregular Fragment, Found in a Dark Passage of the Tower' in the guise of a fragment recovered in remnant form, like many others of this period. Her poem halts midway through a sentence, implying that part of the text was lost as it mouldered in the Tower, decaying into asterisks:

Again! their vengeful look—and now a speechless—
* * * * * * *[22]

Though the title posits the fragmentation of decay and recovery, the 'Advertisement' to the poem claims another kind. Here, Williams imagines a youth fired with inspiration on encountering a long-locked door in the Tower of London, who pictures all the ghosts of people executed in the Tower gathering in that out-of-bounds apartment. His inspiration fires her in turn:

The gloomy wildness of these images struck my imagination so forcibly, that endeavouring to catch the fire of the youth's pencil, this Fragment was produced.[23]

The paratext around Williams's poem pulls it between two fragmentary imaginaries: as a decayed, recovered object from the past, and as a partial (though necessarily inadequate) response to a moment of staggering inspiration. To these models, S. T. Coleridge's poetry adds a sense of the fragment as a text resistant to completion. He never finished his poem 'Christabel' (published in 1816), for example, despite insisting that he had several further parts planned;[24] in the 'Preface' to the poem, he promised 'three parts yet to come, in the course of the present year'.[25] Similarly, his paratextual 'Preface', appended to 'Kubla Khan' in the 1816 edition, excused him from completing the poem with the claim that a Person from Porlock had interrupted him and dispelled his inspiration:

On awaking he appeared to himself to have a distinct recollection of the whole, and taking his pen, ink, and paper, instantly and eagerly wrote down the lines

---

[22] Helen Maria Williams, *Poems* (London: Thomas Cadell, 1786), 2: 43.

[23] Williams, *Poems*, n. pag.

[24] See, for instance, Coleridge to Lord Byron, 22 October 1815: 'the plan of the whole poem was formed and the first Book and half of the second were finished [in 1797] ... It is not yet a Whole: and as it will be 5 Books, I meant to publish it by itself ... ' Samuel Taylor Coleridge, *Collected Letters of Samuel Taylor Coleridge, Volume IV, 1815–1819*, ed. Earl Leslie Griggs (Oxford: Clarendon Press, 1959), 601.

[25] Samuel Taylor Coleridge, *Christabel; Kubla Khan: a Vision; The Pains of Sleep* (London: John Murray, 1816), vi.

136 STEVIE SMITH AND THE APHORISM

that are here preserved. At this moment he was unfortunately called out by a person on business from Porlock, and detained by him above an hour, and on his return to his room, found to his no small surprise and mortification, that ... with the exception of some eight or ten scattered lines and images, all the rest had passed away ...[26]

The paratexts hovering around these Romantic fragments establish and justify their adrift status. The preface to 'Kubla Khan' insists on the text's fragmentary nature, as in fact does the subtitle to Smith's 'Flounder'. Fragmentariness derives, then, from context: in which titles, subtitles, and prefaces inscribe the text as fragmentary, or alternatively outline a past or future continuation into which the text might open up. Without these paratexts, readers might not conceive of the poems as fragments.

Modernist fragments similarly depend on context for their generic status. David Bennett argues that the Modernist fragment was produced 'for and by' its context, 'the little magazine'. He notes that some of modernism's key texts—*The Waste Land*, *Ulysses*, *Finnegans Wake*, much of the *Cantos*—first appeared in little magazines, and usually 'in or as fragments'. *Finnegans Wake* in particular, Bennett reminds us, was published as fragments of a 'Work in Progress'.[27] In his review of Stevie Smith's *A Good Time Was Had By All*, G. W. Stonier positioned Smith's novels in a similar way: her first poetry book, he suggested, was 'a delightful interlude before the next instalment of her odd *Work in Progress*'.[28]

Significantly, however, the portions of Joyce's 'Work in Progress' published in *transition* very seldom present themselves as fragments. The extract published in the April-May issue of 1938 is certainly entitled 'Fragment from "Work in Progress"', but that is the exception rather than the rule.[29] Far more often, it is titled 'Continuation of a Work in Progress'.[30] The majority of instalments, then, minimize their status as parts or excerpts; they imply instead that they go on seamlessly from earlier parts, and, in the moment of publication, fuse with their predecessors to become a larger whole. This is of course misleading: the instalments of 'Work in Progress' were not published in the order they would finally assume in *Finnegans Wake*. In line with the titles' not-altogether-sincere (and not-altogether-merited) faith that the fragments would add up, the language which surrounded 'Work in Progress', in the essays in *Our Exagmination Round His Factification For Incamination Of Work In Progress* (1929), mirrored, despite and alongside a tongue-in-cheek

---

[26] Samuel Taylor Coleridge, *The Collected Works of Samuel Taylor Coleridge 16: Poetical Works I: Poems (Reading Text): Part I*, ed. J. C. C. Mays (Princeton: Princeton University Press, 2001), 511–512.

[27] David Bennett, 'Periodical Fragments and Organic Culture: Modernism, the Avant-Garde, and the Little Magazine', *Contemporary Literature* 30, no. 4 (1989): 480–481.

[28] G. W. Stonier, 'The Music Goes Round and Round', *New Statesman*, 17 April 1937.

[29] James Joyce, 'Fragment from 'Work in Progress', *transition* 27 (April–May 1938): 59–78.

[30] See, for instance, *transition* 2, 3, 4, 5, 6, 7, 8, 13, 22.

reverence, that same faith that every published part of Joyce's text was slotting into a larger whole. Marcel Brion compares the experience of 'Work in Progress' to being 'present at the birth of a world',[31] and Robert Sage argues that 'Joyce's writings, from *Dubliners* to the present book ['Work in Progress'], form an indivisible whole'.[32] Although Victor Llona does refer to the pieces as 'fragments', he ends by looking forward to the completion of the Work, with a religious fervour whose precise relationship to humour is difficult to parse: 'I feel that with the last fragments shall come the revelation'.[33]

If, as Bennett suggests, the little magazine produces the Modernist fragment, these remarks suggest that it also creates the environment for the (future) completion of those fragments. Fragmentariness is not an absolute, unchangeable status, but evolves into completion as the text continues. In their taken-for-granted relationship to a larger whole, the 'fragments' of *Finnegans Wake* draw their significance not from their fragmentary status, but from their capacity to join up with other parts, and the interest attendant on what is thus produced.

Instead of the permanent loss of a whole, then, envisaged by 'Part of an Irregular Fragment' and 'Kubla Khan', the fragmentary instalments of *Finnegans Wake* (like Coleridge's 'Christabel') most visibly associate themselves with an upcoming, emergent whole. A fragment whose significance is firmly located in the past, within a lost whole which can only be imaginatively reconstructed if at all, differs from one with an afterlife—stretching towards a future where it will be completed.

Continuation raises its own problems, however. Assembled together on the page, Schlegel's fragments and Nietzsche's aphorisms move uneasily between isolation and unification. Is each short text a continuation of the last: a space in which it can go on? Or is each text a new beginning, intended to be read independently of what comes before and after? Jacques Derrida announces, in 'Fifty-two Aphorisms for a Foreword', 'An authentic aphorism must never refer to another. It is sufficient unto itself, a world or monad'.[34] Four pages later, he contradicts himself: '... aphorisms can only multiply or be put in a series if they either confirm or contradict one another'.[35] Presented in sequences or collections, short texts find themselves caught between continuity and singularity: their finality of diction exerts one pressure, their arrangement on the page another. Seamus Perry describes the Coleridgean dilemma of the relationship between parts and a larger whole: a collection of aggregated units is undesirable, but a larger whole should

---

[31] Marcel Brion, 'The Idea of Time in the Work of James Joyce', in *Our Exagmination Round His Factification For Incamination Of Work In Progress* (London: Faber and Faber, 1929), 29.

[32] Robert Sage, 'Before Ulysses—And After', in *Our Exagmination*, 149.

[33] Victor Llona, 'I Dont Know What To Call It But Its Mighty Unlike Prose', in *Our Exagmination*, 96, 102.

[34] Jacques Derrida, 'Fifty-two Aphorisms for a Foreword', in *Psyche: Inventions of the Other*, ed. Peggy Kamuf and Elizabeth Rottenberg, trans. Andrew Benjamin (Stanford: Stanford University Press, 2008), 2: 121.

[35] Derrida, 125.

138 STEVIE SMITH AND THE APHORISM

not simply take precedence over its parts.[36] Coleridge's uneasy commentary on Pope in his *Biographia Literaria* pins down this contested relationship between wholes and parts:

> I saw, that the excellence of this kind consisted ... in the logic of wit, conveyed in smooth and strong epigrammatic couplets, as its *form*. Even when the subject was addressed to the fancy, or the intellect ... still a *point* was looked for at the end of each second line, and the whole was as it were ... a *conjunction disjunctive*, of epigrams.[37]

Pope makes a whole out of self-sufficient parts: 'smooth and strong' units, which repudiate the possibility of integrative overtures towards one another. Coleridge cannot quite approve of this 'conjunction' of units which remain 'disjunctive', turning not on any intrinsic interrelation, but on the individual 'point' which seals each epigram into itself. The model of a whole composed of parts which cannot be made to cohere is familiar from a Modernist engagement with the fragmentary which often orients around a collage technique, as Eliot does in *The Waste Land* (1922) and Hope Mirrlees does in *Paris* (1919), positioning modern, urban life as a series of fragmented impressions. Balachandra Rajan positions the Modernist fragment as a performance of striving for wholeness, describing T. S. Eliot's writing as in 'sustained pursuit of a wholeness which gives meaning to experience':[38] the act of gathering fragments together into a single text both confronts the prospect of achieving wholeness of a sort, and explodes the possibility of reconstructing any originary unity. Camelia Elias's taxonomy of the modernist fragment emphasizes its use of juxtaposition,[39] such as the chorus of disconnected voices in Eliot's poem, but this twentieth-century approach to the fragment has its origins in Coleridge's 'mosaic technique'.[40]

As a result, Romantic and Modernist fragments resist easy differentiation; their modes overlap. Although Stevie Smith is writing just after the fragmentary work of the high Modernists, her use of excerpting and aggregation may therefore derive as much from Williams and Coleridge as from T. S. Eliot and Mirrlees. In a 1961

---

[36] Seamus Perry, *Coleridge and the Uses of Division* (Oxford: Clarendon Press, 1999), 194.

[37] Samuel Taylor Coleridge, *The Collected Works of Samuel Taylor Coleridge 7: Biographia Literaria, or, Biographical Sketches of my Literary Life and Opinions I*, ed. James Engell and W. Jackson Bate (Princeton: Princeton University Press, 1983), 18–19.

[38] Balachandra Rajan, *The Form of the Unfinished: English Poetics from Spenser to Pound* (Princeton: Princeton University Press, 1985), 17.

[39] Camelia Elias, 'Clowns of Potentiality: Repetition and Resolution in Gertrude Stein and Emil Cioran', *Cercles* 14 (2005), 41.

[40] See Seamus Perry, 'Coleridge's Literary Influence', in *The Oxford Handbook of Samuel Taylor Coleridge*, ed. Frederick Burwick (Oxford: Oxford University Press, 2009), 668. Perry is quoting Elinor Shaffer's phrase in '*Kubla Khan' and The Fall of Jerusalem: The Mythological School in Biblical Criticism and Secular Literature, 1770–1880* (Cambridge, Cambridge University Press, 1975), 250.

interview with Peter Orr, she describes writing a poem as a careless, playful act, with the kind of reversibility between completeness and openness that underpins Schlegel's fragments:

> one sort of throws it away and goes and digs it up and tosses it into the air and finishes it off or doesn't finish it off. Anyhow, I love doing it.[41]

Smith's grammar effectively equates these two opposing possibilities, finished and unfinished; the unfinished can be offered up as functionally finished, like Schlegel's aphorism-fragments. This reflects Smith's practice in her editing of *The Batsford Book of Children's Verse* (1970). More than a third of the 'poems' she includes in this anthology (thirty-two out of eighty-six) are in fact excerpts from longer texts.[42] The act of excerpting something, Smith hints, makes it enough in itself: a complete text. In this light, 'From the French' and 'Flounder' distinguish themselves from the Modernist fragments of little magazines, which look forwards towards a whole, or stage a failed attempt to add up into a larger narrative. The act of excerpting or writing a fragment, for Smith, makes it self-sufficient: mummifies it into aphoristic solidity.

Collecting Fragments

Like Eliot in *The Waste Land*—like Joyce in his catty books of solecisms by contemporaries,[43] and like Flaubert's collection of platitudes in his *Dictionary of Received Ideas*[44]—Stevie Smith preserved scraps of language. Overhearing is important to her: it offers snatches of words, covertly recorded, stolen and reused. Smith's archives show how she hoarded more and more quotations, on scraps of paper and in her journals:

> Wild weather we're having.
> What!?—Oh, I thought you said 'mild'.[45]

---

[41] Peter Orr, 'Stevie Smith', in *In Search of Stevie Smith*, ed. Sanford Sternlicht (Syracuse: Syracuse University Press, 1991), 31.

[42] Stevie Smith, ed. *The Batsford Book of Children's Verse* (London: Batsford, 1970), 5–7.

[43] See Eloise Knowlton, *Joyce, Joyceans, and the Rhetoric of Citation* (Gainesville: University Press of Florida, 1998), 38.

[44] Roger Shattuck, 'The Alphabet and the Junkyard', in *The Innocent Eye: On Modern Literature and the Arts* (New York: Farrar, Straus and Giroux, 1984), 33.

[45] Pencilled note, Series 2, Box 1, Folder 1, Stevie Smith papers, 1924–1970. Coll. No. 1976.012. McFarlin Library. Department of Special Collections and University Archives. The University of Tulsa.

Guard well her sleeping form!

'And her appropriate laughter'
This is what modern poems are written like

Then spake the American lady, & she said:
'My name is Purrel, I am cast before swine'.

'when she entered anthropology'[46]

A small niece of mine once wrote a little tale with the title "A Bqlir Chesterdroves" (a peculiar chest of drawers)[47]

This becomes Smith's primary mode of writing: the scribbled witticism barely changed when it became her published poem 'Pearl', quoted in full in the introduction. The approach invades even her more formal work projects. Neat schoolgirlish notes in her reading journals give way, as time passes, to straight-up quotations from the texts under study. Even a careful, dignified account of an art exhibition, where the young Smith exerts herself to comment intelligently on the paintings, is disrupted by a sneakily recorded witticism. She draws a line at the bottom of the page and writes underneath: 'Pleistocene, so called Because it was ~~muddy~~ sticky cf. plastocine', creating a secret mischievous identity to run alongside the official version of herself as conscientious scholar.[48]

Unlike Eliot and Flaubert, however, Smith does not use her collected scraps of jokes, puns, and pithy observation to project mingling, disarticulated voices, or a sense of destruction, nor to testify to the linguistic failures of others. Her practice is closer to Joyce's, who, Sara Danius notes, revelled in the middlebrow rhymes and phrases which he collected.[49] In the same way, Smith carefully records jokes, snippets, anecdotes, and portentous phrases as significant or interesting in their own right, most notably in her archive lists of quotations, phrases, and aphorisms titled 'Beyond Words'.[50] A number of these made their way into *Some Are More Human Than Others* (1958), her book of captioned drawings discussed in Chapter 4, and many of the lines jotted down in spare corners turn up, as noted earlier, in *Novel on Yellow Paper:*

So now you shall have some more nice little quotations for your scrap book. Or if you have no scrap book you can shoot them at your friends at your high-class parties ...

[46] Stevie Smith, red notebook, Series 2, Box 9, Folder 1, Stevie Smith papers, University of Tulsa.
[47] Stevie Smith, reading journal, Series 5, Box 1, Folder 6, Stevie Smith papers, University of Tulsa.
[48] Stevie Smith, reading journal, Series 5, Box 1, Folder 6, Stevie Smith papers, University of Tulsa.
[49] Sara Danius, 'Joyce's Scissors: Modernism and the Dissolution of the Event', *New Literary History* 39, no. 4 (2008): 1006.
[50] Stevie Smith, 'Beyond Words', Series 2, Box 1, Folder 7, Stevie Smith papers, University of Tulsa.

Let everything that creeps console itself, for everything that is elevated dies ...

The Dead Sea is very fortunately situated as compared with the German potash deposits inasmuch as its waters for practical purposes contain no sulphates. The sulphates though delightful from the theoretical point of view of the academic chemist have the habit of forming a large number of double salts, which would be the despair of many people.

Jessie: What is a love apple? A love apple is just another name for the tomato.

(*Novel*, 33–34)

Gathering lines from romances, geography books, and the question-and-answer pages of magazines, and presenting them as equivalent, Smith performs the 'total aestheticization of use value' which Susan Stewart associates with the collection.[51] Stripped from their original context, these lines become neat and pretty ('nice'), ready for her reader's 'scrap book'. A scrap book, importantly, does not invite one to read it as a chaotic chorus of voices, like Mirrlees's *Paris*. It promises an orderly management of wisdom: neither claiming to fit its parts together into a single complete whole, nor implicitly lamenting (in the conflicts between the parts) the impossibility of that unitary whole. In other words, Smith presents these snippets from magazine columns and chemistry books with the grandeur of an aphoristic collection. They do not dissolve into Eliotic choruses, but act as aphorisms. They can fit into a scrap-book, or they can be inscribed with aphoristic solidity: shot at friends at parties, like small hard bullets. Smith chooses lines which are technically fragments, but whose rhetorical assertiveness and certainty allows them to deliver an aphoristic punch.

How does the act of collection foster, rather than compromising, the self-sufficiency of short texts which originated as partial and fragmentary? Gary Saul Morson argues that it is the act of 'citation in anthologies' which allows a quotation to '[live] *as* an aphorism precisely in its cited form'.[52] A collection, in other words, is the site in which a line acquires its status as aphorism. Virginia Woolf's short story 'Solid Objects' (1920), about the compulsions which underlie a collection of small objects, offers a twentieth-century language for the complex status of small fragments which claim solid, self-sufficient identities within a larger collection.[53] Digging idly in the sand, John finds an alluring piece of sea-glass:

---

[51] Susan Stewart, *On Longing: Narratives of the Miniature, the Gigantic, the Souvenir, the Collection* (Durham and London: Duke University Press, 1993), 151.

[52] Gary Saul Morson, 'The Aphorism: Fragments from the Breakdown of Reason', *New Literary History* 34, no. 3 (2003): 423.

[53] On Woolf's conception of short stories as themselves 'solid objects', see Laura Marcus, 'The Short Fiction', in *A Companion to Virginia Woolf*, ed. Jessica Berman (Chichester: Wiley-Blackwell, 2016), 34.

142 STEVIE SMITH AND THE APHORISM

> It pleased him; it puzzled him; it was so hard, so concentrated, so definite an object compared with the vague sea and the hazy shore.[54]

John's first encounter with a 'solid object' (for him, pieces of glass, china, and iron) captures the fascination and mystery of the aphoristic encounter. Ben Grant describes how 'the smallness of the [aphoristic] form makes it a tactile object, something we can almost hold in our hand',[55] and Geoffrey Bennington notes that the 'formal "hardness"' of the maxim frequently elicits 'metaphors of jewellery and treasure'.[56] Both aphorism and object are small and contained: 'definite', both in terms of being clearly defined, and in terms of the significance which they seem assertively to claim. Woolf's language suggests the aphorism's 'hardness' (resisting analytic penetration). And, like the aphorism, the piece of glass refuses, in Jacques Derrida's terms, any explanatory 'demonstration': as John gazes at it, his questions about its provenance and significance 'remained unanswered'.[57]

Crucially, the early- to mid-twentieth century witnessed the association of the (literal or metaphorical) solid object with this combination of self-sufficiency and fluidity, concreteness and amorphousness. Walter Benjamin acknowledged, in *The Arcades Project*, 'the wholly irrational character of the object's mere presence at hand', suggesting a paradigm in which the object's obtrusive physicality becomes overwhelming or impossible to assimilate.[58] The object, here, is too solid. It refuses to cohere in the viewer's mind, and therefore hovers on the edge of disintegration. In his essay on 'Solid Objects', Bill Brown quotes Leonard Woolf's observation that the industrial revolution led to an 'intense preoccupation with material things': globalization and modernity saw the world being scoured for resources.[59] Observing that during the First World War the military searched the English countryside for scrap iron to use for bombs (just as John winkles a piece of iron out from under a furze bush in Virginia Woolf's short story), Brown argues that Woolf is exploring the social imperative at this time towards the reappropriation and transformation of waste, aesthetically and practically, into something new.[60] For Brown, therefore, 'Solid Objects' is 'a story not about solidity, but about the fluidity of objects, about how they decompose and recompose themselves as the object of a new fascination'.[61] Wartime scarcity troubled the solidity of objects' and materials'

---

[54] Virginia Woolf, 'Solid Objects', in *A Haunted House: The Complete Shorter Fiction*, ed. Susan Dick (London: Vintage, 2003), 97.

[55] Grant, 4.

[56] Geoffrey Bennington, *Sententiousness and the Novel: Laying Down the Law in Eighteenth-Century French Fiction* (Cambridge: Cambridge University Press, 1985), 56.

[57] Derrida, 124; Woolf, 99.

[58] Walter Benjamin, *The Arcades Project*, trans. Howard Eiland and Kevin McLaughlin (Cambridge, MA: Harvard University Press, 1999), 204–205.

[59] Bill Brown, 'The Secret Life of Things (Virginia Woolf and the Matter of Modernism)', *Modernism/modernity* 6, no. 2 (1999): 17.

[60] Brown, 18–19.

[61] Brown, 3.

FRAGMENTS 'GOING ON'   143

identities; so did new ways of thinking. Douglas Mao identifies the sense, in this period, that 'the particular, the concrete, and the auratic were threatened as never before by habits of generalization and abstraction serving a newly triumphant science'.[62] In the early part of the century, then, the solid object seems to be losing its solidity. It exists equally, according to Jean Baudrillard, as a 'resistant material body ... [and as] a mental realm'.[63] To return to the terms of Chapter 1, the object is both weighty and weightless.

Perhaps as a result of this sense of objects' instability, a 'collecting aesthetic' emerged, Jeremy Braddock finds, at the height of modernism in the 1920s. This manifested both in large art collections and in smaller contexts such as the anthology. While Braddock focuses on questions of 'art's institutional representation', a collection is also a way of reasserting an object's very existence as an object.[64] Susan Pearce notes how the object only gains existence and meaning when collected and positioned in relation to other things.[65] Collecting, then, becomes an instinctive response to entities which both promise and withhold solidity and reliability—such as the aphorism.

Part of this sensation, as 'Solid Objects' depicts it, derives from the fact that John's objects are technically fragments (like the quotations Stevie Smith repeats through her writing), but have been thoroughly, mysteriously formed into aphoristically contained entities. The aphorism's interpretative impenetrability is experienced as opaque, but also, from another angle, unreliable, dissolving, and unpredictable. Collections are the aphorism's natural habitat—the place where, as in Smith's essay 'My Muse', they gather together—since there is, in Derrida's phrase, 'always more than one aphorism'.[66] In this period, the collection of aphorisms is importantly distinct from T. S. Eliot's collection of fragments in *The Waste Land*. Eliot's collecting of fragments *as* fragments nods towards the creation of a singular whole, while performing the impossibility of that endeavour. Collecting aphorisms (or fragments as aphorisms), which insist formally on their own wholeness, is a process of repeatedly insisting on or reinscribing that promised wholeness, precisely because it does not materialize as we expect it to.

So John's reaction to his piece of sea-glass in 'Solid Objects' (the first object in what would become a collection) mirrors the reaction to the aphorism which oscillates in and out of wholeness. 'It pleased him; it puzzled him ... '. On one

---

[62] Douglas Mao, *Solid Objects: Modernism and the Test of Production* (Princeton: Princeton University Press, 1998), 6–7.

[63] Jean Baudrillard, 'The System of Collecting', in *The Cultures of Collecting*, ed. John Elsner and Roger Cardinal (London: Reaktion Books, 1994), 7.

[64] Jeremy Braddock, *Collecting as Modernist Practice* (Baltimore: Johns Hopkins University Press, 2012), 2.

[65] Susan M. Pearce, *On Collecting: An Investigation into Collecting in the European Tradition* (London and New York: Routledge, 1995), 14.

[66] Derrida, 125. See also Andrew Hui, *A Theory of the Aphorism* (Princeton and Oxford: Princeton University Press, 2019), 12, on the aphorism as a dialectical play between fragments and systems.

hand, John is 'pleased', or satisfied: a need has been fulfilled. On the other, he is 'puzzled': not fully satisfied, retaining the sense—like the publisher's reader 'E.B', struggling to get to grips with Smith's poems—that he is missing something, or that something is missing.

Solid but amorphous, the object reflects the way that the fragment moves in and out of an aphoristic identity: it may please or puzzle depending on the lens through which it is viewed. Preserving a fragment in a collection can give it the solid status of aphorism, framed as enough in itself without the promise of continuation. And yet, as John's experience hints, the aphorism draws its specific effects from the nod it makes to the fragmentary: the possibility, held in play, that this tiny enigmatic text might in fact have been left unfinished. Its brevity leaves its audience wanting more: John stares longer at his piece of glass than he or his friend can explain.

Aphorism: Going On

So, overwhelmingly, small texts spark the desire for more: either for more of the same text (a fragment which may be continued or lengthened), or for more texts like it. The rhythm of the collection, particularly the aphoristic collection, hinges not only on keeping the fascinating object in place, but on ensuring that there is something to divert us from it: in other words, offering more, an opportunity to go on. Collection also involves an act of passing on, from the already-collected object to a new source of interest. In her aphorisms in *X*, with which this book opened, Smith whisks the reader on from one aphorism to the next. Her aphorisms are devastating, resigned, callous. They cut the poet down to size, dismiss him or her as a person of no significance—but the text goes on, from aphorism to aphorism, before the reader has time to dwell on or react to these brutal revelations:

> Poetry is very strong and never has any kindness at all. She is Thetis and Hermes, the Angel, the white horse and the landscape. All Poetry has to do is to make a strong communication. All the poet has to do is to listen. The poet is not an important fellow. There will always be another poet.[67]

In Woolf's 'Solid Objects', the object drives John, with the same brisk dispatch, to move on to the next collected thing, and the next. The piece of china he retrieves from behind the railings goes on the mantelpiece with the glass:

---

[67] Vernon Watkins, Patrick Kavanagh, Hugh MacDiarmid, and Stevie Smith, 'Poets on Poetry', in *An Anthology from X: A Quarterly Review of Literature and the Arts, 1959–1962*, ed. David Wright (Oxford: Oxford University Press, 1988), 69.

As his eyes passed from one to another, the determination to possess objects that even surpassed these tormented the young man.[68]

With two objects on the mantelpiece, his eyes can '[pass] from one to another'. But inherent in the capacity of the individual object (and now the newly formed collection) to sate John's need is a further dissatisfaction. John is 'tormented' by the urge to add to his collection, which signifies lack instead of completeness and solidity. He is filled, in Werner Muensterberger's terms, with 'a chronic restiveness that can be curbed only by more finds or yet another acquisition'.[69]

When Muensterberger associates collection with the 'need to achieve *allness*', he implicitly demonstrates the impossibility of any such endpoint.[70] Sylvia Plath claimed that Stevie Smith's writing sparked the same insatiable compulsion, when she described herself in a letter to the older writer as 'a desperate Smith-addict'.[71] This language of addiction emerges in reviews of Smith's *Selected Poems* (1962) as a way of accounting for her strangeness. A 1962 review in the *TLS* concludes that 'she is one of those who attract addicts, leaving many merely indifferent',[72] while *The Tablet* suggested that the addictive quality of Smith's poems derives from the fact that they 'are so odd, so unnerving, so vehemently different ... those who are addicted to them cannot see why everyone does not share their addiction, and those who do not like them cannot see why anyone should'.[73] The reviewer casts a taste for Smith's eccentric, undervalued works as something exclusive, closed off to the common run of people. Woolf's 'Solid Objects' similarly encourages the reader to sympathize with John: his capacity to see beauty and value in strange places, and to set himself against the world in fulfilling this desire, casts him as a misunderstood genius. Smith's addictive, pleasing-but-puzzling poems and John's solid objects both posit a reader-collector aroused by eccentricity, drawn to an oddness not everyone can appreciate, who cannot now be satiated—whose reading only sparks a craving for more.

Like the drug Plath implies, for those who have become hooked, Smith's wares induce not satisfaction but a need for more. Because they stall and confuse the reader—because the disconcerting simplicity of a poem like 'Croft' (CP, 218), discussed in Chapter 1, resists any critical summation—they engender a perpetual sense that, in the next encounter, fulfilment will surely be reached. Plath and others read Smith's work in the same obsessive, passing-on spirit with which a collector amasses their artefacts. Smith's inclusion in John Gross's and Geoffrey

---

[68] Woolf, 100.
[69] Werner Muensterberger, *Collecting: An Unruly Passion* (Princeton: Princeton University Press, 1994), 3.
[70] Muensterberger, 39.
[71] Sylvia Plath to Stevie Smith, Series 1, Box 7, Folder 2, Stevie Smith papers, University of Tulsa.
[72] 'Light but not Slight', *Times Literary Supplement*, 28 December 1962, 1006.
[73] 'Angle Shot', *The Tablet* 217, 15 June 1963, 656.

Grigson's books of aphorisms and epigrams points to her collectability. Grigson, his blurb tells us, 'has been copying out epigrams since his undergraduate days. This new Faber Book is the result.'[74] Smith becomes part of a personal as well as a public collection, part of a dedicated (even obsessive) life's collecting project.

The response to the aphorism's claim to totality, either by authors or by readers, seems therefore to be a counter-totalizing: collecting more aphorisms, in an instinctive attempt to gather all the truth possible. To meet this need, to be aphoristically collectable, Smith makes her small products abundantly available. Her early critics often focused on the numerousness of her poems. While the early reader 'E.B' lamented that her poems were 'so many',[75] John Bayley wrote in the *Listener*: 'It is an excellent thing that there are so many poems, in whose bizarre copiousness we can immerse ourselves ... '.[76] Bayley's is a mixed compliment. The 'excellent thing' is not the poems themselves, but their 'bizarre copiousness' in which one can be 'immerse[d]': a word which suggests drowning or losing oneself, the oblivion of addiction.

Wanting 'more', however, carries a double valence. On one hand, the collector wants more of the same, which is why their collection goes on growing. On the other, the collector collects objects precisely in order to own them, to keep them in one place, so that they can be returned to and re-experienced. Smith constantly stages and re-stages her poems: not just literally, in her performances, but by studding her essays and novels with them, creating mini-anthologies in pieces such as 'Too Tired For Words' and 'Simply Living', which use selections of her poems to illustrate their points (MA, 111–118, 108–110). Her long-form writing is itself a site of collection; it offers the reader a chance to return to a poem again and again. 'To an American Publisher' asks, wearily, if perhaps such repetition and return might allow her to dismount the writing treadmill for a while:

> You say I must write *another* book? But I've just written this one.
> You liked it so much that's the reason? Read it again then.
> (CP, 310)

But you cannot read something again unless you have stopped reading it; returning to something necessitates that you have departed, even momentarily, and this ethic of loss or departure is part of the collection. To return to 'Solid Objects', Woolf positions the pleasure of the solid object in the fact that it can in fact be abandoned. John's piece of glass, like the aphorism, can be '[l]ooked at again and again.'[77] To

---

[74] Geoffrey Grigson, ed. *The Faber Book of Epigrams and Epitaphs* (London: Faber & Faber, 1977).
[75] 'E.B', reader's report, Series 2, Box 4, Folder 17, Stevie Smith papers, University of Tulsa.
[76] John Bayley, 'Obscure Crucifixions', *The Listener*, 25 September 1975, 409.
[77] Woolf, 98.

look at something 'again and again' involves regularly looking away. Its very self-sufficiency creates the urge to pass from it. And we witness this act of endlessly passing by in the way critics tend to engage with Smith. Arthur Rankin, author of the first book-length study of Smith, exemplifies a tendency in Smith criticism to echo the form of the aphorism collection: he resorts to serving up one poem after another to his readers, with minimal interrogation or analysis.[78] In doing so, he highlights one aspect of her aphoristic aesthetic: the tension between feeling that the poem is enough in itself, that there is nothing more to add—and at the same time, feeling propelled onwards, to make another attempt at understanding and articulation.

I contend, however, that Smith invites this particular mode of reading. In a 1942 letter to John Hayward, she describes her writing process in terms of overproduction, texts which pile up rather than each demanding sustained engagement: 'I was so inspired ... that I wrote six more poems and did 24 new drawings, and now I am terribly tied up and my room at the office looks like a paper chase'.[79] This is abundant language as escapism. The sense is of Smith's language as enabling not communication, but an effect achieved through sheer verbal volume: to use her most famous line, not waving but drowning. Passing from one poem to another becomes a mode of taking refuge, seeking repeated solace in language which is too 'bizarre' to be penetrable for meaning, but which soothes in its tonal authority.

Quoted lines appear, therefore, at moments of high emotion in Smith's novels, in order to flatten them out, or at junctions where the protagonist expresses a fear that her reader may be losing interest. After several pages of her views on imperialism, Pompey in *Over the Frontier* (1938) offers a long extract from a military memoir 'to make a nice break and a 'change' for you, dear Reader' (*Frontier*, 101). Acts of anthologization have a calming, refreshing effect, like the excursion or day-trip which Pompey's phrasing suggests; they manage and contain situations which threaten to become too intense. After describing the exquisite agony of spraining her knee, Pompey offers her reader liniment in the form of four poems on the Crucifixion:

> At random there are these poems:
> the hill is all bald stone
> And now and then the hangers gave a groan
> Up in the dark, three shapes with arms outspread ...
> ... Then there is also this:
> Large throne of Love! royally spread

---

[78] Arthur C. Rankin, *The Poetry of Stevie Smith: 'Little Girl Lost'* (Gerrards Cross: Colin Smythe Ltd, 1985).

[79] Frances Spalding, *Stevie Smith: A Critical Biography* (London: Faber and Faber, 1988), 161.

148   STEVIE SMITH AND THE APHORISM

> With purple of too rich a red ...
> ... and this:
> The third hour's deafen'd with the cry
> Of 'Crucify Him, crucify' ...
> ... and this:
>> Drop, drop, slow tears,
>> And bathe those beauteous feet ... [ellipses mine]
>
> (*Frontier*, 68–69)

Presenting poem after poem without annotation, strung together thinly with the repeated 'and this', Pompey offers more than was needed: the 'unnecessary', to echo Chapter 1, the surplus to requirements which nevertheless compels.

The burgeoning of a collection of small objects—the desire of the reader to have more and more units, felt also and fulfilled by the writer who goes on offering them up—reflects a relationship between the fragmentary and the whole. Collecting these broken bits (fragments) turns them into something solid (aphorisms). But in aggregate, presented together, their juxtaposition fuels (as well as fulfils) a rhythm of going-on between them. As we move paratactically from one aphorism to the next in a collection, we both do and do not read the units as sequential to each other.

And this brings us to the other kind of 'more', the type of going-on which Smith's longer poems in particular offer: a lengthening of a short text, your own or belonging to others, beyond its original bounds. Smith does not just gather scraps from other writers, but incorporates them into her writing, as a prompt to kickstart a poem. She installs fragments of Coleridge's (itself-fragmentary) poem 'Christabel' (1816) into her poem 'Eulenspiegelei':

> The Mastiff old did not awake,
> Yet she an angry moan did make.
> And what can ail the Mastiff Bitch?
> Never till now she utter'd Yell
> Beneath the eye of Christabel.
> Perhaps, it is the Owlet's Scritch:
> For what can ail the Mastiff Bitch?
>
> (S. T. Coleridge, 'Christabel')[80]
>
> Oh what can ail the gravid bitch
> That howls upon the midnight stroke?
>
> ('Eulenspiegelei', CP, 105)

---

[80] Coleridge, *Collected Works*, 488.

Smith's practice of collecting fragments which might one day be lengthened or repurposed in her own poems echoes James Joyce's strategy with his 'epiphanies'. Gathering overheard fragments or personal meditations between 1901–1902 and 1904,[81] he constructed them into an overarching if unsustainable aesthetic,[82] outlined in *Stephen Hero* (1904–1906):

> He [Stephen] was passing through Eccles' St one evening, one misty evening, with all these thoughts dancing the dance of unrest in his brain when a trivial incident set him composing some ardent verses which he entitled a 'Vilanelle of the Temptress'. A young lady was standing on the steps of one of those brown brick houses which seem the very incarnation of Irish paralysis. A young gentleman was leaning on the rusty railings of the area. Stephen as he passed on his quest heard the following fragment of colloquy out of which he received an impression keen enough to afflict his sensitiveness very severely.
> The Young Lady—(drawling discreetly) ... O, yes ... I was ... at the ... cha ... pel ...
> The Young Gentleman—(inaudibly) ... I ... (again inaudibly) ... I ...
> The Young Lady—(softly) ... O ... but you're ... ve ... ry ... wick ... ed ...
> This triviality made him think of collecting many such moments together in a book of epiphanies.[83]

Stephen imagines this moment as complete in itself: a unitary epiphany, to be collected in a book with others like it. But this fragment also 'set [Stephen] composing': a small incident, recorded and made textual as a fragment, without context, past, or future, is or may be the seed from which outgrowth might occur.[84] This contested relationship between units of text—where something was felt to be finished but went on nevertheless, was succeeded by further units—models the particular relationship between the opening stanzas of many of Smith's poems, and the rest of these texts. In this poetic structure, the opening tends towards an

---

[81] A. Walton Litz, 'Epiphanies: Introduction', in James Joyce, *Poems and Shorter Writings*, ed. Richard Ellman, A. Walton Litz, and John Whittier-Ferguson (London: Faber & Faber, 1991), 157.

[82] See Michael Sayeau, *Against the Event: The Everyday and the Evolution of Modernist Narrative* (Oxford: Oxford University Press, 2013), 44: the epiphanies 'represent the fulfillment of Conrad's intimation of a literature put out of work, moving busily but to no end, simulating the received eventual structure but without actually offering the development or revelation that is supposed to come with it'.

[83] James Joyce, *Stephen Hero*, ed. Theodore Spencer (London: Jonathan Cape, 1956), 216.

[84] In A. Walton Litz's account, however, these 'epiphanies' do not so much generate more writing as find homes in longer fictions: 'The epiphanies are like an artist's *trouvailles*: their significance lies in the writer's recognition of their potentialities, his faith that a revealing context will eventually be found'. A. Walton Litz, 'Introduction', 159.

150 STEVIE SMITH AND THE APHORISM

aphorism which reluctantly allows itself to be misidentified as a fragment (something which could and therefore does go on, as the poem continues) but retains its aphoristic resistance to interrogation.

Many of Stevie Smith's poems carry this same sense that they were finished after the first verse, but unenthusiastically continued. 'Our Bog is Dood' similarly continues itself beyond the play on 'our dog is dead' (or, possibly, according to J. Edward Mallot, 'our god is good')[85] by asking pedantically probing questions which know that they can never be answered to anyone's satisfaction.

> Our Bog is dood, our Bog is dood,
> They lisped in accents mild,
> But when I asked them to explain
> They grew a little wild.
> How do you know your Bog is dood
> My darling little child? (CP, 302)

The children go wild because Smith's speaker is transgressing the rules of their form: a sealed declaration does not allow questions. The poem offers the same experience of satisfied dissatisfaction found when one passes between objects/aphorisms in a collection. Attempting to probe further into the phrase 'Our Bog is Dood', the poem's narrator finds herself up against another piece of suggestive but sealed language.

> Then tell me, darling little ones,
> What's dood, suppose Bog is?
> Just what we think, the answer came,
> Just what we think it is.
> They bowed their heads. Our Bog is ours,
> And we are wholly his. (CP, 302)

The sealed line 'Our Bog is dood, our Bog is dood' with which the poem opens provokes a desire for more. The 'more' the speaker gets is the 'more' of the aphoristic collection rather than the fragment: she moves from one version of the same to the next, rather than managing sequential development. In response, the poem's narrator stages an act of withdrawal: she leaves the children behind, and imagines them being drowned by a sudden surge of the sea. She enters, in other words, into the dynamic of the aphoristic collection. John's eyes rove between his items in 'Solid Objects': passing between them involves constantly alternating which one he departs from. Equally, passing from one aphorism to another is both an act of

---

[85] J. Edward Mallot, 'Not Drowning But Waving: Stevie Smith and the Language of the Lake', *Journal of Modern Literature* 27 no. 1/2 (2003): 187.

FRAGMENTS 'GOING ON' 151

moving towards and of moving away. The repeated experience one wishes to have, as one moves through the collection of aphorisms, involves an act of departure, as well as a return to sameness.

Like 'Our Bog is Dood', 'Mr Over' raps out its punchline by the fourth line. The whole setup of that first stanza is directed towards this jokey payoff:

> Mr Over is dead
> He died fighting and true
> And on his tombstone they wrote
> Over to You. (CP, 299)

Yet the poem must limp on for several other stanzas, by which time the poem has turned into something completely different: a musing on death, faith, and sin:

> And who pray is this You
> To whom Mr Over is gone?
> Oh if we only knew that
> We should not do wrong. (CP, 299)

Smith continues the poem by opening up the punchline 'Over to You'. She interrogates the word 'You', lingers on it until the joke turns to despair. Throughout, one cannot forget the poem's beginnings in a punch of self-contained wordplay. That is its memorable section. Continued on, the poem becomes, in part, a text about the failure of levity to last; the impingement of dreary ongoing thought on something which might have withdrawn at its peak, but instead flattens into dolour. Unlike Mr Over himself, who died 'fighting and true', the poem is not allowed to depart on a high. Doggedly, it goes on.

Thoughts about the Person from Porlock

These questions of continuation against the possibility of departure accelerate in Smith's three-page poem 'Thoughts about the Person from Porlock' (1962), a text interested in this very question surrounding the aphorism: of when one gets to leave, to depart from a situation which has offered all it can, against social pressure to continue. Smith's poem springboards from Coleridge's 'Kubla Khan' (1816), as Smith cogitates over the merciful interruption offered to that earlier poet by the Person from Porlock, saving him from the charge that he ran out of inspiration and providing an excuse for leaving 'Kubla Khan' in a 'fragmentary' state:

> He was weeping and wailing, I am finished, finished,
> I shall never write another word of it

152   STEVIE SMITH AND THE APHORISM

> When along comes the Person from Porlock
> And takes the blame for it. (CP, 445)

Her poem deals with the pressure to write more when faced with writer's block; it describes a longing to be allowed to stop talking, to have someone 'bring my thoughts to an end' (CP, 446). She couches interruption of this sort as a gift: a withdrawal before one can overstay one's welcome, before others (and oneself) can grow weary. When Hans-Jost Frey describes conversation as interruption, he reveals how interruption humanely regulates the presence of the individual in the social space, allowing them to stop, justifiably, before they have embarrassed themselves by going on too long.[86]

With no sign of her own person from Porlock, however, Smith's speaker has to go on, to extort more from a text which has already made its brief original point: that Coleridge had run out of inspiration for 'Kubla Khan' even before the Person from Porlock knocked. She finds ways to coax the narrative into continuation, fusing 'Person' and 'Porlock' to produce 'Porson'. 'Porlock' also provides a location ('He lived at the bottom of Porlock Hill'), and, through its rhyme, an occupation for the Person's grandmother ('a Warlock'). Wordplay can take the narrative a certain distance, spin it out a little bit longer. Quickly, however, the speaker begins to dry up:

> And he lived at the bottom of the hill as I said
> And had a cat named Flo,
> And had a cat named Flo. (CP, 446)

The Muse has flown; the poem stalls into a prosaic repetition of randomly invented facts. By going on, the speaker tries to engender 'flo[w]', to persuade the poem to keep going. Smith's notebook drafts make this process very clear:

> As ~~I think~~ he {certainly} knew, {for sure} come Person or not
> He was finished with Kubla Khan.
> ~~Yes, He~~ {Yes, he knew he} was finished with Kubla Khan
> He would never write another word of it
> [another draft:]
> As he knew ahem oh yes he knew
> As already he knew[87]

---

[86] Hans-Jost Frey, *Interruptions*, trans. Georgia Albert (New York: State University of New York Press, 1996), 6.

[87] Stevie Smith, black notebook, Series 2, Box 9, Folder 1. Stevie Smith papers, University of Tulsa. Braces indicate sections which have been added to the manuscript by hand; parts scored out have been crossed out in the manuscript.

The jaunty, singalong repetitions, as the draft coughs and agrees with itself, fill the textual space, bulking out the line: one can hear Smith trying but not quite succeeding in catching on to a rhythm which would carry the text forward productively. Her speaker signals that she cannot simply stop or abandon the poem as a fragment. She must generate more, for if the poem were to get going, to fall into an inspired track, then perhaps it might create its own conditions in which a respectable, closing-off ending could take place. The speaker becomes increasingly desperate to enforce an end which would allow her to escape with dignity. But she tries first the Biblical line which might close prayer, 'For ever and ever amen', then an imperious apostrophizing speech-act, 'O Person from Porlock', to no avail. This formal language of closure tends in other contexts to 'create ... a sense of ... finality and stability'.[88] Yet these devices fail to bring the poem to a close. In spite of these pre-formed phrases which should clean up and tuck away anxiety, the poem dribbles on. Smith's repeated, failed kickstarts towards an ending offer the poem its eventual subject matter: what happens when nothing remains to be said, but one goes on anyway.

The constant continuations of 'Thoughts about the Person from Porlock' signal that it is marking time just a little bit longer. To an extent, this is an act of courtesy, a decision not to bolt the scene or go away before the narrative has 'gone somewhere', to wait until the (or an) end. Courteously hanging around, from a particular angle, becomes a way of keeping up appearances, or keeping one's moral end up. In the same instance, however, Smith flags up her own over-extension: we can never forget that this continuation is excess, a refusal to give in to the fragmentary but an inability to find the grooves of a successful whole. Lengthening a text ironically makes it more fragmentary: it abandons the brevity of the aphorism, but fails to become something complete.

'Thoughts about the Person from Porlock' explores what happens when closure becomes unavailable to the writer. Its nightmare-scape revolves around not being allowed to withdraw: to have to stay on, embarrassing yourself by going on too long, sharing more (and more intimately) than you intended. Rather than the tactful rhythm of burgeoning offered by the collection of solid, enclosed units like aphorisms—where one may come, and go, and return, and freely add more texts with a paratactic flexibility, since each is already finished in itself—this is the 'more' of the fragment: gaping open, eliciting an anxious obligation to lengthen and lengthen it until an appropriate ending is found.

Smith associated interruption—both from outside, like the Person from Porlock, and the self-interruption of the aphorism, boldly making a claim while stopping short—with completion. Frey underscores this approach when he writes 'What breaks off justifiably has ended. The discourse that is able to say why it

---

[88] Beverly Coyle, *A Thought to Be Rehearsed: Aphorism in Wallace Stevens's Poetry* (Ann Arbor: UMI Research Press, 1983), 3.

154   STEVIE SMITH AND THE APHORISM

breaks off is not fragmentary'.[89] Having an excuse for breaking off (like an interruption) preserves one from the charge of fragmentariness. Stopping before you are ready to end, before you have crossed into excess, you can go away with dignity. The fragment, conversely, cannot go away. It has exhausted itself, so it cannot continue, and fails to blossom into a final completed whole. But neither can it depart while it hangs on to the faint hope of future conclusion.

Smith's writing is fascinated by this fragmentary space, like that of 'Porlock': where the writer runs out of steam before reaching a point at which they can gracefully finish, and therefore has to helplessly generate more and more in the hope of finding an appropriate end. Smith herself was often terribly tired, having had very poor health as a child (although her friends suggested that she sometimes played up to this image as frail and fatigued in order to get what she wanted).[90] But the writer who becomes too tired to finish properly and neatly invites both her empathy and her contempt. She contextualizes 'The Deserter' with an explanation that its speaker was 'a deserter to ill health', who took to his bed instead of dedicatedly pushing on. The speaker emphasizes his helplessness:

> The world has come upon me, I used to keep it a long way off,
> But now I have been run over and I am in the hands of the hospital staff.
> They say I have not been run over as a matter of fact it's imagination,
> But they all agree I should be kept in bed under observation.
> I must say it's very comfortable here, nursie has such nice hands,
> And every morning the doctor comes and lances my tuberculous glands.
> He says he does nothing of the sort, but I have my own feelings about that,
> And what they are if you don't mind I shall continue to keep under my hat.
> My friend, if you call it a friend, has left me; he says I am a deserter to ill health,
> And that the things I should think about have made off for ever, and so has my wealth ... (CP, 295)

This is the babbling we recognize from 'Porlock': a strained nervous system, afraid to pause or to dwell on the 'feelings' which must be kept 'under [his] hat' instead of confronted. The deserter has run out of steam, but is keeping up appearances

---

[89] Frey, 72.
[90] See, for instance, Elisabeth Lutyens, *A Goldfish Bowl* (London: Cassell, 1972), 313.

by claiming he has 'been run over': interrupted, in other words, in the middle of his trajectory while walking. The person run over is a victim of circumstance, not at fault, rudely interrupted and therefore forgiven.

Granting the Deserter of her poem no such excuse, Smith criticizes him in her essay 'Too Tired For Words':

> ... [tiredness] can provide an excuse for not writing at all. One hugs one's disabilities, one cultivates them, one becomes—like the wretch I have put in the next poem—a deserter to ill health. (The wretch was a writer but now he lies in his hospital bed—and let the Muse go hang). (MA, 113–114)

Smith claims she sees through the speaker's trick: he says he has been interrupted but really he has simply let the Muse 'hang' in purgatorial suspension. It is difficult to know how seriously to take Smith's criticism; there is an element we are meant to find absurd, I think, in the disjunction between the poem's narrative and that of its framing story. She begins the essay by suggesting that forcing oneself on to finish something might be creatively productive:

> One forces oneself, one gets a bit feverish (and much more tired) and eventually, out of the strain and exasperation, the words come headlong ... the scene shifts wonderfully in the light of the words that are, by reason of the tiredness, just a bit off-beam. (MA, 111)

Forcing oneself onwards towards an appropriate moment for withdrawal, then, can be productive, Smith thinks. She laments, in an interview, that it was 'wicked' of Coleridge not to push on with 'Christabel' and try to reach a proper, dignified conclusion.[91] Poor Coleridge seems to have felt it was wicked too. His letters show him making excuses, casting about for ideal circumstances in which to bring the poem to an end. 'By the Sea side I hope to finish my Christabel', he writes to Thomas Boosey, of that very un-sea-sidey poem, in August 1816.[92] But he never finished his Christabel, and even the text now extant took several years to write. Gaps elapsed between the writing of the first part (written 1798–1799), the second part (1800), and the conclusion to the second part (1801).[93] The conclusion to Part II, J. C. C. Mays notes, does not appear in any manuscript of the poem. Coleridge included it in a letter to Robert Southey on 6 May 1801, as a description of his son Hartley; it may not have joined 'Christabel' until as late as 1816, when the poem was published.[94]

---

[91] Jonathan Williams, 'Much Further Out Than You Thought', in *In Search of Stevie Smith*, 42.
[92] Coleridge, *Collected Letters IV*, 663.
[93] Coleridge, *Collected Works*, 478.
[94] Coleridge, *Collected Works*, 503.

156   STEVIE SMITH AND THE APHORISM

This disjunctive, fragmented history hints that, even in its final form, 'Christabel' is a text internally marked by evidence of its own uncomfortable relationship with closure. Wordsworth felt that Coleridge should have stopped writing the poem after the first part: mood, tone, and image shift significantly across the poem. Mays, editing Coleridge, echoes this view, suggesting that Part II was added 'to an essentially complete fragment'.[95] But Coleridge overextended the poem, and trapped himself—like the speaker of 'Thoughts About the Person from Porlock'— in a situation where he needed to push on to a new end, but could not. Though in 1820, he was still insisting that he could 'no doubt' finish Christabel if only he could find himself 'easy in mind',[96] the text hangs open in the form of a fragment, unable quite to end: causing Coleridge guilt, annoying Wordsworth.

So, in a manuscript notebook, Stevie Smith made an abortive attempt to continue the poem for Coleridge:

> Christabel has left the castle
> Because of the snake-lady, she lost the battle
> She hates snakes and has gone to the sea
> But oh it is so wintry
> There she has met an aged elf
> Who say, Christabel be true to yourself
> …
> Take this stone, Princess
> (For so you should be
> A princess, in a far [illegible])
> Look to the stone and look in it, see,
> It will tell you when [illegible] your heart[97]

Smith's attempt to finish 'Christabel' smacks, on one hand, of the benevolent busybody: keeping it going, hurrying it towards a tidy ending. Coleridge left his protagonist in Geraldine's thrall: when Smith takes up the narrative, Christabel has 'lost the battle', and abruptly 'has left the castle' (we do not learn how). Smith's version is breezy; it skips over tedious details surrounding Christabel's escape and gets her somewhere more exciting. Instead of completing the poem on its own terms, she uses the core images of fairytale to kickstart a new beginning: an entirely new generic direction. As in 'Thoughts about the Person from Porlock', Smith introduces chunks of familiar textual structures to induce continuation (elf, magic stone, princess, in the way that 'Porlock' used apostrophes and snatches of prayer).

[95] Coleridge, *Collected Works*, 479.
[96] Samuel Taylor Coleridge to Thomas Allsop, 30 March 1820, in *Collected Letters of Samuel Taylor Coleridge, Volume V, 1820–1825*, ed. Earl Leslie Griggs (Oxford: Clarendon Press, 1971), 31.
[97] Stevie Smith, red notebook, Series 2, Box 9, Folder 1, Stevie Smith papers, University of Tulsa.

The poem's rhetorical similarity to 'Porlock', however, which revolves around the elusiveness of any ending, should warn us that this continuation of the poem has no intention of helping to end it. Drawing the text drastically away from the narrative direction that Coleridge set up, Smith establishes her continuation in a zone which is entirely tonally and narratively subsequent to 'Christabel's extant form. Christabel lost the battle; she left the castle; everything is over. In that flat space, Smith continues the poem.

This narrative sabotage points to a less conscientious, ending-oriented aspect to her interest in continuing this fragment: Smith's artistic attraction towards staging the failure of texts when they are continued past the point at which they needed to stop. The short, complete text, terminating before it has said everything possible, and before it could begin to grate, finds it embarrassing to keep going. When Smith's poems continue past their self-determining point of termination, they perform their own resistance to this going-on by staging a withdrawal of effort. Her continuation of Coleridge's poem lazily stacks up ready-made textual blocks, and the poem 'Duty was his Lodestar' signals that it is phoning its plot in:

> Duty was my Lobster, my Lobster was she,
> And when I walked out with my Lobster
> I was happy.
> But one day my Lobster and I fell out,
> And we did nothing but
> Rave and shout.
>
> Rejoice, rejoice, Hallelujah, drink the flowing champagne,
> For my darling Lobster and I
> Are friends again.
>
> Rejoice, rejoice, drink the flowing champagne-cup,
> My Lobster and I have made it up. (CP, 290)

Based on a mishearing of 'lobster' for 'lodestar', the poem describes someone befriending a lobster, falling out with it, and then reconciling within a few short stanzas. No reasons or explanations are offered. We are never allowed to forget that this tiny joke, based on a small mishearing, was initially enough in itself. Lengthened into a whole poem, the flimsiness of the narrative reads like an amused grumble against its own necessity. The small, finished joke should have been allowed to stay as it was: aphorism not fragment.

Overextended in this way, reader and writer find themselves working in a twilight zone, in which everything important has already happened. The main weight of the text has already been discharged in the very first stanza; everything subsequent is belated, existing only in the penumbra of that initial short text. Aphorism bows out graciously because it knows it has failed, or will fail, to be properly heeded. To go on elaborating, explaining, and justifying seems to indicate an embarrassing (and vain) hope that the right, effective words might still, somehow, be found.

Conclusion
To Go On

I shall know when to stop, and I shall stop. And whatever I write then will be Volume Two.

> (Stevie Smith, *Novel*, 179)

The secret of remaining satisfied is to make it a rule to leave the table long before you have had enough.

> (Katherine Mansfield, 'Bites from the Apple'[1])

Stevie Smith spends her poetic career, and her personal life, wrestling with the question of whether to go on, or whether to stop: to simply go away. Toying continually with the option of death, her poems may end early. 'I'll indicate tomorrow / Just why this course is not for you to follow' promises her poem 'From My Notes for a Series of Lectures on Murder', without ever delivering this explanation (CP, 68). Alternatively, like 'The Stroke', the poems may continue unexpectedly past their assumed ending (CP, 657). Yet, claiming towards the end of *Novel on Yellow Paper*, 'I shall know when to stop', Pompey Casmilus focuses in on an idealized point of termination: when the time has come to end, neither too late nor too early.

Knowing when to stop, in this first quotation, becomes a sign of an often feminized self-control: the moderation of knowing when to withdraw. Smith's self-portrayal as an eccentric outsider in *Novel on Yellow Paper*, through Pompey, comes via a tactical (and tactful) removal of herself: 'I wish only to be a visitor', she remarks (*Novel*, 182).

Pompey's way of being, and Smith's via Pompey, becomes inextricable from a performance of careful social manners. Not that Smith was well-behaved—she annoyed her friends and her aunt, behaved childishly and eccentrically, sang at inappropriate moments—but as Chapter 4 suggests, manners fascinated her, especially when connected with prudence, frugality, and a genteel capacity to overlook or disregard. These are the manners which Katherine Mansfield plays on in aphorism 46 of 'Bites of the Apple' (*c*.1911), her unpublished collection of aphorisms. Like a young Victorian lady, urged to cultivate a delicate appetite, she imagines leaving the table (going away) before she is sated. Doing so, however, is the only

---

[1] Katherine Mansfield, 'Aphorisms', in *The Edinburgh Edition of the Collected Works of Katherine Mansfield, Volume 3: The Poetry and Critical Writings of Katherine Mansfield*, ed. Gerri Kimber and Angela Smith (Edinburgh: Edinburgh University Press, 2014), 420.

Stevie Smith and the Aphorism. Noreen Masud, Oxford University Press.
© Noreen Masud (2022). DOI: 10.1093/oso/9780192895899.003.0007

160   STEVIE SMITH AND THE APHORISM

way to guarantee that she remains satisfied. At the heart of this paradox is a play between 'remaining' and 'leav[ing]': going away, underserved, somehow allows one to go on, feeling fully served.

No coincidence, I suggest, that Mansfield wrote this wrestle with desire and satisfaction, leaving and staying, self-restraint and self-fulfilment, in the form of an aphorism. Reading Smith as aphoristic allows us to see that aphorism, too, has been concerned throughout its history with the same questions of want, fulfilment, and termination. Chapter 1 teased out the implications of Karl Kraus's aphoristic statement that an aphorism is either half a truth or one-and-a-half truths: appearing either less than whole or more than whole, depending on the angle of view. The dilemma, both in Smith and in the aphoristic form with which she engages, is precisely this question of when to go on and when to stop and go away—and how, and if, both can somehow be achieved in the same gesture. In her nursing-home revelation, little Pompey in *Novel on Yellow Paper* realizes that she can go on because she can go away any time she wants (*Novel*, 123). Going on becomes possible *because* one has choices, can move in any direction, not because one has no other choice.

So going on is always ghosted, for Smith, by its alternative: the departure which was invariably considered and which therefore didn't happen. Poems such as 'She got up and went away' allow the going-away fantasy to take its fullest form:

> She got up and went away
> Should she not have? Not have what?
> Got up and gone away.
>
> Yes, I think she should have
> Because it was getting darker.
> Getting what? Darker. Well,
> There was still some
> Day left when she went away, well,
> Enough to see the way. (CP, 726–727)

This is 'going away' as archetype: a pure strong gesture, stripped of context and plot. The whole poem feeds off—and issues from, with everything of importance already discharged in the first line—the image of a decisive but unidentified, unsituated, unexplained departure. A kind of disturbance, a fuzziness on the line in this poem, prevents even the frugal information on offer from being fully heard or understood. The speakers mishear and misunderstand each other: 'Not have what?' 'Getting what?' From the clear, definite, quiet but unapologetic first line, darkness closes in upon this poem. We are working in a post-apocalyptic landscape of remnants (like the survival of the 'ineradicable' line 'Not Waving But

Drowning', in Rodney Ackland's imaginary),[2] the era of the 'too late' in which this book has so often positioned Smith's centre of gravity: dealing with the last traces of light, of day; on a fizzing radio which won't transmit properly; where information is painfully limited, and incomprehensible even when it is heard. The staccato exchange gives way to something even less coherent, more garbled:

> And it was the last time she would have been able ...
> Able? ... to get up and go away.
> It was the last time the very last time for
> After that she could not
> Have got up and gone away any more. (CP, 727)

In those last three lines, the iambic metre which funnelled in readerly attention in the third line—'Got up and gone away', returned to again in the ninth line ('Enough to see the way')—breaks down completely. Punctuation, grammar, and subject positions all vanish in this flattened, disjointed rhythm. Events become as indeterminate as landscape. 'After that', the speaker tells us. After what? Objects, events, and places vanish from this poem. What is the event which would have stopped her going away? What, indeed, is she going away from?

In its purity of gesture—departure without destination, withdrawing firmly from the world—Smith's speaker exemplifies perfectly Sitwell's origin-story of eccentricity: 'any dumb but pregnant comment on life, any criticism of the world's arrangement, if expressed by only one gesture, and that of sufficient contortion, becomes eccentricity'.[3] Smith's figure makes a departure which is a pure, extreme, contorted gesture, a leaving par excellence: a 'dumb but pregnant comment' on a place arranged so as to become intolerable, which cannot be lived in any longer.

The figure goes away, definitely and firmly. But the poem goes on. Its garbling and repetitions become ways to continue it, to keep (as Chapter 5 explored) the poetic show on the road. Going on stands in for the going away which has already happened, has been described in the very first line, but which continues to be the substance of the whole poem. The poem itself is a remnant, something whose 'going on' marks an absence.

Stevie Smith did not publish this poem in her lifetime. In that sense, she excluded it from her writing—removed it from a territory in which it could mark something, be lucidly stated and available. But other poems which Smith did publish, some very early in her career, experiment with the capacity of 'going' to mark

---

[2] Rodney Ackland, 'Bear up Chaps,' *Spectator* 223, 30 August 1969, 272.
[3] Edith Sitwell, *English Eccentrics* (London: The Folio Society, 1994), 4.

162   STEVIE SMITH AND THE APHORISM

both presence and absence. The final stanza of 'The Deathly Child', for instance, makes this clear:

> Over the café tables the talk is going to and fro,
> And the people smile and they frown, but they do not know
> That the deathly child walks. Ah who is it that must go?[4]

'Going', in the first line, inscribes 'go' with the solid substance of the present-continuous, reinscribing it insistently as the focus of that line. That final 'go', however, is the 'go' of death: the invitation to depart the mortal world, abruptly and in ways unspecified, with the deathly child. The same word does double service; the two kinds of going become muddled together. When in 'Noble and Ethereal' the protagonist 'bravely turned away' from the river-edge (CP, 140), his decision to continue with life appears more like a rejection of it, and the poem stops there.

This book has been arguing for a way of reading Smith which finds a simultaneity in her 'going on' and 'going away': where they can be the same thing, or one discovered to be the other; where an assertion of presence can become concomitant with a final withdrawal. The aphorism, as a form, performs this particular work, which makes it key to Smith's writing. I have argued that the aphorism accommodates Smith's unique twists between going away and going on: cancelling a declaration even as it is emphatically made. Smith's choice, or that of her characters, seems to be that of the world (working, striving, having an effect, being important), or that of departure (lightness, insignificance, superficiality, uselessness, withdrawal from labour). Smith's poetic, I argue, presents that choice as false. Weight and importance become resituated even in something purposeless, useless and trivial: not in a camp, frivolous repurposing of waste for the approval of a social clique, but in a gesture which sabotages the possibility of social approval.

Aphorism engages with ending in multiple ways, as this book has argued. It may invite return, since it cannot be engaged with fully in one sitting; it may be continued on, past its natural end, and use that unsatisfactory situation to protest its continued existence. Aphorism engages uneasily with excess: though the aphorism seems a performance of neatness, there is also a model of the aphorism as an excessive form. It may overflow its bounds, like Smith's overspilling final lines; it may alternatively be 'unnecessary', like Smith's guerrilla recordings of phrases and overheard snatches, and like Karl Kraus's lists of aphorisms titled 'Waste'. Aphorism's brevity, coupled with its monumental truth-claims, means that it is always anticipating and guarding against its own inappropriate excess, a snapshot of the social failure which might ensue if thunderous revelation was really to be heard

---

[4] Stevie Smith, *Two in One: Selected Poems and The Frog Prince and Other Poems* (London: Longman, 1971), 100.

and heeded. So aphorisms leave the scene with anti-social promptness, fearing that they've already said too much, embarrassed themselves.

Mansfield's aphorism reminds us that the only way to stay satisfied is to manage one's own desires. Aphorism, as the twentieth-century aphorist and raconteur Quentin Crisp implies in *Doing It With Style* (1981), is a way of not asking for anything: of disowning the possibility that you could be making a demand on your audience:

> most people are profoundly indifferent to your pain and suffering ... The only justification for introducing such subjects into a conversation is for purposes of entertainment, and then you must make it clear from the outset that your story is being offered for people's amusement and not for their sympathy. Even at that, the story should be condensed into a single anecdote or epigram.[5]

Doing It With Style is a guide to manners, and Crisp offers aphorism as a tool for the social management of pain: to clean it up at the edges, of the mess of human affect. Aphorism means that a sad story can be told without eliciting or demanding sadness from its hearers. It becomes a site in which one can claim, or perform the claiming of, something that will not be granted, in the knowledge that it is safe to make this claim because it will be refused. Aphorism is often about the impossibility of being granted what you would like (attention, sympathy, belief) for which you make a bid stripped of its affective capacity. Even Nietzsche's bloody, mountainous aphorisms display this control, this knowing acknowledgement that the aphorism brings no fulfilment:

> *Fettered Heart, Free Spirit.*—When one firmly fetters one's heart and keeps it prisoner, one can allow one's spirit many liberties: I said this once before. But people do not believe it when I say so, unless they know it already.[6]

Nietzsche has had to make this observation (based again, we note, around the rhythms of restraint and release) twice. He has said it before, he tells us, to no effect, and now he says it again, with not much more hope that he will be heeded. This, I suggest, is another kind of aphoristic 'going on'. Aphorism's defusal of emotional and real-world impact means that it presents itself despite its (signalled) knowledge of its own redundancy, its inevitable failure to be heeded.

This is the gesture at work in Smith's selection of 'Voice from the Tomb' poems. Brief, punchy, and cross, their voices protest against their own marginalization, but prevent us from taking them seriously or even sympathizing. The subtitle in

---

[5] Quentin Crisp and Donald Carroll, *Doing It With Style* (London: Eyre Methuen, 1981), 51.
[6] Friedrich Nietzsche, *Beyond Good and Evil: Prelude to a Philosophy of the Future*, trans. Helen Zimmern (Edinburgh: Darien Press, 1907), 88.

164 STEVIE SMITH AND THE APHORISM

'Voice from the Tomb (5)' witheringly dismisses its speaker's potentially very valid grievance as absurd, but also frames it for presentation:

> *a Soul earthbound by the grievance*
> *of never having been important*
>
> You never heard of me, I dare
> Say. Well, I'm here. (CP, 536)

This model of the aphorism as a form for the marginalized, speaking in a way that does not elicit a hearing, casts light on a range of twentieth-century women writers. Mina Loy—poet, artist, Futurist, feminist, lampshade designer, and aphorist—illustrates this choreography of declaration and withdrawal throughout her strange, tonally insistent oeuvre. In her 'Aphorisms on Futurism' (1914), for instance:

> THE velocity of velocities arrives in starting.
> IN pressing the material to derive its essence, matter becomes deformed.
> AND form hurtling against itself is thrown beyond the synopsis of vision.[7]

Even as aphorism's imperious form lets Loy make an emphatic (if opaque) claim, she collapses her literary performances into everyday banality. In a 1960 interview, she comments on her outsider status within the literary world of her youth ('The *Little Review*, I was reading about it somewhere, they wouldn't have anything to do with me ... '), and as part of the same breath hints that her writing might be worthless or meaningless: 'I'd only written these things for the **sake** of the sounds of the words. It was like making jewelry or something'.[8] Loy casts her own work as jewellery-making: sadly seen as counting, when done by a woman, as decorative domestic craft rather than art. Humble domestic tinkering with gemstones becomes a gesture not replacing, not complicating, but simultaneous with the lapidary brilliance which underlay her 'Aphorisms on Futurism': Loy undermines the declarations she makes.

The model of aphorism further identifies Ivy Compton-Burnett's use of the form in her novels, largely published between the 1920s and the 1960s. Smith and Compton-Burnett have a long association: even before Kay Dick published *Ivy and Stevie* (1983), a short volume of interviews with the two writers, reviewers picked out similarities between them. Writing in *Books of the Month*, Herbert Van

---

[7] Mina Loy, *The Lost Lunar Baedeker* (Manchester: Carcanet, 1997), 149.

[8] Mina Loy, 'Mina Loy Interview with Paul Blackburn and Robert Vas Dias', in *Mina Loy: Woman and Poet*, ed. Maeera Shreiber and Keith Tuma (Orono, Maine: National Poetry Foundation, 1998), 214.

Thal managed Smith's apparent eccentricity by remarking, 'doubtless one becomes as absorbed in her style, just as one acquires the taste for reading the works of Miss Compton-Bennett [sic] when once you have mastered her full reasonings.'[9] A 1967 review in the *Times Literary Supplement* felt that the archaic social context which Smith evokes in her poetry 'almost recalls Miss Ivy Compton-Burnett.'[10] The critical language emerging here revolves around the acquired taste, the alien feminine, the skewed or out-of-time. *Harper's Bazaar* showed its working most clearly when, in 1964, it published the remark 'Stevie Smith is one of those dear English ladies (Ivy Compton-Burnett is another) who invites the reader to tea, and who leads him, in a surprisingly short time, to wonder whether he is going to leave the house alive.'[11] Compton-Burnett and Smith enter a tradition of sweet old ladies whose smiles are slightly too wide, who lure in the (young, male) reader in order to predate on him.

Despite her ambivalence towards such ideas of association and literary lineage, Stevie Smith admired Ivy Compton-Burnett greatly. She reviewed two of her novels (*Two Worlds and Their Ways* (1949) and *Darkness and Day* (1951)) and praised, in her unpublished essay 'Modern English Literature', 'the incomparable, the fabulous Miss Ivy Compton-Burnett, whose exquisite dialogue carries everything with it of character plot and feeling [sic], whose children and servants are so especially superb, with all told and never a word lost.'[12] This sense of a frugal use of language, with nothing wasted even as everything is openly admitted ('all told'), foregrounds Compton-Burnett's striking taste for the aphorism.[13] Shaped around family life, the books follow similar patterns: tyrannical heads of household, who are pedantic about small details of conduct and expense, and subordinates who, as Penelope Lively notes, retaliate with 'elegant and crushing verbal skills.'[14] It is in this power hierarchy that the aphorism asserts itself. The powerless members of her families speak aphoristically, the powerful tyrants speak colloquially. The patriarchs meet the aphoristic remarks of their victims with jollity, a performance of an amiable inability to understand or respond to such threateningly gnomic sentiments. In *Manservant and Maidservant* (1947), for instance, the children of the tyrannical Horace remark, in front of him, on the ragged quality of the clothes which they had been forced to wear far past the point of respectability:

'I don't suppose people looked at us in them,' said Marcus.
'It may be proper to suppose they did not,' said Sarah, 'but it was not the truth.'

---

[9] Herbert Van Thal, 'New Novels', *Books of the Month*, September 1949.
[10] 'Waving And Drowning', *Times Literary Supplement*, 19 January 1967.
[11] Elrond, 'Book Bazaar', *Harper's Bazaar*, September 1964, 299.
[12] Stevie Smith, 'Modern English Literature', 13, Series 2, Box 3, Folder 9, Stevie Smith papers, University of Tulsa.
[13] On the response of contemporary critics to Compton-Burnett's aphoristic style, see Elizabeth Sprigge, *The Life of Ivy Compton-Burnett* (London: Victor Gollancz Ltd, 1973), 43.
[14] Penelope Lively, 'Introduction', in *Manservant and Maidservant* (Oxford: Oxford University Press, 1983), x.

'They look at us less in these,' said Tamasin. 'They seemed to prefer the sight that was less suitable for them.'

'It is people's disadvantages that people think about,' said Sarah, 'even children's.'

'What a pack of little cynics!' said Horace.[15]

Sarah, the oldest child, is just thirteen, but her remarks are precisely constructed. They possess the aphorism's quality of apparent generality but clear, pointed relevance to the situation at hand. The aphorism possesses plausible deniability: if it is challenged, if its content is addressed head-on, it can maintain the excuse that it was a general statement and not a comment on the current situation. Aphorism allows Sarah to say something without really saying it.

Here, the aphorism marks a moment of disappointment. It protests against its own sidelining in terms and form so coded that we cannot respond or act on what it says. Rather than claiming authority, the 'aphorism' refers most, I think, to a kind of speech which performs a peculiar acrobatic: even as it states something authoritatively, it deletes the grounds on which authority might take effect. The aphorism sweeps up after itself. When it is done, it gets up and goes away.

The aphorism allows escape through virtuosity: a display of rhetorical skill which insists that its speaker or writer is not to be touched. Aphorism can make it impossible for someone to question you or to argue. For that reason, even as it presents itself as an authoritative form, the use of aphorism can equally signal resignation. The powerful person's aphorism (especially in the case of proverb, as Chapter 3 suggested) shuts down argument because he or she assumes the next step will be obedience. When the powerless use aphorisms, conversely, they do so because they are too tired to argue—they know they won't convince their listeners, not wholly, or rather will not be properly understood by their readers—and so they use a form which shuts down (or renders absurd) further argument.[16] It is a form of speech which comes back to the speaker, rather than resting with the listener as something to be responded to. Using aphorism releases you from the responsibility of having to answer questions. It bespeaks an absolute faith in your own declaration, even as you signal that you have no faith in the world to listen, understand, or act in response. Revelation, in Smith's 'Recognition not Enough', is inadequate to effect meaningful change:

> Sin recognised—but that—may keep us humble,
> But oh, it keeps us nasty. (CP, 450)

---

[15] Ivy Compton-Burnett, *Manservant and Maidservant* (Oxford: Oxford University Press, 1983), 136.

[16] Compare with Herbert Spencer's rueful reflection, deepening this connection between aphorism and eccentricity, on the common belief that 'If you show yourself eccentric in manners or dress, the world ... will not listen to you'. Detractors of eccentricity count this as risk: the aphorism uses this threat to its own advantage. Herbert Spencer, 'Manners and Fashion', in *Essays: Scientific, Political, and Speculative, Vol 1* (London: Williams and Norgate, 1868), 98.

In this way, the aphorism limits its own power. It does not open up a dangerous space of threat for the listener, which might lead to aggression or violence. It is the rhetorical equivalent of having your say and then immediately leaving the room. It reduces itself to sass. Aphorism states itself (goes on) in the moment that it departs from view or use (goes away). The aphorism remains behind when the speaker has departed: it is a remnant, a scar or a tombstone, signalling the wound, or the disappointment, or the loss. Like a scar, or the navel in Elisabeth Bronfen's *The Knotted Subject*,[17] it seems like a door but cannot be entered. Like such a scar, or such a tombstone, aphorism is hard to the touch.

This new conception of the aphorism lets us nuance moments where authors use aphorism in their work. Rather than signalling a superior didacticism, it may instead be a placeholder for pain, a way of saying something without really saying it, a way of abdicating responsibility for what you say, a way of saying something even though you have lost faith in its real-world power.[18] More than a few aphorisms are in fact about that dilemma:

... All the good maxims exist in the world: we only fail to apply them.

[Pascal][19]

If it were true, what in the end would be gained? Nothing but another truth. Is this of such great advantage? We have enough old truths still to digest, and even these we would not be able to endure if we did not sometimes flavor them with lies.

[Lichtenberg][20]

One uses aphorism when time is limited; when one is afraid that people will not stick around to listen to the full version. It is a form which accommodates femaleness, queerness, illness, outsiderhood, unhearability. Aphorism signals embarrassment, and represents an attempt to be less embarrassing: to manage its own excess by being neat and amusing, to minimize the affective force of its inconvenient complaint. When that undertow of social exclusion and awkwardness becomes legible, aphorism itself becomes embarrassing. Auden grew embarrassed by the aphoristic final line of a stanza in 'September 1, 1939', 'We must love one another or die',

---

[17] Elisabeth Bronfen, *The Knotted Subject: Hysteria and Its Discontents* (Princeton: Princeton University Press, 1998), 37.

[18] For another exploration of 'wit's relation to despair' in women's writing—focusing on Mina Loy's phonemic play and punning, and its failure to 'console or suffice'—see Sean Pryor, *Poetry, Modernism, and an Imperfect World* (Cambridge: Cambridge University Press, 2017), 123.

[19] Blaise Pascal, *Pensées and Other Writings*, ed. Anthony Levi, trans. Honor Levi (Oxford: Oxford World's Classics, 1999), 114.

[20] Georg Christoph Lichtenberg, *Georg Christoph Lichtenberg: Philosophical Writings*, ed. and trans. Steven Tester (Albany: State University of New York Press, 2012), 67.

168 STEVIE SMITH AND THE APHORISM

omitting or altering its gauchely bald claim at various stages after initial publication.[21] Far from indicating an increasingly autocratic attitude in Auden, which is Richard Badenhausen's argument,[22] Auden's use of aphorism may relate instead to a juggling of outsider status: an unease about whether to locate himself at the centre or in the margins, a simultaneous inhabitation of dignity and absurdity which agonizes over its right to take up space.

The aphorism's accommodation of a speaker who is or feels fundamentally at odds with the basic structures of everyday, taken-for-granted life and ways of living with other people, in ways that it may be or have been physically or emotionally unsafe to reveal unmediated, dovetails with Stevie Smith's choice to remain 'on the edge' of life, of the world, so that she could get out, as she said to Kay Dick, easily if she needed to.[23] The aphorism lingers on the edge of the community, the edge of conversation: the closing quip which shuts down proceedings, so that its speaker can gracefully (and perhaps gratefully) withdraw.

Smith's poems about hiding or sabotaging the written text, described in Chapter 1, ring true in the light of these concerns about loss and outsiderhood. Poems such as 'The Weak Monk' or texts which ask but do not answer 'What is she writing?' raise again the question of textual function and legibility. The aphorism may not just be something which it is impossible to use, but perhaps even something which it is impossible even to hear. Smith's short poem 'The Songster' depicts the gestures, the performance of speech without substance, which remains unhearable and unreadable:

> Miss Pauncefort sang at the top of her voice
> (Sing tirry-lirry-lirry down the lane)
> And nobody knew what she sang about
> (Sing tirry-lirry-lirry all the same). (CP, 20)

We do not hear Miss Pauncefort singing, but we hear singing about her. The singing we hear in the second line may at first sight seem to be her own. By the time we reach the fourth line, it becomes clear that it is instead singing from elsewhere which she is lip-syncing. The singing masquerades as hers, ultimately overrides her, urges us to sing along 'all the same' regardless of Miss Pauncefort, who may be suffering as her own voice remains unheard. Chapter 4 discussed how, in Smith's sketchbooks, her figures do not seem to mouth the words which they are supposedly saying. Here, the situation reverses.

---

[21] Edward Mendelson, *Early Auden, Later Auden: A Critical Biography* (Princeton and Oxford: Princeton University Press, 2017), 401–402.

[22] Richard Badenhausen, 'Double Take: Auden in Collaboration', in *W. H. Auden in Context*, ed. Tony Sharpe (Cambridge: Cambridge University Press, 2013), 357.

[23] Kay Dick, *Ivy and Stevie* (London: Allison & Busby, 1983), 70.

Figure C.1 Miss Pauncefort. Stevie Smith, *The Collected Poems and Drawings of Stevie Smith*, ed. Will May (London: Faber & Faber, 2015), 20. By permission of Faber and Faber Ltd and New Directions Publishing Corp.

The picture accompanying 'The Songster' positions Miss Pauncefort in the ranks of ardently declarative women in Smith's drawings, described in the introduction. It shows Miss Pauncefort with mouth wide open, hands behind her back: a good, trained singing posture which without the singing looks ridiculous or parodic (see Figure C.1). There is comedy in doing the gestures without the result; there is also pathos, and valiance.

Miss Pauncefort's dilemma, read as an act of aphoristic statement-without-power, allows us to develop critical accounts of Smith's subversive capacity. Finding aphorism in Smith makes us aware of the particular kind of work she is doing. Once we recognize her aphoristic impulse in her shorter texts, once we attend to what aphorism can do in different hands, we are able to perceive what is happening even in her longer texts: a bold statement which is also a going-away. It builds on the question we implicitly bring to Smith: what are her texts for? What are her allusions, her humour, her lightness, her pictures trying to achieve? Smith's difficulty resides in the fact that the whole point of her poems is a failure to have a rhetorical effect, disguised as something which we understand (lazily) as aimed entirely towards having a rhetorical effect.

170   STEVIE SMITH AND THE APHORISM

This is a peculiar difficulty: where something simple insists on itself but flatly refuses penetration. Smith is hard—hard to read, hard to interpret, hard to use—in more ways than one. Her language loops around refrain, cliché, quotation, aphorism, the lurid bits of proverb: language gone hard, through repeated exposure, like a baguette left out. And this sense of 'hard language' as something stale is useful: something waste or wasted. Smith's poetry has been discarded by critics even as they praise her; her language invites people to dismiss it, too simple to be interpreted, too troubling to be simply enjoyed. Her writing presents itself as something whose time has already passed, which is always-already archaic in its unusable references to obscure Victorian novels and outfitters' catalogues: running too late.

If aphorisms come too late, as witnessed in Chapter 2, they also come too early, located in an unrecoverable past. We exist only in hindsight in relation to an aphorism: its truth can only be apprehended when looking back, too late. This twilight time (again I am reminded of the weather of 'She got up and went away') is a limbo, in which everything has already been said.

This study of aphorism in Stevie Smith, as a declaration which is also a departure, has implications for our reading of women's writing of the early- to-mid-twentieth century. Jan Montefiore outlines how Smith has been passed down through a feminist critical tradition, in which the female poet is firstly marginal because female, and secondly marginal because considered inferior to the female novelist.[24] Montefiore identifies the contradiction which emerges, for readers, where this female marginality comes into conflict with the immense ambition implied by the act of writing poetry. As a result, Smith has been read as subversive, playful, tricksy: secretly moving out of this marginal position, finding ways to seize social and rhetorical power, as James Najarian suggested, while seeming to disavow any interest in it.[25] In contrast, to see her as not subversive—as earnestly saying the thing, and just as earnestly departing, enabled by the double-move of aphorism—complicates our view of women's writing. One does not need to be 'subversive' to present the world as something which one accepts completely, but at the same time unquestioningly and unflinchingly departs from. So in other words we may find—not aphorism itself, in all cases, but the sleight-of-hand which characterizes aphorism's idiosyncratic withdrawal from the scene. Aphorism offers a way of underlining the unacceptability of the status quo without bidding for power, without believing that the truth it declares will be attended to. It is no coincidence, then, that Smith's critical stock has increased in the last decade, precisely as our political understanding of speech has become more nuanced: as we have come to terms with a social context in which truth or untruth, provided they are clearly

---

[24] Jan Montefiore, *Feminism and Poetry: Language, Experience, Identity in Women's Writing* (London and New York: Pandora, 1987), 2.
[25] James Najarian, 'Contributions to Almighty Truth: Stevie Smith's Seditious Romanticism', *Twentieth-Century Literature* 49, no. 4 (2003): 472.

and emphatically declared, make no difference either way. That is the world which Smith acknowledges, visible in the 1930s as now, and on whose edge she holds herself.

The aphorism is waste (a waste of time, wasted bits discarded from a longer text). Yet it is also frugality: those bits saved, recycled, fished out of the waste bin in the belief that they might some day be worth holding on to. In that sense, as Chapter 1 hinted, the aphorism is a site of faith. We return, again and again, in the vain but compelling hope that something might be revealed: that the thing which draws our attention, unyieldingly, might one day come into focus in a way that we can grasp.

I said to my cousin, on another occasion when we had gone horseback riding
together: Do you like Death?

Caz said: He is nothing to write home about.

The wind blew then, and the sun shone, and the clouds came, and the shadows
moved across the grass; the bay leaves burnt green in the Greek pool.

—Stevie Smith, *The Holiday*

Mary Grace
1922–2018

Faisal Masud
1954–2019

Morvern
c. 2011–2022

Bibliography

Ackland, Rodney. 'Bear up Chaps'. *Spectator* 223, 30 August 1969, 271–272.

Adorno, Theodor. *Minima Moralia: Reflections on a Damaged Life*, translated by E.F.N Jephcott. London and New York: Verso, 2005.

Adorno, Theodor W. 'Parataxis: On Hölderlin's Late Poetry'. In *Notes to Literature*, Volume 2, edited by Rolf Tiedemann, translated by Shierry Weber Nicholsen, 109–149. New York: Columbia University Press, 1992.

Agamben, Giorgio. *Infancy and History: On The Destruction of Experience*, translated by Liz Heron. London and New York: Verso, 2007.

Anderson, Linda. 'Gender, Feminism, Poetry: Stevie Smith, Sylvia Plath, Jo Shapcott'. In *The Cambridge Companion to Twentieth-Century Poetry*, edited by Neil Corcoran, 173–186. Cambridge: Cambridge University Press, 2007.

'Angle Shot'. *The Tablet* 217, 15 June 1963, 656.

'aphorize, v'. OED Online. June 2017. Oxford University Press. http://www.oed.com/view/Entry/9152 (accessed September 19, 2017).

Arewa, E. Ojo, and Alan Dundes, 'Proverbs and the Ethnography of Speaking Folklore'. *American Anthropologist* 66, no. 6, pt.2 (1964): 70–85.

Auden, W. H. *As I Walked Out One Evening: Songs, Ballads, Lullabies, Limericks and other Light Verse*, edited by Edward Mendelson. London: Faber & Faber, 1995.

Auden, W. H. *Collected Poems*, edited by Edward Mendelson. London: Faber and Faber, 1991.

Auden, W. H., and Louis Kronenberger. *The Faber Book of Aphorisms*. London: Faber and Faber, 1970.

Auden, W. H. *The Prolific and the Devourer*. Hopewell: Ecco Press, 1981.

Bacon, Francis. 'The Advancement of Learning'. In *Francis Bacon: The Major Works*, edited by Brian Vickers, 120–299. Oxford: Oxford University Press, 2002.

Badenhausen, Richard. 'Double Take: Auden in Collaboration'. In *W. H. Auden in Context*, edited by Tony Sharpe, 347–358. Cambridge: Cambridge University Press, 2013.

Barbera, Jack. 'The Relevance of Stevie Smith's Drawings'. *Journal of Modern Languages* 12, no. 2 (1985): 221–236.

Barbera, Jack, and William McBrien. *Stevie: A Biography of Stevie Smith*. London: Macmillan, 1986.

Barlow, Shirley A. *The Imagery of Euripides*. London: Methuen & Co, 1971.

Barthes, Roland. 'The Photographic Message'. In *Image Music Text*, translated by Stephen Heath, 15–31. London: Fontana Press, 1977.

Barthes, Roland. 'Rhetoric of the Image'. In *Image Music Text*, translated by Stephen Heath, 32–51. London: Fontana Press, 1977.

Baudrillard, Jean. 'The System of Collecting'. In *The Cultures of Collecting*, edited by John Elsner and Roger Cardinal, 7–24. London: Reaktion Books, 1994.

Baumbach, Manuel, Andrej Petrovic, and Ivana Petrovic. 'Archaic and Classical Greek Epigram: An Introduction'. In *Archaic and Classical Greek Epigram*, edited by Manuel Baumbach, Andrej Petrovic, and Ivana Petrovic, 1–19. Cambridge: Cambridge University Press, 2010.

174 BIBLIOGRAPHY

Baumert, Ruth. 'Fear, Melancholy, and Loss in the Poetry of Stevie Smith'. In *The Abject of Desire: The Aestheticization of the Unaesthetic in Contemporary Literature and Culture*, edited by Monika Mueller and Konstanze Kutzbach, 197–219. Amsterdam and New York: Rodopi, 2007.

Bayley, John. 'Obscure Crucifixions'. *The Listener*, 25 September 1975, 409.

BBC Arts. 'WH Auden and Stevie Smith in the Pub in 1965'. BBC.co.uk. http://www.bbc.co.uk/programmes/p034md2x (accessed 15 February 2021).

BBC Third Programme. 'Poets in Public: W. H. Auden and Stevie Smith Introducing and Reading Their Own Poems'. British Library, NP884.

Bedient, Calvin. *Eight Contemporary Poets*. London: Oxford University Press, 1974.

Benjamin, Walter. *The Arcades Project*. Translated by Howard Eiland and Kevin McLaughlin. Cambridge, MA: Harvard University Press, 1999.

Benjamin, Walter. 'The Storyteller'. In *Illuminations*, translated by Harry Zorn, 83–107. London: Pimlico, 1999.

Bennett, David. 'Periodical Fragments and Organic Culture: Modernism, the Avant-Garde, and the Little Magazine'. *Contemporary Literature* 30, no. 4 (1989): 480–502.

Bennington, Geoffrey. *Sententiousness and the Novel: Laying Down the Law in Eighteenth-Century French Fiction*. Cambridge: Cambridge University Press, 1985.

Bergonzi, Bernard. 'Tones of Voice'. *The Guardian*, 16 December 1966.

Bergson, Henri. *Laughter: An Essay on the Meaning of the Comic*. Translated by Cloudesley Brereton and Fred Rothwell. London: Macmillan, 1921.

Betjeman, John. 'Something Funny'. *Daily Telegraph and Morning Post*, 12 December 1958, 15.

Blackham, H. J. *The Fable as Literature*. London and New York: Bloomsbury, 2013.

Blake, William. *Blake: The Complete Poems*, edited by W. H. Stevenson. Harlow: Pearson Education, 2007.

BLAST 1. London: John Lane, 1914.

Bluemel, Kristin. 'The Dangers of Eccentricity: Stevie Smith's Doodles and Poetry'. *Mosaic: An Interdisciplinary Critical Journal* 31, no. 3 (1998): 111–132.

Bluemel, Kristin. *George Orwell and the Radical Eccentrics: Intermodernism in Literary London*. New York: Palgrave Macmillan, 2004.

Bluemel, Kristin. '"Suburbs are not so bad I think": Stevie Smith's Problem of Place in 1930s and '40s London'. *Iowa Journal of Cultural Studies* 3, no. 1 (2003): 96–114.

Bowen, Elizabeth. 'Bright-Plumaged Brood'. *The Tatler and Bystander*, 5 October 1949, 32–33.

Boyiopoulos, Kostas, and Michael Shallcross. 'Introduction'. In *Aphoristic Modernity: 1880 to the Present*, edited by Kostas Boyiopoulos and Michael Shallcross, 1–20. Leiden: Brill, 2020.

Braddock, Jeremy. *Collecting as Modernist Practice*. Baltimore: Johns Hopkins University Press, 2012.

Brion, Marcel. 'The Idea of Time in the Work of James Joyce'. In *Our Exagmination Round His Factification For Incamination Of Work In Progress*, 23–33. London: Faber and Faber, 1929.

Brockbank, Russell. *Manifold Pressures: Motoring Misadventures of Major Upsett*. London: Temple Press, 1958.

Bronfen, Elisabeth. *The Knotted Subject: Hysteria and Its Discontents*. Princeton: Princeton University Press, 1998.

Brown, Bill. 'The Secret Life of Things (Virginia Woolf and the Matter of Modernism)'. *Modernism/modernity* 6, no. 2 (1999): 1–28.

BIBLIOGRAPHY 175

Bryant, Marsha. *Women's Poetry and Popular Culture*. New York: Palgrave Macmillan, 2011.

Bryson, Norman. *Word and Image: French Painting of the Ancien Régime*. Cambridge: Cambridge University Press, 1981.

Burke, Kenneth. 'Literature as Equipment for Living'. In *The Philosophy of Literary Form: Studies in Symbolic Action*, 2nd edn, 293–304. Baton Rouge: Louisiana State University Press, 1967.

Burnett, Anne Pippin. *Catastrophe Survived: Euripides' Plays of Mixed Reversal*. Oxford: Clarendon Press, 1971.

Burra, Peter. 'Fiction'. *Spectator* 157, 18 September 1936, 474.

Cannon, Christopher. 'Proverbs and the Wisdom of Literature: *The Proverbs of Alfred* and Chaucer's *Tale of Melibee*'. *Textual Practice* 24, no. 3 (2010): 407–434.

'Cats'. *Times Literary Supplement*, 18 September 1959, 535.

Chesterton, G. K. 'Critics and Conversation'. In *G. K. Chesterton at the Daily News: Literature, Liberalism and Revolution, 1901–1913*, Volume 1, edited by Julia Stapleton. London: Pickering & Chatto, 2012, 86–89.

Cixous, Hélène, Keith Cohen, and Paula Cohen. 'The Laugh of the Medusa'. *Signs* 1, no. 4 (1976): 875–893.

Coleridge, Samuel Taylor. *Christabel; Kubla Khan: a Vision; The Pains of Sleep*. London: John Murray, 1816.

Coleridge, Samuel Taylor. *Collected Letters of Samuel Taylor Coleridge, Volume IV, 1815–1819*, edited by Earl Leslie Griggs. Oxford: Clarendon Press, 1959.

Coleridge, Samuel Taylor. *Collected Letters of Samuel Taylor Coleridge, Volume V, 1820–1825*, edited by Earl Leslie Griggs. Oxford: Clarendon Press, 1971.

Coleridge, Samuel Taylor. *The Collected Works of Samuel Taylor Coleridge 7: Biographia Literaria, or, Biographical Sketches of my Literary Life and Opinions I*, edited by James Engell and W. Jackson Bate. Princeton: Princeton University Press, 1983.

Coleridge, Samuel Taylor. *The Collected Works of Samuel Taylor Coleridge 16: Poetical Works I: Poems (Reading Text): Part I*, edited by J. C. C. Mays. Princeton: Princeton University Press, 2001.

Compton-Burnett, Ivy. *Manservant and Maidservant*. Oxford: Oxford University Press, 1983.

Cox, C. B. 'Scots and English'. *Spectator*, 17 February 1967.

Coyle, Beverly. *A Thought to Be Rehearsed: Aphorism in Wallace Stevens's Poetry*. Ann Arbor: UMI Research Press, 1983.

Crisp, Quentin, and Donald Carroll. *Doing It With Style*. London: Eyre Methuen, 1981.

Crossan, John Dominic. *In Fragments: The Aphorisms of Jesus*. San Francisco: Harper & Row, 1983.

Culbertson, Diana. *The Poetics of Revelation: Recognition and the Narrative Tradition*. Macon GA: Mercer University Press, 1989.

Culler, Jonathan. *Theory of the Lyric*. Cambridge, MA, and London: Harvard University Press, 2015.

Cullerne-Browne, Clive. 'Letter from Anywhere'. *Hampstead and Highgate Express*, 14 November 1958.

D'Israeli, Isaac. *A Dissertation on Anecdotes; by the Author of Curiosities of Literature*. London: Kearsley and Murray, 1793.

Danius, Sara. 'Joyce's Scissors: Modernism and the Dissolution of the Event'. *New Literary History* 39, no. 4 (2008): 989–1016.

176 BIBLIOGRAPHY

Davison, Irene. *Etiquette for Women: A Book of Modern Manners and Customs*. London: C. Arthur Pearson Ltd, 1928.

Dentith, Simon. 'Thirties Poetry and the Landscape of Suburbia'. In *Rewriting the Thirties: Modernism and After*, edited by Keith Williams and Steven Matthews, 108–123. London and New York: Longman, 1997.

Derrida, Jacques. 'Aphorism Countertime'. In *Psyche: Inventions of the Other*, Volume 2, edited by Peggy Kamuf and Elizabeth Rottenberg, 127–142. Translated by Nicholas Royle. Stanford: Stanford University Press, 2008.

Derrida, Jacques. 'Fifty-two Aphorisms for a Foreword'. In *Psyche: Inventions of the Other*, Volume 2, edited by Peggy Kamuf and Elizabeth Rottenberg, 117–126. Translated by Andrew Benjamin. Stanford: Stanford University Press, 2008.

Dick, Kay. *Ivy and Stevie*. London: Allison & Busby, 1983.

Diepeveen, Leonard. *The Difficulties of Modernism*. London and New York: Routledge, 2003.

Dillon, Brian. 'Brief Encounters: The Pleasure of Aphorisms'. *Frieze* 74 (2003), https://frieze.com/article/brief-encounters, n. pag.

Dillon, Brian. *Essayism*. London: Fitzcarraldo Editions, 2017.

Doelman, James. 'Epigrams and Political Satire in Early Stuart England'. *Huntington Library Quarterly* 69, no. 1 (2006): 31–46.

Dowson, Jane, and Alice Entwistle. *A History of Twentieth-Century British Women's Poetry*. Cambridge: Cambridge University Press, 2005.

'E.B', reader's report, Stevie Smith papers, 1924–1970. Coll. No. 1976.012. McFarlin Library. Department of Special Collections and University Archives. The University of Tulsa. Series 2, Box 4, Folder 17.

Eco, Umberto. 'Wilde: Paradox and Aphorism'. In *On Literature*, translated by Martin McLaughlin, 62–83. London: Vintage, 2006.

Elias, Camelia. 'Clowns of Potentiality: Repetition and Resolution in Gertrude Stein and Emil Cioran'. *Cercles* 14 (2005): 41–56.

Elrond. 'Book Bazaar'. *Harper's Bazaar*, September 1964.

Emerson, Ralph Waldo. *Essays*. Boston: Houghton Mifflin, 1883.

Erasmus. *Collected Works of Erasmus, Adages [i] to Iv100*, translated by Margaret Mann Phillips. Toronto: University of Toronto Press, 1982.

'etiquette, n'. OED Online. June 2017. Oxford University Press, http://www.oed.com/view/Entry/64853?redirectedFrom=etiquette (accessed 17 February 2021).

Euripides. *The Complete Euripides, Volume IV: Bacchae and Other Plays*, edited by Peter Burian and Alan Shapiro. Oxford: Oxford University Press, 2009.

Euripides. *Orestes and Other Plays*, edited and translated by Philip Vellacott. Harmondsworth: Penguin, 1972.

Euripides. *Medea and Other Plays*, translated by James Morwood. Oxford: Oxford World's Classics, 1998.

F. M. 'Among the New Books'. *Natal Witness Saturday Magazine* (Pietermaritzburg, South Africa), 25 April 1959.

Faber, Marion. 'The Metamorphosis of the French Aphorism: La Rochefoucauld and Nietzsche'. *Comparative Literature Studies* 23, no. 3 (1986): 205–217.

Fagg, John. *On the Cusp: Stephen Crane, George Bellows, and Modernism*. Tuscaloosa: The University of Alabama Press, 2009.

Ferrebe, Alice. *Literature of the 1950s: Good, Brave Causes*. Edinburgh: Edinburgh University Press, 2012.

Fox, Michael V. *Proverbs 10–31: A New Translation with Introduction and Commentary.* New Haven and London: Yale University Press, 2009.

François, Anne-Lise. *Open Secrets: The Literature of Uncounted Experience.* Stanford: Stanford University Press, 2008.

Frey, Hans-Jost. *Interruptions,* translated by Georgia Albert. New York: State University of New York Press, 1996.

Frost, Robert. *The Poetry of Robert Frost,* edited by Edward Connery Lathem. London: Vintage, 2001.

Geary, James. *The World in a Phrase: A Brief History of the Aphorism.* New York: Bloomsbury, 2005.

Gilbert, W. S. 'Preface'. In *The 'Bab' Ballads: Much Sound and Little Sense,* v–vi. London: John Camden Hotten, 1869.

Gingrich, Arnold. *Esquire Cartoon Album.* London: Heinemann, 1958.

Glendinning, Victoria. *Edith Sitwell: A Unicorn Among Lions.* London: Phoenix, 1993.

Goldhill, Simon. *Reading Greek Tragedy.* Cambridge: Cambridge University Press, 1986.

Gombrich, E. H. *Meditations on a Hobby Horse and Other Essays on the Theory of Art.* London: Phaidon Press, 1963.

Grant, Ben. *The Aphorism and Other Short Forms.* London and New York: Routledge, 2016.

Gray, Richard T. *Constructive Destruction: Kafka's Aphorisms: Literary Tradition and Literary Transformation.* Tübingen: Niemeyer, 1987.

Greene, Richard. *Edith Sitwell: Avant-Garde Poet, English Genius.* London: Virago, 2011.

Gregory, Eileen. *H.D. and Hellenism: Classic Lines.* Cambridge: Cambridge University Press, 1997.

Grigson, Geoffrey, ed. *The Faber Book of Epigrams and Epitaphs.* London: Faber & Faber, 1977.

Grimm, Jacob and Wilhelm. *Household Stories,* translated by E. H. Wehnert. London: David Bogue, 1857.

Gross, John, ed. *The Oxford Book of Aphorisms.* Oxford: Oxford University Press, 1983.

Gross, John. 'Ruthless Rhymes'. Observer, 11 December 1966.

Halleran, Michael R. 'Episodes'. In *A Companion to Greek Tragedy,* edited by Justina Gregory, 167–182. Malden, MA and Oxford: Blackwell, 2005.

Halliday, Mark. 'Stevie Smith's Serious Comedy'. *Humor* 22, no. 3 (2009): 295–315.

Harries, Elizabeth Wanning. *The Unfinished Manner: Essays on the Fragment in the Later Eighteenth Century.* Charlottesville and London: University Press of Virginia, 1994.

Harvey, Robert C. 'How Comics Came to Be'. In *A Comics Studies Reader,* edited by Jeet Heer and Kent Worcester, 25–45. Jackson: University Press of Mississippi, 2009.

H.D. *Collected Poems 1912–1944,* edited by Louis L. Martz. New York: New Directions, 1984.

Heaney, Seamus. 'Introduction'. In *Beowulf: A New Translation,* translated by Seamus Heaney, ix–xxx. London: Faber & Faber, 1999.

Heath, Malcolm. *The Poetics of Greek Tragedy.* Stanford, CA: Stanford University Press, 1987.

Hoffman, Daniel. 'Two Cases of Double Vision'. *New York Times,* 6 December 1970.

Horder, Mervyn, to Stevie Smith. Stevie Smith papers, 1924–1970. Coll. No. 1976.012. McFarlin Library. Department of Special Collections and University Archives. The University of Tulsa. Series 1, Box 3, Folder 2.

Horovitz, Michael. 'Of Absent Friends'. In *In Search of Stevie Smith,* edited by Sanford Sternlicht, 147–165. Syracuse: Syracuse University Press, 1991.

178 BIBLIOGRAPHY

Hotz-Davies, Ingrid. '"My Name is Finis": The Lonely Voice of Stevie Smith'. In *In Black and Gold: Contiguous Traditions in Post-War British and Irish Poetry*, edited by C. C. Barfoot, 219–234. Amsterdam and Atlanta, GA: Rodopi B.V., 1994.

'How to Be Happy'. *Home Notes*, 12 July 1930.

Hui, Andrew. *A Theory of the Aphorism*. Princeton and Oxford: Princeton University Press, 2019.

Huk, Romana. 'Eccentric Concentrism: Traditional Poetic Forms and Refracted Discourse in Stevie Smith's Poetry'. *Contemporary Literature* 34, no. 2 (1993): 240–265.

Huk, Romana. 'Poetic Subject and Voice as Sites of Struggle: Toward a "Postrevisionist" Reading of Stevie Smith's Fairy-Tale Poems'. In *Dwelling in Possibility: Women Poets and Critics on Poetry*, edited by Yopie Prins and Maeera Shreiber, 147–165. Ithaca and London: Cornell University Press, 1997.

Huk, Romana. *Stevie Smith: Between the Lines*. Basingstoke: Palgrave Macmillan, 2005.

Huk, Romana. 'On "the Beat Inevitable": The Ballad'. In *A Companion to Poetic Genre*, edited by Erik Martiny, 117–138. Oxford: Wiley Blackwell: 2012.

'Humour'. *Times Literary Supplement*, 8 May 1937.

James, Stephen. 'Stevie Smith, "A Most Awful Twister"'. *Essays in Criticism* 66, no. 2 (2016): 242–259.

Joyce, James. *Finnegans Wake*, edited by Robbert-Jan Henkes, Erik Bindervoet, and Finn Fordham. Oxford: Oxford University Press, 2012.

Joyce, James. 'Fragment from 'Work in Progress'. *transition* 27 (April–May 1938): 59–78.

Joyce, James. *Stephen Hero*, edited by Theodore Spencer. London: Jonathan Cape, 1956.

Kennedy, Clare. *Paradox, Aphorism and Desire in Novalis and Derrida*. London: MHRA, 2008.

Kinney, Arthur F. *Dorothy Parker*. Boston: Twayne, 1978.

Knowlton, Eloise. *Joyce, Joyceans, and the Rhetoric of Citation*. Gainesville: University Press of Florida, 1998.

Kraus, Karl. 'Abfälle'. *Die Fackel* 198, 12 March 1906.

Kraus, Karl. *Half Truths and One-and-a-Half Truths: Karl Kraus: Selected Aphorisms*, edited and translated by Harry Zohn. Manchester: Carcanet, 1986.

Larkin, Philip. 'Frivolous and Vulnerable'. In *Required Writing: Miscellaneous Pieces 1955–1982*, 153–158. London: Faber & Faber, 1983.

Lassner, Phyllis. 'A Cry for Life: Storm Jameson, Stevie Smith, and the Fate of Europe's Jews'. In *Visions of War: World War II in Popular Literature and Culture*, edited by M. Paul Holsinger and Mary Anne Schofield, 181–190. Bowling Green: Bowling Green State University Popular Press, 1992.

Lassner, Phyllis. *British Women Writers of World War II: Battlegrounds of their Own*. London and Basingstoke: Macmillan, 1998.

Lawrence, D. H. *Apocalypse and the Writings on Revelation*, edited by Mara Kalnins. Cambridge: Cambridge University Press, 1980.

Lewis, Philip E. *La Rochefoucauld: The Art of Abstraction*. Ithaca and London: Cornell University Press, 1977.

Lichtenberg, Georg Christoph. *Georg Christoph Lichtenberg: Philosophical Writings*, edited and translated by Steven Tester. Albany: State University of New York Press, 2012.

Liebenberg, Jacobus. *The Language of the Kingdom and Jesus*. Berlin: Walter de Gruyter, 2001.

'Light but not Slight'. *Times Literary Supplement*, 28 December 1962, 1006.

BIBLIOGRAPHY   179

Litz, A. Walton. 'Epiphanies: Introduction'. In James Joyce, *Poems and Shorter Writings*, edited by Richard Ellman, A. Walton Litz, and John Whittier-Ferguson, 157–160. London: Faber & Faber, 1991.

Lively, Penelope. 'Introduction'. In Ivy Compton-Burnett, *Manservant and Maidservant*, v–xii. Oxford: Oxford University Press, 1983.

Livingstone, Niall, and Gideon Nisbet. *Epigram*. Cambridge: Cambridge University Press, 2010.

Llona, Victor. 'I Dont Know What To Call It But Its Mighty Unlike Prose'. In *Our Exagmination Round His Factification For Incamination Of Work In Progress*, 93–102. London: Faber and Faber, 1929.

Lloyd, Michael. *The Agon in Euripides*. Oxford and New York: Oxford University Press, 1992.

Loriot. *Dog's Best Friend*. London: Hammond Hammond, 1958.

Loy, Mina. *The Lost Lunar Baedeker*. Manchester: Carcanet, 1997.

Loy, Mina. 'Mina Loy Interview with Paul Blackburn and Robert Vas Dias'. In *Mina Loy: Woman and Poet*, edited by Maeera Shreiber and Keith Tuma. Orono, Maine: National Poetry Foundation, 1998. 205–243.

Lüthi, Max. *The European Folktale: Form and Nature*, translated by John D. Niles. Philadelphia: Institute for the Study of Human Issues, 1982.

Lüthi, Max. *Once Upon A Time: On the Nature of Fairy Tales*, translated by Lee Chadeayne and Paul Gottwald. New York: Frederick Ungar, 1970.

Lutyens, Elisabeth. *A Goldfish Bowl*. London: Cassell, 1972.

MacNeice, Louis. *Modern Poetry*. Oxford: Oxford University Press, 1938.

Mallot, J. Edward. 'Not Drowning But Waving: Stevie Smith and the Language of the Lake'. *Journal of Modern Literature* 27, no. 1/2 (2003): 171–187.

Mann, Joel E. *Hippocrates, On the Art of Medicine*. Leiden and Boston: Brill, 2012.

Mansfield, Katherine. 'Aphorisms'. In *The Edinburgh Edition of the Collected Works of Katherine Mansfield, Volume 3: The Poetry and Critical Writings of Katherine Mansfield*, edited by Gerri Kimber and Angela Smith, 416–421. Edinburgh: Edinburgh University Press, 2014.

Mao, Douglas. *Solid Objects: Modernism and the Test of Production*. Princeton: Princeton University Press, 1998.

Marangoni, Kristen. '"Not Waving": Miscommunication Between Stevie Smith's Poems and Drawings'. In *Picturing the Language of Images*, edited by Nancy Pedri and Laurence Petit, 163–176. Newcastle upon Tyne: Cambridge Scholars Publishing, 2013.

Marcus, Laura. 'The Short Fiction'. In *A Companion to Virginia Woolf*, edited by Jessica Berman, 29–39. Chichester: Wiley-Blackwell, 2016.

Masud, Noreen. '"Ach ja": Stevie Smith's Escheresque Metamorphoses'. *Cambridge Quarterly* 45, no. 3 (2016): 244–267.

May, Will. 'An Eye for an I: Constructing the Visual in the Work of Stevie Smith'. In *From Self to Shelf: The Artist Under Construction*, edited by Sally Bayley and William May, 76–86. Newcastle: Cambridge Scholars Publishing, 2007.

May, Will. 'Drawing Away from Lear: Stevie Smith's Deceitful Echo'. In *Edward Lear and the Play of Poetry*, edited by Matthew Bevis and James Williams, 316–338. Oxford: Oxford University Press, 2016.

May, Will. *Stevie Smith and Authorship*. Oxford: Oxford University Press, 2010.

May, Will. 'The Untimely Stevie Smith'. *Women: A Cultural Review* 29, no. 3–4 (2018): 381–397.

180 BIBLIOGRAPHY

May, Will. 'Verbal and Visual Art in Twentieth-Century British Women's Poetry'. In *The Cambridge Companion to Twentieth-Century British and Irish Women's Poetry*, edited by Jane Dowson, 42–61. Cambridge: Cambridge University Press, 2011.

Mendelson, Edward. *Early Auden, Later Auden: A Critical Biography*. Princeton and Oxford: Princeton University Press, 2017.

Mieder, Wolfgang. *American Proverbs: A Study of Texts and Contexts*. Bern: Peter Lang, 1989.

Mieder, Wolfgang. '"Ever Eager to Incorporate Folk Proverbs": Wilhelm Grimm's Proverbial Additions in the Fairy Tales'. In *The Brothers Grimm and Folktale*, edited by James M. McGlathery with Larry W. Danielson, Ruth E. Lorbe, and Selma K. Richardson, 112–132. Urbana and Chicago: University of Illinois Press, 1988.

Miller, Betty. *Farewell Leicester Square*. London: Robert Hale, 1941.

Mitchell, W. J. T. 'Beyond Comparison'. In *A Comics Studies Reader*, edited by Jeet Heer and Kent Worcester, 116–123. Jackson: University Press of Mississippi, 2009.

Montefiore, Jan. *Feminism and Poetry: Language, Experience, Identity in Women's Writing*. London and New York: Pandora, 1987.

Moretti, Franco. *Modern Epic: The World System from Goethe to García Márquez*, translated by Quintin Hoare. London and New York: Verso, 1996.

Morson, Gary Saul. 'The Aphorism: Fragments from the Breakdown of Reason'. *New Literary History* 34, no. 3 (2003): 409–429.

Mourant, Chris. 'We Moderns: Katherine Mansfield and Edwin Muir in the *New Age*'. In *Aphoristic Modernity: 1880 to the Present*, edited by Kostas Boyiopoulos and Michael Shallcross, 94–112. Leiden: Brill, 2020.

Muensterberger, Werner. *Collecting: An Unruly Passion*. Princeton: Princeton University Press, 1994.

Muldoon, Paul. *The End of the Poem: Oxford Lectures on Poetry*. London: Faber & Faber, 2006.

Munton, Alan. '"You must remain broken up": Wyndham Lewis, Laughter, and the Subjective Aphorism'. In *Aphoristic Modernity: 1880 to the Present*, edited by Kostas Boyiopoulos and Michael Shallcross, 113–132. Leiden: Brill, 2020.

Muratore, Mary J. 'Deceived by Truth: The Maxim as a Discourse of Deception in *La Princesse de Clèves*'. *Zeitschrift für Französische Sprache und Literatur* 104 (1994): 29–37.

Najarian, James. 'Contributions to Almighty Truth: Stevie Smith's Seditious Romanticism'. *Twentieth-Century Literature* 49, no. 4 (2003): 472–493.

National Gallery Trafalgar Square Catalogue. 86th edn. London, 1929.

Nehamas, Alexander. *Nietzsche: Life as Literature*. Cambridge, MA and London: Harvard University Press, 1985.

Nel, Philip Johannes. *The Structure and Ethos of the Wisdom Admonitions in Proverbs*. Berlin and New York: Walter de Gruyter, 1982.

Nicholson, Bob. 'Jonathan's Jokes: American Humour in the Late-Victorian Press'. *Media History* 18, no. 1 (2012): 33–49.

Nietzsche, Friedrich. *Beyond Good and Evil*, edited and translated by Marion Faber. Oxford: Oxford University Press, 1998.

Nietzsche, Friedrich. *Beyond Good and Evil: Prelude to a Philosophy of the Future*, translated by Helen Zimmern. Edinburgh: Darien Press, 1907.

Nietzsche, Friedrich. *Human, All Too Human*, translated by Marion Faber and Stephen Lehmann. London: Penguin, 1994.

Nietzsche, Friedrich. *On The Genealogy of Morals*, translated by Douglas Smith. Oxford: Oxford University Press, 1996.

Novitz, David. *Pictures and their Use in Communication: A Philosophical Essay*. The Hague: Martinus Nijhoff, 1977.

Oesterley, W. O. E. *The Book of Proverbs: With Introduction and Notes*. London: Methuen, 1929.

Orr, Peter. 'Stevie Smith'. In *In Search of Stevie Smith*, edited by Sanford Sternlicht, 31–37. Syracuse: Syracuse University Press, 1991.

Ovid. *Metamorphoses: Volume I*, translated by Frank Justus Miller. London: William Heinemann, 1960.

Pagliaro, Harold E. 'Paradox In The Aphorisms Of La Rochefoucauld And Some Representative English Followers'. *PMLA* 79, no. 1 (1964): 42–50.

Parker, Dorothy, George S. Chappell, and Frank Crowninshield. *High Society: Advice as to Social Campaigning, and Hints on the Management of Dowagers, Dinners, Debutantes, Dances, and the Thousand and One Diversions of Persons of Quality*. New York and London: The Knickerbocker Press, 1920.

Parker, Dorothy. 'Preface [to Men, Women and Dogs]'. In James Thurber, *Vintage Thurber: Volume I*, 245–247. Harmondsworth: Penguin, 1983.

Pascal, Blaise. *Pensées and Other Writings*, edited by Anthony Levi, translated by Honor Levi. Oxford: Oxford World's Classics, 1999.

Pearce, Susan M. *On Collecting: An Investigation into Collecting in the European Tradition*. London and New York: Routledge, 1995.

Pearson's Weekly 1539, 10 January 1920.

Pero, Allan. 'A Fugue on Camp'. *Modernism/modernity* 23, no. 1 (2016): 28–36.

Perris, Simon R (2011). 'What Maketh The Messenger? Reportage in Greek Tragedy'. In ASCS 32 *Proceedings*, edited by Anne Mackay, available at http://www.ascs.org.au/news/ascs32/Perris.pdf (accessed 28 January 2021).

Perry, Seamus. *Coleridge and the Uses of Division*. Oxford: Clarendon Press, 1999.

Perry, Seamus. 'Coleridge's Literary Influence'. In *The Oxford Handbook of Samuel Taylor Coleridge*, edited by Frederick Burwick, 661–676. Oxford: Oxford University Press, 2009.

P. G. B. K, *Granta* 46, 5 May 1937.

'Picture Books'. *Spectator* 201, 21 November 1958, 730.

Piette, Adam. 'Travel Writing and the Imperial Subject in 1930s Prose: Waugh, Bowen, Smith, and Orwell'. In *Issues in Travel Writing: Empire, Spectacle, and Displacement*, edited by Kristi Siegel, 53–65. New York: Peter Lang, 2002.

Plain, Gill. *Women's Fiction of the Second World War: Gender, Power and Resistance*. Edinburgh: Edinburgh University Press, 1996.

Plath, Sylvia, to Stevie Smith. Stevie Smith papers, 1924–1970. Coll. No. 1976.012. McFarlin Library. Department of Special Collections and University Archives. The University of Tulsa. Series 1, Box 7, Folder 2.

Pope, Ged. *Reading London's Suburbs: From Charles Dickens to Zadie Smith*. London: Palgrave Macmillan, 2015.

Pound, Ezra. 'A Retrospect'. In *Modernism: An Anthology of Sources and Documents*, edited by Vassiliki Kolocotroni, Jane Goodman and Olga Taxidou, 373–382. Edinburgh: Edinburgh University Press, 1998.

Pryor, Sean. *Poetry, Modernism, and an Imperfect World*. Cambridge: Cambridge University Press, 2017.

182   BIBLIOGRAPHY

Pumphrey, Martin. 'Play, Fantasy, and Strange Laughter: Stevie Smith's Uncomfortable Poetry'. In *In Search of Stevie Smith*, edited by Sanford Sternlicht, 97–113. Syracuse: Syracuse University Press, 1991.

Rajan, Balachandra. *The Form of the Unfinished: English Poetics from Spenser to Pound*. Princeton: Princeton University Press, 1985.

Randall, Bryony. '"Give him your word": Legal and Literary Interpretation in Stevie Smith's "The Story of a Story"'. *Law and Literature* 21, no. 2 (2009): 234–256.

Rankin, Arthur C. *The Poetry of Stevie Smith: 'Little Girl Lost'*. Gerrards Cross: Colin Smythe Ltd., 1985.

Rare Bits 36, 5 August 1882.

Reader, Simon. 'Social Notes: Oscar Wilde, Francis Bacon, and the Medium of Aphorism'. *Journal of Victorian Culture* 18, no. 4 (2013): 453–471.

Rees-Jones, Deryn. *Consorting with Angels: Essays on Modern Women Poets*. Tarset: Bloodaxe, 2005.

Ricks, Christopher. *Keats and Embarrassment*. Oxford: Clarendon Press, 1974.

Ricks, Christopher. *T. S. Eliot and Prejudice*. London: Faber and Faber, 1988.

Riley, Denise. 'On the Lapidary Style'. *d i f f e r e n c e s* 28, no. 1 (2017): 17–36.

Risteen, Eleanor Gordon. 'Daddy, Mummy and Stevie: The Child-Guise in Stevie Smith's Poetry'. *Modern Poetry Studies* 11 (1983): 232–244.

Robinson, Peter. 'Aphoristic Gaps and Theories of the Image'. In *Aphoristic Modernity: 1880 to the Present*, edited by Kostas Boyiopoulos and Michael Shallcross, 21–36. Leiden: Brill, 2020.

de La Rochefoucauld, François. *Collected Maxims and Other Reflections*, translated by E. H. and A. M. Blackmore and Francine Giguère. Oxford: Oxford University Press, 2007.

Roth, Wolfgang. *Numerical Sayings in the Old Testament: A Form-Critical Study*. Leiden: Brill, 1965.

Roth, Wolfgang M. W. 'The Numerical Sequence x/x + 1 in the Old Testament'. *Vetus Testamentum* 12, no. 3 (1962): 300–311.

Sage, Robert. 'Before Ulysses—And After'. In *Our Exagmination Round His Factification For Incamination Of Work In Progress*, 147–170. London: Faber and Faber, 1929.

Sandy, Mark. '"A Ruin Amidst Ruins": Modernity, Literary Aphorisms, and Romantic Fragments'. In *Aphoristic Modernity: 1890 to the Present*. Edited by Kostas Boyiopoulos and Michael Shallcross, 37–52. Leiden: Brill, 2020.

Sayeau, Michael. *Against the Event: The Everyday and the Evolution of Modernist Narrative*. Oxford: Oxford University Press, 2013.

Sayers, Dorothy L. *Gaudy Night*. London: Hodder & Stoughton, 1970.

Schlegel, Friedrich. *Lucinde and the Fragments*, translated by Peter Firchow. Minneapolis: University of Minnesota Press, 1971.

Scott, R. B. Y. *The Way of Wisdom in the Old Testament*. London and New York: Macmillan, 1971.

Seaford, Richard. *Euripides: Bacchae*. Warminster: Aris & Phillips, 1996.

Sedgwick, Eve Kosofsky. 'Paranoid Reading and Reparative Reading, or, You're So Paranoid, You Probably Think This Essay Is About You'. In *Touching Feeling: Affect, Pedagogy, Performativity*, 123–152. London: Duke University Press, 2003.

Segal, Charles. 'Introduction [to *Bacchae*]'. In *The Complete Euripides, Volume IV: Bacchae and Other Plays*, edited by Peter Burian and Alan Shapiro, 201–231. Oxford: Oxford University Press, 2009.

Sellers, Susan. *Myth and Fairy Tale in Contemporary Women's Fiction*. Basingstoke: Palgrave, 2001.

BIBLIOGRAPHY   183

Severin, Laura. 'Becoming and Unbecoming: Stevie Smith as Performer'. *Text and Performance Quarterly* 18, no. 1 (1998): 22–36.

Severin, Laura. *Poetry Off the Page: Twentieth-Century British Women Poets in Performance.* Farnham: Ashgate, 2004.

Severin, Laura. *Stevie Smith's Resistant Antics.* Madison: University of Wisconsin Press, 1997.

Shattuck, Roger. 'The Alphabet and the Junkyard'. In *The Innocent Eye: On Modern Literature and the Arts,* 32–39. New York: Farrar, Straus and Giroux, 1984.

Siegel, Sandra. 'Wilde's Use and Abuse of Aphorisms'. *Newsletter of the Victorian Studies Association of Western Canada* 12, no. 1 (1986): 16–26.

Sims Steward, Julie. 'Ceci n'est pas un Hat: Stevie Smith and the Refashioning of Gender'. *South Central Review* 15, no. 2 (1998): 16–33.

Sims Steward, Julie. 'Pandora's Playbox: Stevie Smith's Drawings and the Construction of Gender'. *Journal of Modern Literature* 22, no. 1 (1998): 69–91.

Sims Steward, Julie. 'The Problem of the Body in Stevie Smith's Body of Work'. *South Atlantic Review* 70, no. 2 (2005): 72–95.

Siné. *Scatty: British Cats, French Cats and Cosmopolitan Cats.* London: Max Reinhardt, 1958.

Sitwell, Edith. *English Eccentrics.* London: The Folio Society, 1994.

Smith, Stevie. 'Beyond Words'. Stevie Smith papers, 1924–1970. Coll. No. 1976.012. McFarlin Library. Department of Special Collections and University Archives. The University of Tulsa. Series 2, Box 1, Folder 7.

Smith, Stevie. 'The Castle', typescript. Stevie Smith papers, 1924–1970. Coll. No. 1976.012. McFarlin Library. Department of Special Collections and University Archives. The University of Tulsa. Series 2, Box 2, Folder 9.

Smith, Stevie. Fairytale, unfinished. Stevie Smith papers, 1924–1970. Coll. No. 1976.012. McFarlin Library. Department of Special Collections and University Archives. The University of Tulsa. Series 5, Box 1, Folder 7.

Smith, Stevie. 'Father, I have had enough'. Stevie Smith papers, 1924–1970. Coll. No. 1976.012. McFarlin Library. Department of Special Collections and University Archives. The University of Tulsa. Series 2, Box 1, Folder 11.

Smith, Stevie. *A Good Time Was Had by All.* London: Jonathan Cape, 1937.

Smith, Stevie. *The Holiday,* typescript. Stevie Smith papers, 1924–1970. Coll. No. 1976.012. McFarlin Library. Department of Special Collections and University Archives. The University of Tulsa. Series 2, Box 2, Folders 15–17.

Smith, Stevie. 'The House of Over-Dew', introduction. Stevie Smith papers, 1924–1970. Coll. No. 1976.012. McFarlin Library. Department of Special Collections and University Archives. The University of Tulsa. Series 2, Box 1, Folder 4.

Smith, Stevie. 'I rode with my darling ... ', typescript. Stevie Smith papers, 1924–1970. Coll. No. 1976.012. McFarlin Library. Department of Special Collections and University Archives. The University of Tulsa. Series 2, Box 2, Folder 10.

Smith, Stevie. Interview with Patrick Garland. Stevie Smith papers, 1924–1970. Coll. No. 1976.012. McFarlin Library. Department of Special Collections and University Archives. The University of Tulsa. Series 3, 1:24A.

Smith, Stevie. Letter to Helen Fowler, 30 May 1952. Stevie Smith papers, 1924–1970. Coll. No. 1976.012. McFarlin Library. Department of Special Collections and University Archives. The University of Tulsa. Series 1, Box 3, Folder 7.

184   BIBLIOGRAPHY

Smith, Stevie. 'Modern English Literature'. Stevie Smith papers, 1924–1970. Coll. No. 1976.012. McFarlin Library. Department of Special Collections and University Archives. The University of Tulsa. Series 2, Box 3, Folder 9.

Smith, Stevie. Note, pencilled. Stevie Smith papers, 1924–1970. Coll. No. 1976.012. McFarlin Library. Department of Special Collections and University Archives. The University of Tulsa. Series 2, Box 1, Folder 1.

Smith, Stevie. Notebook, black. Stevie Smith papers, 1924–1970. Coll. No. 1976.012. McFarlin Library. Department of Special Collections and University Archives. The University of Tulsa. Series 2, Box 9, Folder 1.

Smith, Stevie. Notebook, red. Stevie Smith papers, 1924–1970. Coll. No. 1976.012. McFarlin Library. Department of Special Collections and University Archives. The University of Tulsa. Series 2, Box 9, Folder 1.

Smith, Stevie. 'Oh stubborn race of Cadmus' seed ... ', performance introductions. Stevie Smith papers, 1924–1970. Coll. No. 1976.012. McFarlin Library. Department of Special Collections and University Archives. The University of Tulsa. Series 2, Box 2, Folder 11.

Smith, Stevie. 'The Poet and the Pussycat'. Stevie Smith papers, 1924–1970. Coll. No. 1976.012. McFarlin Library. Department of Special Collections and University Archives. The University of Tulsa. Series 2, Box 5, Folder 5.

Smith, Stevie. Reading journal. Stevie Smith papers, 1924–1970. Coll. No. 1976.012. McFarlin Library. Department of Special Collections and University Archives. The University of Tulsa. Series 5, Box 1, Folder 6.

Smith, Stevie. 'World of Books', typescript. Stevie Smith papers, 1924–1970. Coll. No. 1976.012. McFarlin Library. Department of Special Collections and University Archives. The University of Tulsa. Series 2, Box 6, Folder 20.

Smith, Stevie. *Novel on Yellow Paper*, typescript. U DP-156-1, Stevie Smith Papers 1935–1969, Hull History Centre.

Smith, Stevie. 'Art'. In *London Guyed*, edited by William Kimber, 153–164. London: Hutchinson, 1938.

Smith, Stevie. 'At School'. In *Me Again: The Uncollected Writings of Stevie Smith*, edited by Jack Barbera and William McBrien, 119–124. London: Virago, 1981.

Smith, Stevie, ed. *The Batsford Book of Children's Verse*. London: Batsford, 1970.

Smith, Stevie. 'Beside the Seaside: A Holiday with Children'. In *Me Again: The Uncollected Writings of Stevie Smith*, edited by Jack Barbera and William McBrien, 13–25. London: Virago, 1981.

Smith, Stevie. *British Poets of Our Time: Stevie Smith, Adrian Mitchell: Poems Read by the Authors*, edited by Alan Brownjohn and Charles Osborne. Argo Record Company, 1973.

Smith, Stevie. *Cats in Colour*. London: Batsford, 1959.

Smith, Stevie. *The Collected Poems and Drawings of Stevie Smith*, edited by Will May. London: Faber & Faber, 2015.

Smith, Stevie. 'History or Poetic Drama?' In *Me Again: The Uncollected Writings of Stevie Smith*, edited by Jack Barbera and William McBrien, 148–152. London: Virago, 1981.

Smith, Stevie. *The Holiday*. London: Virago, 1979.

Smith, Stevie. 'The Ironing-Board of Widow Twanky'. *Queen* 219, 20 December 1961, 11.

Smith, Stevie. 'Is There A Life Beyond The Gravy?' In *Me Again: The Uncollected Writings of Stevie Smith*, edited by Jack Barbera and William McBrien, 60–73. London: Virago, 1981.

Smith, Stevie. 'A London Suburb'. In *Me Again: The Uncollected Writings of Stevie Smith*, edited by Jack Barbera and William McBrien, 100–104. London: Virago, 1981.

BIBLIOGRAPHY 185

Smith, Stevie. *Me Again: The Uncollected Writings of Stevie Smith*, edited by Jack Barbera and William McBrien. London: Virago, 1981.

Smith, Stevie. 'My Muse'. In *Me Again: The Uncollected Writings of Stevie Smith*, edited by Jack Barbera and William McBrien, 125–126. London: Virago, 1981.

Smith, Stevie. *Novel on Yellow Paper*. London: Virago, 2015.

Smith, Stevie. *Over the Frontier*. London: Virago, 1980.

Smith, Stevie. 'Party Views'. *Listener* 77, 25 May 1967, 690–691.

Smith, Stevie. 'Simply Living'. In *Me Again: The Uncollected Writings of Stevie Smith*, edited by Jack Barbera and William McBrien, 108–110. London: Virago, 1981.

Smith, Stevie. *Some Are More Human Than Others*. London: Peter Owen, 1990.

Smith, Stevie. *Stevie Smith Reads and Comments on Selected Poems*, introduced by Iain Crichton Smith. Recorded 30 July 1965. Marvell Press, 1965, LP.

Smith, Stevie. 'Syler's Green: A Return Journey'. In *Me Again: The Uncollected Writings of Stevie Smith*, edited by Jack Barbera and William McBrien, 83–99. London: Virago, 1981.

Smith, Stevie. 'A Turn Outside'. In *Me Again: The Uncollected Writings of Stevie Smith*, edited by Jack Barbera and William McBrien, 335–358. London: Virago, 1981.

Smith, Stevie. *Two in One: Selected Poems and The Frog Prince and Other Poems*. London: Longman, 1971.

Smith, Stevie. 'What Poems Are Made Of'. In *Me Again: The Uncollected Writings of Stevie Smith*, edited by Jack Barbera and William McBrien, 127–129. London: Virago, 1981.

Snider, Alvin. 'Francis Bacon and the Authority of Aphorism'. *Prose Studies* 11, no. 2 (1988): 60–71.

Sommerstein, Alan H. 'Tragedy and Myth'. In *A Companion to Tragedy*, edited by Rebecca Bushnell, 163–180. Oxford: Blackwell, 2005.

Sontag, Susan. *As Consciousness is Harnessed to Flesh: Diaries 1964–1980*, edited by David Rieff. London: Penguin, 2012.

Sontag, Susan. 'Notes on "Camp"'. In *Against Interpretation*, 275–292. London: Vintage, 2001.

Sontag, Susan. *Regarding the Pain of Others*. London: Penguin, 2003.

Sophocles. *The Three Theban Plays: Antigone, Oedipus the King, Oedipus at Colonus*, translated by Robert Fagles. Harmondsworth: Penguin, 1984.

Spackman, Barbara. 'Machiavelli and Maxims'. *Yale French Studies* 77 (1990): 137–155.

Spalding, Frances. *Stevie Smith: A Critical Biography*. London: Faber and Faber, 1988.

Spencer, Herbert. 'Manners and Fashion'. In *Essays: Scientific, Political, and Speculative, Vol 1*, 61–115. London: Williams and Norgate, 1868.

Sprigge, Elizabeth. *The Life of Ivy Compton-Burnett*. London: Victor Gollancz, 1973.

Stedman, Jane W. *W. S. Gilbert: A Classic Victorian and his Theatre*. Oxford: Oxford University Press, 1996.

Stern, J. P. *Lichtenberg: A Doctrine of Scattered Occasions*. Bloomington: Indiana University Press, 1959.

Stevenson, Sheryl. 'Stevie Smith's Voices'. *Contemporary Literature* 33, no. 1 (1992): 24–45.

Stewart, Susan. *On Longing: Narratives of the Miniature, the Gigantic, the Souvenir, the Collection*. Durham and London: Duke University Press, 1993.

Stonier, G. W. 'The Music Goes Round and Round'. *New Statesman*, 17 April 1937.

Strathman, Christopher A. *Romantic Poetry and the Fragmentary Imperative: Schlegel, Byron, Joyce, Blanchot*. Albany: State University of New York Press, 2006.

186 BIBLIOGRAPHY

Swann, Bruce W. *Martial's Catullus: The Reception of an Epigrammatic Rival*. Zürich and New York: George Olms, 1994.

Tatar, Maria. 'Beauties vs. Beasts in the Grimms' *Nursery and Household Tales*'. In *The Brothers Grimm and Folktale*, edited by James M. McGlathery, with Larry W. Danielson, Ruth E. Lorbe, and Selma K. Richardson, 133–145. Urbana and Chicago: University of Illinois Press, 1988.

Tatar, Maria. *The Hard Facts of the Grimms' Fairy Tales*. Princeton: Princeton University Press, 2003.

Tester, Steven. 'Introduction'. In Georg Christoph Lichtenberg, *Georg Christoph Lichtenberg: Philosophical Writings*, edited and translated by Steven Tester, 1–28. Albany: State University of New York Press, 2012.

Teverson, Andrew. *Fairy Tale*. Abingdon: Routledge, 2013.

Thurber, James. *Vintage Thurber: Volume I*. Harmondsworth: Penguin, 1983.

'Tit-Bits'. *Tit-Bits* 1, 22 October 1881, 1.

Tucker, Lauryl. 'Progeny and Parody: Narcissus and Echo in Stevie Smith's Poems'. *Twentieth-Century Literature* 60, no. 3 (2014): 336–366.

Van Thal, Herbert. 'New Novels'. *Books of the Month*, September 1949.

van Tongeren, Paul J. M. *Reinterpreting Modern Culture: An Introduction to Friedrich Nietzsche's Philosophy*. West Lafayette, Indiana: Purdue University Press, 2000.

[Marquis of] Vauvenargues, Luc de Clapiers. *The Reflections and Maxims*, translated by F. G. Stevens. London: Humphrey Milford, 1940.

Verbeke, Demmy. 'On Knowing Greek (And Latin): Classical Elements in the Poetry of Stevie Smith'. *International Journal of the Classical Tradition* 16, no. 3/4 (2009): 467–483.

Walasek, Helen. *The Best of Punch Cartoons*. London: Prion, 2008.

Wallace, Jennifer. *The Cambridge Introduction to Tragedy*. Cambridge: Cambridge University Press, 2007.

'Wastrels, Pirates, Poets in Paperbacks'. *San Francisco News-Call Bulletin*, 6 June 1964.

Watkins, Vernon, Patrick Kavanagh, Hugh MacDiarmid, and Stevie Smith. 'Poets on Poetry'. In *An Anthology from X: A Quarterly Review of Literature and the Arts, 1959–1962*, edited by David Wright, 63–69. Oxford: Oxford University Press, 1988.

'Waving And Drowning'. *Times Literary Supplement*, 19 January 1967.

Wilde, Oscar. 'The Importance of Being Earnest'. In *Complete Works of Oscar Wilde*, introduced by Merlin Holland, 357–419. London: HarperCollins, 2003.

Wilde, Oscar. *The Picture of Dorian Gray*. In *Complete Works of Oscar Wilde*, introduced by Merlin Holland, 17–159. London: HarperCollins, 2003.

Wilde, Oscar. 'A Woman of No Importance'. In *Complete Works of Oscar Wilde*, introduced by Merlin Holland, 465–514. London: HarperCollins, 2003.

Willans, Geoffrey, and Ronald Searle. *The Dog's Ear Book*. London: Max Parrish, 1958.

'Without Title'. *Times Literary Supplement*, 12 September 1936, 727.

Williams, Dorian. *Horses in Colour*. London: Batsford, 1959.

Williams, Helen Maria. *Poems*. Volume 2. London: Thomas Cadell, 1786.

Williams, Jonathan. 'Much Further Out Than You Thought'. In *In Search of Stevie Smith*, edited by Sanford Sternlicht, 38–49. Syracuse: Syracuse University Press, 1991.

Woodhouse, Barbara. *Dogs in Colour*. London: Batsford, 1960.

Woolf, Virginia. 'Solid Objects'. In *A Haunted House: The Complete Shorter Fiction*, edited by Susan Dick, 96–101. London: Vintage, 2003.

Woolf, Virginia. *A Room of One's Own and Three Guineas*, edited by Morag Shiach. Oxford: Oxford University Press, 2008.

Wright, David, to Stevie Smith. Stevie Smith papers, 1924–1970. Coll. No. 1976.012. McFarlin Library. Department of Special Collections and University Archives. The University of Tulsa. Series 1, Box 11, Folder 7.

Yeazell, Ruth Bernard. *Picture Titles: How and Why Western Paintings Acquired Their Names*. Princeton and Oxford: Princeton University Press, 2015.

Zajko, Vanda, and Miriam Leonard. *Laughing with Medusa: Classical Myth and Feminist Thought*. Oxford: Oxford University Press, 2008.

Zipes, Jack. *Fairy Tales and the Art of Subversion*. London and New York: Routledge, 2012.

Index

Please note that, given the messiness and overlap of various published editions, each of Smith's works appears in its own right, rather than nested within a specific collection.

Ackland, Rodney 1–2
Adorno, Theodor 22–3
anagnorisis 66–70
aphorism
    contradiction, internal 19–25 *see also* Smith,
        Stevie, language and literary registers,
        symmetrical
    definitions of 2–5, 134
    as distinct from fragment 133–9
    as distinct from maxim 3–4, 31–2, 47
    eccentricity of 13–15
    truth, claims to 2–7, 23–5, 31–46, 104
    usefulness and uselessness 11–19, 29, 40 n.21,
        45–6, 162
    white space around 19–21
Auden, W. H. 131–3, 167–8

Bacon, Francis 2–5
ballad 105–6
Barthes, Roland 109–10
Benjamin, Walter 92
Bowen, Elizabeth 8
Brockbank 113

Cannon, Christopher 73
Catullus 58, 105
Coleridge, S. T.
    Biographia Literaria (1817) 138
    'Christabel' 135, 148, 155–7
    'Kubla Khan' 151–2
Compton–Burnett, Ivy 164–6
Crisp, Quentin 163

Derrida, Jacques 9 n.40
    'Aphorism Countertime' 73
    'Fifty-two Aphorisms for a Foreword' 4–5,
        43–4, 48, 59, 137
D'Israeli, Isaac 76–7
Dog's Best Friend (1958) 114
Dog's Ear Book, The (1958) 113–14
Dunn, Sheila 113

Eliot, T. S. 143
epigram 57–60

epitaph 57, 72–7
Erasmus 78 n.1
Esquire Cartoon Album (1958) 109
Euripides
    Bacchae 57–8, 61–6, 69–72
    Children of Heracles, The 62
    Electra 69
    Herakles 62
    Iphigenia in Aulis 62
    Phoenician Women 62

fairytale
    Cinderella 92
    as distinct from fable 87 n.27
    Goose Girl, the 93–6
    Grimms' Fairy Tales (1857) 80–2, 86
    protagonists of 84
    relation to proverb 80, 85
    Snow White 93–4
    threes, importance of 92, 99–100
Fowler, Helen 107
France, Anatole 22
Frost, Robert 6
Futurism 164 *see also* modernism

Gide, André 54
Gilbert, W. S. 105–6
Gombrich, E. H. 104

Homer 80–1, 84
Horder, Mervyn 103, 109
Horses in Colour (1959) 127
Huk, Romana 24, 27–8, 83–4

Imagism 60 *see also* modernism

Joyce, James
    Finnegan's Wake (1939) 35, 137
    Stephen Hero (1904–6) 149
    Ulysses (1922) 75
    'Work in Progress' 136–7

Kavanagh, Patrick 19–21
Kraus, Karl 3, 35, 160–3

INDEX 189

Lawrence, D. H. 99–100
Lichtenberg, Georg Christoph 167
Loy, Mina 164

MacDiarmid, Hugh 19–21
Mansfield, Katherine 159–60, 163
maxim 77, 111, 142
  as distinct from aphorism 3–4, 31–2, 47
Mieder, Wolfgang 86
Miller, Betty 88
modernism 5–6, 22, 30, 75, 165
Moretti, Franco 75

newspapers and periodicals
  Harper's Bazaar 165
  Home Notes 111, 121
  Listener 146
  'little magazines' 136–9
  Little Review 164
  New Statesman 7
  New Yorker 115
  Peg's Paper 13
  Punch 103
  Rare Bits 10
  Spectator 11, 66, 109, 119
  Tablet 8, 145
  Times Literary Supplement 66, 109, 165
  Tit-Bits 10
  X: A Quarterly Review 11, 19–21, 144
Nietzsche, Friedrich 16, 21–3, 134, 163

Parker, Dorothy 10 n.42, 111–12, 119
Pascal, Blaise 16, 54, 167
Plath, Sylvia 145
proverb 77, 86, 170
  Book of Proverbs 88, 91, 96–9
  as distinct from aphorism 81
  usefulness and uselessness of 81, 88–91

quotation *see* Smith, Stevie, language and literary
  registers, quotation

radio 85, 94
Rankin, Arthur 147

Sayers, Dorothy L. 90
Sedgwick, Eve Kosofsky 44–6
Segal, Charles 70
Sitwell, Edith 13–14, 161
Smith, Stevie
  doodles and illustrations 7, 15–16, 26
    'Angela has passed out' 127
    captions 107, 130

appropriate and inappropriate 112, 115,
  120–2, 125–8
catalogue, captions to 123–5
image, relationship with 103–6
laughing while composing 112
'Croft, in the loft' 33–6, 34*f*
'Father, I have had enough' 40–1, 42*f*
'His eyes are blue' 122*f*
'How Cruel is the Story of Eve' 17*f*
'How Slowly Time Lengthens' 38–9, 39*f*
'I am Antigone and I shall bury my
  brother!' 56
'I could eat you' 121*f*
'I will tell you everything' 118*f*
'Lord Say-and-Seal' 118, 119*f*
'Love is everything' 18*f*
'Moi, c'est moralement que j'ai mes
  élégances' 18*f*
'My mother was a fox' 119–22, 120*f*, 126
'Sometimes it holds its head on one
  side' 125, 126*f*
'So what!' 114, 115*f*
'Such an animal is not responsive to
  love' 108*f*
'The Countess of Egremont does not wish
  for visitors' 117
'These girls are full of love' 117, 117*f*
'The Songster' 168–9, 169*f*
'The Weak Monk' 36, 37*f*
'Think!' 117
fragments
  collections of 103, 140–3, 146–9
  as distinct from aphorism 133–9
  as modernist 136–9
interviews given by 12, 107, 130, 139,
  164–5
language and literary registers
  anti–Semitic 27–8, 82, 89
  appropriate and inappropriate (embarrass-
    ing, excessive) 112, 115, 120–2, 125–8,
    129–32
  camp 9, 32
  classically inflected 44, 54, 55–77, 80–1,
    84, 105 *see also* Catullus; Euripides;
    Homer; Sophocles
  comedic (frivolous, humorous, irreverent,
    light, playful, whimsical) 7–9, 16–17,
    21–3, 28, 35, 89–92, 110–12, 130, 133,
    140, 151, 157, 169
  complete and incomplete 51, 131–9, 146,
    149, 153–7, 166
  death–related 7, 14–16, 32–3, 44, 59, 74,
    129–30, 159, 162 *see also* epitaph

190 INDEX

Smith, Stevie (*Continued*)
    eccentric ('dotty') 8, 145
    feminist 26–7, 56, 170
    flat 48–9, 54
    hard (firm, stiff, impenetrable) 1, 16, 20, 23, 32–4, 41, 54, 60–5, 147, 170
    imperious 12, 164
    insistent (assertive, resistant) 1–2, 19–20, 23, 32–4, 44, 72, 130–1, 134, 150, 157, 170
    late (undelivered) 55, 65–73, 83, 87, 161, 170
    pithy (brief, dense, weighty) 9–10, 17–18, 31–4, 47, 56, 59–60, 63, 130–2, 140
    predicative 32–4
    quotation 90, 139, 170
    religious 15–16, 40–3, 129–30, 151–3, 156, 170 *see also* proverb, Book of Proverbs
    repetitive 32–3, 40, 80–4, 87–9, 94–5
    rhyming 21–3, 31–3, 43, 50, 129
    rhythmical 6, 31, 43–6, 93, 161
    self-cancelling (light, self-effacing, disposable, insignificant, invisible, ordinary, withholding, withdrawing) 2, 11–14, 20, 24–5, 32, 35–8, 44–8, 60, 97, 117, 126–8, 131, 150, 161–4, 170
    sexual 31, 45
    symmetrical 2, 31
    tragic 1, 7, 23, 50–4
    truth-claiming 2, 33–46, 50–2, 101
  performances by 13, 85, 132
private life and persona of 12–13, 62
    eccentricity and ex-centricity of 13–16, 61, 159–61, 165, 168–70
writing
    'Advice to Young Children' 88, 130
    'All Things Pass' 10–11, 23
    'Art' 122–5
    'A Turn Outside' 94
    Batsford Book of Children's Verse (1970) 57, 91, 98, 139
    'Behind the Knight' 7
    'Beside the Seaside: A Holiday with Children' 88–9
    'Beware the Man' 6
    'Beyond Words' 103, 140
    Cats in Colour (1959) 107–10, 114, 122, 125–7
    'Come, Death' 59
    'Cool as a Cucumber' 78–80, 83–4
    'Croft' 33–6, 34*f*
    'Dear Little Sirmio' 105
    'Dido's Farewell to Aeneas' 44, 57–9
    'Duty was his Lodestar' 157

editing of 85–6, 90, 93, 94 n.41, 103, 125
'Eulenspiegelei' 148
'Everything is Swimming' 105
'Flounder' 129, 139
'From My Notes for a Series of Lectures on Murder' 159
'From the Coptic' 130
'From the Country Lunatic Asylum' 6
'From the French' 130, 139
'From the Greek' 58–60, 130
'From the Italian' 130
'God the Eater' 16
'Hast Du dich verirrt?' 79
'How Cruel is the Story of Eve?' 15–17, 17*f*
'How do you see?' 7
'How Slowly Time Lengthens' 38–9, 39*f*
'If I lie down' 32–3, 36
'I had a dream' 55
'In Canaan's Happy Land' 129–30
'I rode with my darling ...' 83, 86
'Is There a Life Beyond the Gravy?' 94–5
'Lightly Bound' 7
'Lord Say-and-Seal' 58, 118
'Magna est Veritas' 75–7
'Man is a Spirit' 21
'Modern English Literature' 165
'Mr Over' 7, 151
'My Hat' 7
'My Muse' 43, 51, 143
'Never Again' 40–3, 46, 49, 52
'Noble and Ethereal' 162
'No Categories!' 2
'Not Waving but Drowning' 1–2, 7, 106, 118, 160–1
Novel on Yellow Paper (1936) 77, 97, 101–2, 124–5, 159
  anti-Semitism 27
  autobiographical nature of 62, 159
  death 44, 50–2, 160
  editing of 93
  Euripides, reference to 57–72 *see also* Euripides
  fragments 133, 140–1
'O Happy Dogs Of England' 132–3
'Oh stubborn race of Cadmus' seed ...' 55–6
'O Lord!' 64–5
'Our Bog is Dood' 150–1
Over the Frontier (1938) 27, 82, 85, 88–9, 102, 147–8
'Parents' 16, 21
'Pearl' 11, 140
'Poet!' 6

'Professor Snooks Does His Worst with a Grecian Fragment' 57, 67
'Recognition Not Enough' 9, 166
'Reversionary' 33
reviews of 1, 7–8, 11, 30, 66, 109, 112, 115, 119, 125–6, 136, 146 *see also* newspapers and periodicals
'She got up and went away' 160–1, 170
'Simply Living' 146
Some Are More Human Than Others (1958) 17, 56, 103, 107–14, 117–20, 125–7, 140
'Spanky Wanky' 45–6, 128
'Suicide's Epitaph' 74
'The Bereaved Swan' 14, 129
The Best Beast (1969) 115
'The Castle' 85, 116
'The Deathly Child' 162
'The Dedicated Dancing Bull and the Water Maid' 7
'The Deserter' 154
'The English Visitor' 50–3
'The Fool' 79
'The Forlorn Sea' 83
'The Frog King' 87
'The Frog Prince' 8–9, 106
The Holiday (1949) 18, 79–81, 84, 87–91, 94–102
'The House of Over-Dew' 48–9
'The Ironing Board of Widow Twanky' 92–5
'The Leader' 7
'"The Persian"' 105
'The Poet and the Pussycat' 82–3

'The Poet Hin' 30
'The Repentance of Lady T' 36
'The Songster' 133, 168–9
'The Stroke' 130, 159
'The Weak Monk' 36–8, 168
'This Englishwoman' 9
'Thoughts about the Person from Porlock' 151–6 *see also* Coleridge, S. T.
'To An American Publisher' 146
'Too Tired for Words' 146, 155
'Voice from the Tomb (5)' 163–4
'What Poems Are Made Of' 59
'World of Books' 85
'Yes, I know' 130–1
Sontag, Susan 124
Sophocles
   Oedipus Coloneus 57–8
   Oedipus the King (*Oedipus Tyrannos*) 68–70
Spalding, Frances 114–16
Stevens, Wallace 43, 46

Thurber, James 115–21, 116*f*

Vorticism 5 *see also* modernism
voyeurism 116, 121

Watkins, Vernon 19–21
Wilde, Oscar 46–7, 112
Williams, Helen Maria 135
Woodhouse, Barbara 127
Woolf, Virginia 31
   'Solid Objects' (1920) 141–6, 150
   Three Guineas (1938) 56
Wright, David 11–12, 19